Ephemeral Architecture

In memory of Conxi Papió

Ephemeral Architecture
1000 projects & 1000 ideas

ISBN 978-84-15967-70-5
Edited by Àlex Sànchez Vidiella
First published in 2016 in English, Spanish and French by Promopress Editions

Selection of contents and text:
Àlex Sànchez Vidiella
Foreword © Xevi Bayona
English translation: Karen Chalmers
Grahic design: spread: David Lorente with Claudia Parra and Conxi Papió

Front Cover
La Ville Intelligente. Jakob + MacFarlane, 2011
© Jakob+MacFarlane - Nicolas Borel.
Bar Bucky. DUS Architects, 2010
© DUS Architectsrototyping
Mobile Craft Module. Adam Marcus + Variable Projects, 2015
© Prototyping Mobility Studio, Joseph Chang, Jeffrey Maeshiro

Back Cover
Elastic Plastic Sponge. Ball-Nogues Studio, 2009 © Chris Ball.
The Movement Café. M. Myerscough.
Luke Morgan + Studio Myerscough, 2012
© Gareth Gardner, Studio Myerscough.
Antoine. Bureau A, 2014
© Bureau A, Dylan Perrenoud.

Promopress is a brand of:
Promotora de Prensa Internacional S.A.
C/ Ausiàs Marc 124
08013 Barcelona, Spain
Phone: +34 93 245 14 64
Fax: +34 93 265 48 83
email: info@promopress.es
www.promopresseditions.com
Facebook: Promopress Editions
Twitter: Promopress Editions @PromopressEd

Printed in Slovenia

EPHEMERAL ARCHITECTURE

100 projects 1000 ideas

Àlex S. Vidiella ed.

promopress

architecture. (From the Latin architectūra).
nf. The art of designing and constructing buildings.

ephemeral. (From the Greek. ἐφήμερος, of one day).
adj. Momentary, short-lived.

Ephemeral Architecture

XEVI BAYONA

We can look up the definitions of "ephemeral" and "architecture", but, as Aristotle said in Metaphysics, "the whole is greater than the sum of its parts."

Architecture is present in everybody's daily life and can be used to trace the physical map of society so that people can engage in their everyday activities. In a world where change and transformation are the norm, long-term construction needs are no longer the sole aim when it comes to serving this changing society. This synergy between architectural and construction techniques, as well as the fact that the structures do not need to be permanent, is the essence of ephemeral architecture: boundaries widen and proposals are created in fields that go beyond those which define their terms.

Understanding art as a manifestation of human activity through which a personal and selfless vision is expressed, which interprets the real or imagined using fine art, linguistic or sound resources, ephemeral architecture incorporates art as an inseparable ingredient of this manifestation, approaching and blurring the boundaries between art and architecture.

Ephemeral architecture makes it possible to create spaces where people can gather to watch a show and, paradoxically, there is always the possibility that ephemeral architecture itself becomes the show. This is the case when pavilions are designed to create the ideal setting for a show, as well as with lighting architecture which, perhaps, aims to become the entertainment itself. Ephemerality implies the opportunity to build in spaces designed for other uses, questioning their original role, temporarily occupying a public space in order to transform it, or to modify enclosed spaces to attract an audience in an unusual way.

As a temporary construction, ephemeral architecture must have the capacity to energise a place, changing how it is perceived, or highlighting the building or public space itself, either by covering or emphasising it. As it is not permanent, each assembly represents the construction of a prototype without the prerequisite of durability. Ephemeral architecture acquires the quality of being an experimental search in itself, which accentuates the importance of the actual structure and the material that forms it, where the construction process determines or even becomes the essence of the final result. This material is, in some cases, so determinative that it becomes the architect of its own formalism. Understanding the will to give shape to and explore the most remote potential of a particular material, means that the project is born from the material itself, exploring its possibilities to the limit. In *Land-Art*, natural material is the norm, the requirement, and the subject matter from which the project is born and develops.

As they are not durable installations, the lack of budget can inspire or instigate imaginative proposals. Sometimes, to please the senses or for no other purpose than to reject immobility, these can generate excitement without the means available years ago, using ingenuity to add value to materials that are economical and abundant.

Ephemeral architecture now plays a relevant role in our society; it gives imaginative responses capable of energising places, exciting and inspiring at the same time as offering opportunities to shine in an industry that is currently devoid of excitement and inspiration. Architecture with a best before date and with the single premise that it will not endure physically... or maybe it will, because, as William Wordsworth wrote: "Though nothing can bring back the hour / Of splendour in the grass, of glory in the flower / We will grieve not, rather find / Strength in what remains behind." An exercise in existential modesty where it is evident that nothing lasts forever but it is important that everything has, in due time, a beautiful meaning in an ever-changing world.

Editor Àlex Sánchez Vidiella has worked extensively to collect the most representative ephemeral projects from the last five years or so. The book contains a wide range of different interventions, visually divided into different categories: land-art, pavilions, stands, functional interventions, installations and projects. This book represents a varied analysis of the most recent scene in the ephemeral architecture sphere.

Xevi Bayona graduated in Architecture from the University of Barcelona in 2008, having also studied at the Faculty of Architecture at Porto. In 2009 he completed a post-graduate course in Landscaping at the University of Barcelona, and in the same faculty, in 2012, completed a Master's degree in Theory and Architectural Practice with his dissertation "La Girona dels Carrers Escala". He taught at Girona's University of Architecture between 2009 and 2013. He has won two FAD awards as well as numerous national and international architecture and art awards and competitions.

Contents

Index of Authors

1—4

La Ville Intelligente

JAKOB + MACFARLANE

PARIS, FRANCE, 2011

AREA
370 m^2

CLIENT
ORANGE GROUP + ARTEVIA

PHOTO
© A. FAINSILBER, BERNARD TSCHUMI, G. CHAMAYOU, JAKOB + MACFARLANE, NICOLAS BOREL

1 The original structure represents a pavilion designed to host the exhibition *HelloDemain* at the *Cité des Sciences et de l'Industrie*, in the Parc de la Villette.

The exhibition's main pavilion
reflects the technological
advances that dominate
the urban futuristic scene.
It is very close to La Geode
2 and the L'Ourcq canal.

The architects designed
La Ville Intelligente as the Paris
of the future. A technological
exchange through which the
3 different paths of visitors cross.

The structure of the pavilion,
like a road network that
envelops the metropolis of the
future, has multiple entrances
and exits to a new space where
the public rediscovers streets,
4 squares, furniture and objects.

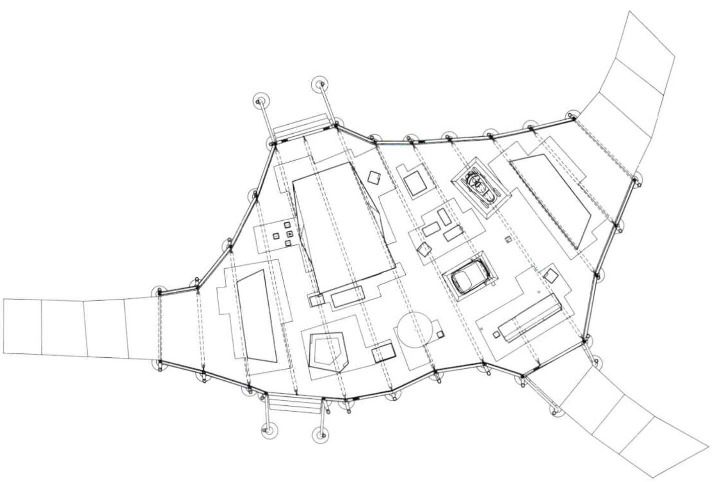

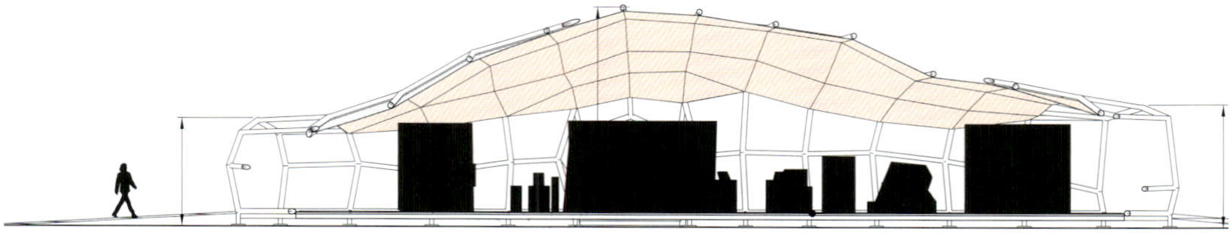

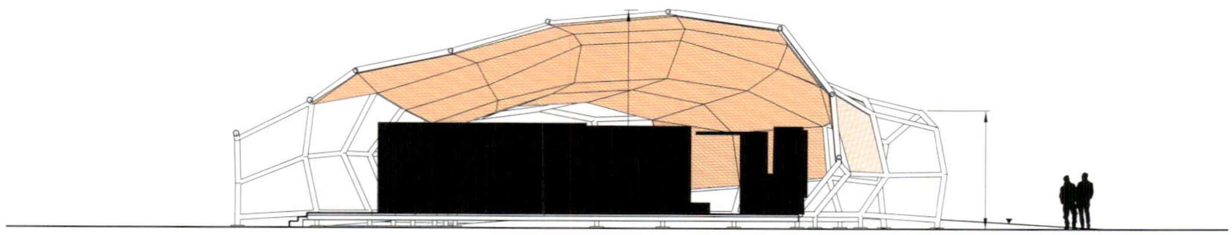

5 The choice of colour for this structure was not casual. The architects decided that La Ville Intelligente should represent Orange's corporate identity.

6 The construction shows the frame formed by a tubular structure of enamelled steel. This helps to tension a cover that serves as a shell, enveloping the architecture.

7 Large flat pieces of screwed steel were used for the flooring so that it could be walked over by visitors. The entire tubular structure is secured at the ends of the pieces.

8 Enamelled and painted in different shades of orange, the structure occupies an area of 370 m^2. The building stands out from its surroundings thanks to the pre-stretched canvas and its original structural design.

9 The porticos are interlaced with cross pieces that form an interconnected network of portals that function as receptions.

10 The welded steel tubes form irregular parallel polyhedrons. The loads are distributed using metal flooring. The textile cover is stitched to the tubular structure with cord.

The Movement Café

MORAG MYERSCOUGH, LUKE MORGAN +
STUDIO MYERSCOUGH

LONDON, UNITED KINGDOM, 2012

AREA
140 m^2

CLIENT
N/A

PHOTO
© GARETH GARDNER,
STUDIO MYERSCOUGH

11 In The Movement Café, you can spend an afternoon reading outdoors, eat, have a drink or order a vegan ice cream in the small booth next to the recycled container which also functions as the café.

12 Vividly coloured geometric shapes and bright prints are the main attraction of this project, as the size of the decorative structure far exceeds that of the café.

13 An old recycled container is transformed into a modern café that closes its doors at night. It is also protected by the scaffolding that surrounds it, also functioning as a decorative element.

14 The skilled interaction between scaffolding, various wooden slats and a recycled container demonstrate that basic, old and cheap materials can be used to build a structure that is modern, functional and very successful.

15 The construction and decoration of this place is very simple: it consists of recycled containers, re-usable scaffolding, brightly painted wooden walls, comfortable cushions and a couple of tables in the central area.

16 Organic and local food and drinks are served at The Movement Café and ice cream parlour. Profits were donated to organisations that help London's most disadvantaged communities.

17 The scaffolding is decorated with wooden slats that show a poem by Lemn Sissay, the official tweeter for the London 2012 Olympic Games The words are strategically arranged at the top of the café.

18 The area around Greenwich train station was completely changed when the Morag Myerscough studio was commissioned to decorate it. The site was original and the cost of the construction had to be very economical. It was built in 16 days to coincide with the opening of the Olympic Games.

19—20

19 The Movement Café includes a meeting place, a café, a social centre and a theatre, all surrounded by seats and cushions to welcome the visitor.

20 The cushions for resting or drinking coffee are made from material similar to that used for kites. It is water-resistant and they are always outside.

THE MOVEMENT CAFÉ—MORAG MYERSCOUGH, LUKE MORGAN + STUDIO MYERSCOUGH

Nomad

BUREAU A

PARIS, FRANCE, 2015

AREA
N/A

CLIENT
MUSÉE DU QUAI BRANLY

PHOTO
© BUREAU A

With the Nomad project, the architects sought to create a relaxed atmosphere in the gardens of the Quai Branly museum during the summer months.

22 Second hand caravans, coloured carpets and some original stools are the elements the architects have used to create a dynamic cultural space that is accessible to all.

23 The nucleus of this original project consists of five re-used caravans used as a mobile disco, nursery, ice cream parlour, stage and information point.

24 Once the summer rush is over, the nomadic caravans live up to their name and abandon the museum garden to look for a new home.

25 Created with recycled items, the five nomadic pavilions allow visitors to have a pleasant time surrounded by culture, architecture and various events.

26 Once the exhibition is over, the items that were used are removed without leaving a trace in the spaces where they were located during the three months of summer.

27 Wooden tables, which are clearly inspired by the works within the museum's walls, caravans and mobile pavilions, carpets and comfortable seats.

28 Nomadism is becoming increasingly rooted in different cultures and this exhibition seeks to create a communal environment in the different installation locations.

29 Stools and items which have been used previously are used to create a whole new atmosphere; one that welcomes whoever wishes to enjoy a summer evening outdoors.

30 Informal architecture, homogeneous distribution and a space that's surrounded by nature completely transforms the garden, which becomes a hub for social gatherings.

Temple of Agape

MORAG MYERSCOUGH, LUKE MORGAN + STUDIO MYERSCOUGH

LONDON, UNITED KINGDOM, 2014

AREA
84 m²

CLIENT
SOUTHBANK CENTRE

PHOTO
© GARETH GARDNER

31 This is a temporary installation created for the Southbank Centre's *Festival of Love*. It represents love for humanity, one of the seven classical Greek themes of love represented at the festival.

32 A showcase of love in its fullness is created by a series of performances, installations and workshops. The intention is to celebrate the legitimacy of marriage for everyone.

33 Colours are the main attraction of this installation which is designed to demonstrate that love can be found everywhere, even in a project created with scaffolding and pieces of wood. All the paints used are water soluble.

34 The project's journey starts with large colourful neon letters and motifs around the entrance. This tempts the visitor to enter and stroll through the different areas where the main focus is on simplicity and large spaces.

35 Inside the temple, Martin Luther King's words "I have decided to stick with love", the main inspiration for the project, are written. A large number of words related to love decorate the installation with bright colours.

36 All the information is presented chronologically and schematically through the superimposed curves. These control the general shape of the installation. Spatiality and chromaticity are the two main distinguishing features.

37 The journey starts with large colourful neon letters and motifs around the entrance, which tempt the visitor to enter and stroll through the different areas where the main focus is on simplicity and large spaces.

38 The temple is 8 metres high and 10.5 metres wide. It is built with a scaffolding structure decorated with hand-painted fabrics and over 300 wooden panels.

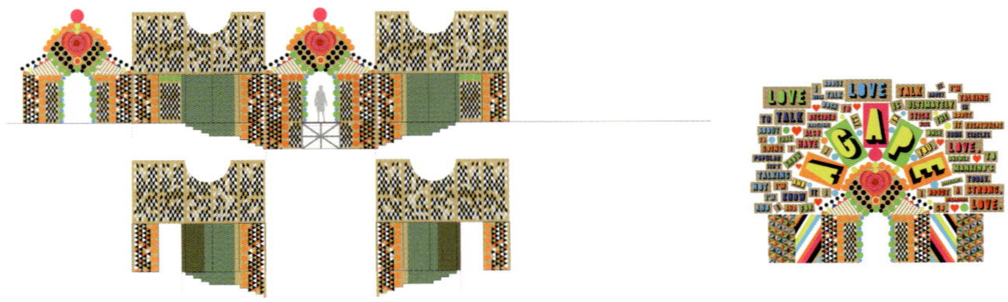

39 The client's requirement was the creation of a project that would look attractive to visitors. This was achieved with a combination of neon colours, wooden panels and scaffolding structure that created a space that was unique, surprising and original.

40 A series of multi-coloured geometric patterns cover the interior walls, while a black tiled pattern showed the route through the installation.

Bucky Bar

DUS ARCHITECTS

ROTTERDAM, NETHERLANDS, 2010

AREA
N/A

CLIENT
STUDIO FOR UNSOLICITED ARCHITECTURE (SUA), NETHERLANDS ARCHITECTURE INSTITUTE (NAI)

PHOTO
© 2B ARCHITECTES, DRACE, LUIS ASÍN LAPIC

41 This intervention was created for an outdoor event for the *Architecture of Consequence* event held in Rotterdam, in association with the Studio for Unsolicited Architecture.

42 The event is a spontaneous street party to celebrate the American inventor Buckminster Fuller's ideas. He showed how minimum-energy geodesic domes could open a path towards a more environmentally sustainable future.

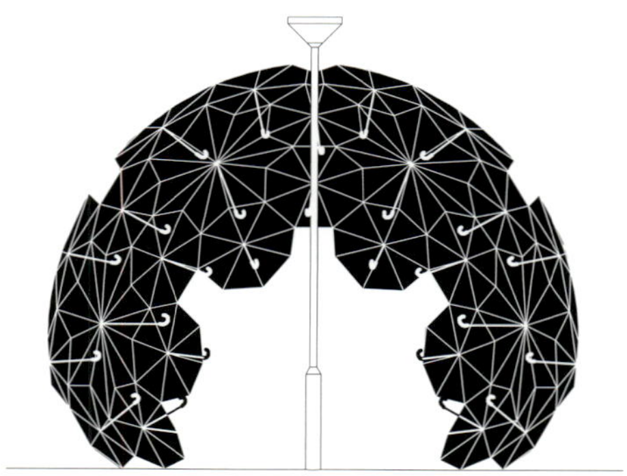

43 The ephemeral bar was made using umbrellas of the same colour and size in order to create a geodesic dome.

44 The architects asked the audience of this performance to bring orange umbrellas in with them. This was intended to create an ephemeral haven using umbrellas that were available around a lamp post.

45 This ephemeral dome is a life size model of what it could be in a more sustainable future: a demonstration of the power of space to create spontaneous meetings and improvised shelters.

46 Re-using ordinary materials assumes a new social value linked to the creation of unexpected spaces which can give rise to new activities in public areas.

47 In this spontaneous celebration, almost 300 visitors and participants in the event were able to have conversations, debates and games with complete freedom.

48 The term "unsolicited architecture" used by DUS Architects refers to buildings that arise from necessity and social projects that seek the architect's professional autonomy.

49 This project shows how architecture combines research and design with strategic focuses and the exclusive use of materials in multiple combinations.

50 DUS architects wanted to portray public architecture as the stage for all life's events through five "unsolicited positive proposals" for the future of the city of Rotterdam.

Wanderlust

JAKOB + MACFARLANE

PARIS, FRANCE, 2015

AREA
N/A

CLIENT
N/A

PHOTO
© ROLAND HALBE

51 Wanderlust is a project included in a previous one called *The Docks – City of fashion and design*, designed to create a fusion of leisure and entertainment spaces.

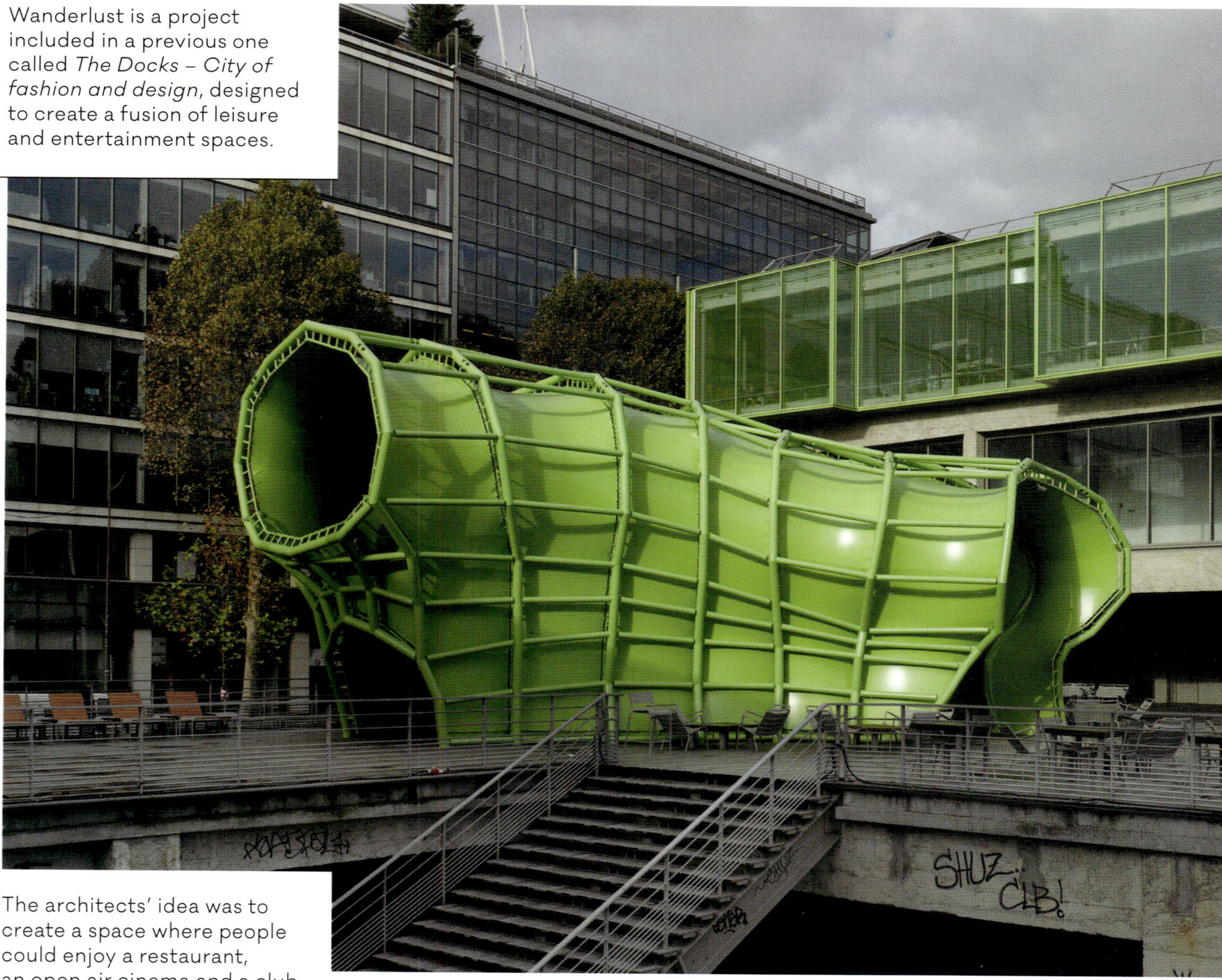

52 The architects' idea was to create a space where people could enjoy a restaurant, an open air cinema and a club, creating a place to spend a lively and complete night.

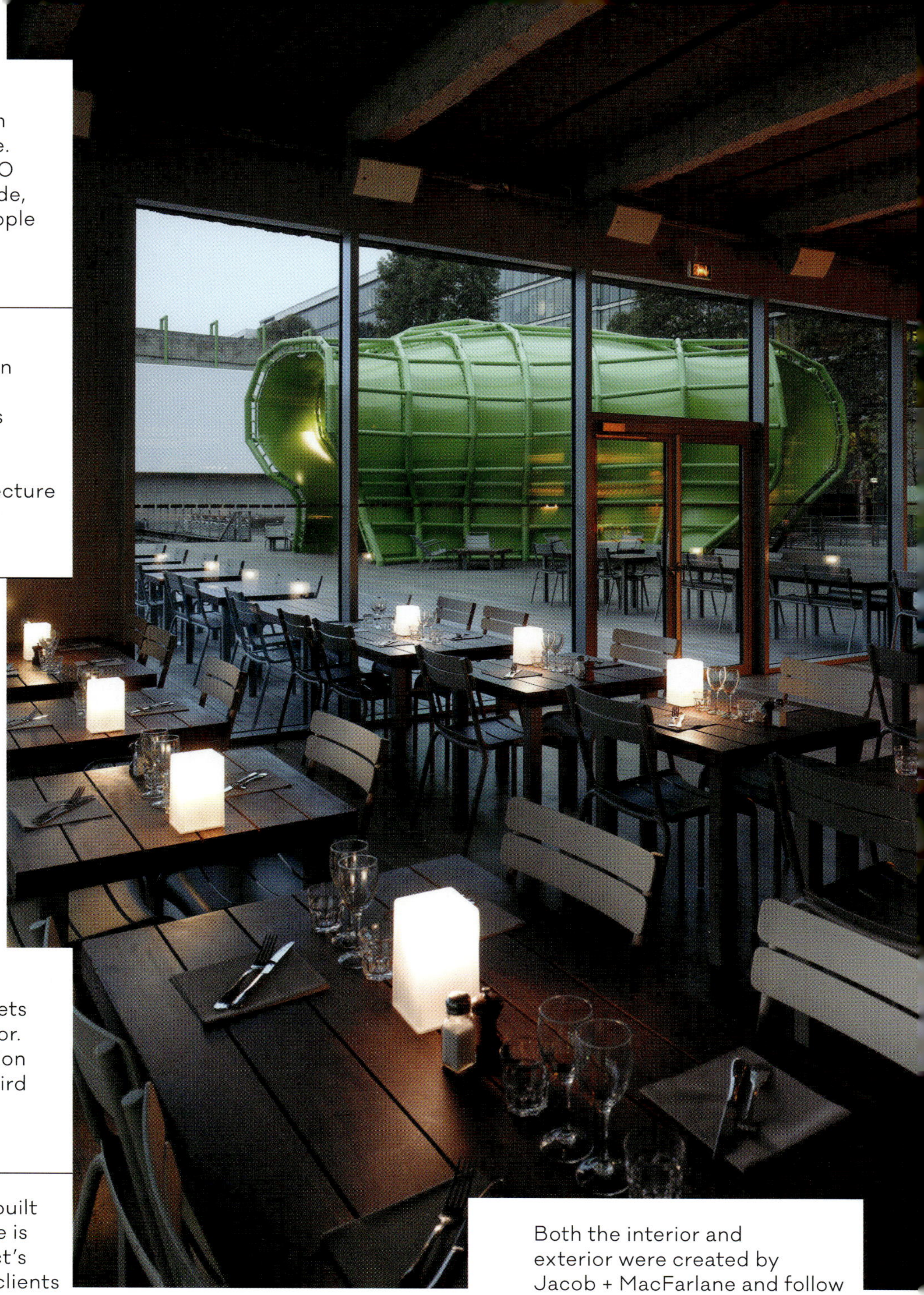

The exterior space that
functions as a dining room
has space for 400 people.
There is also space for 100
people in the cinema. Inside,
there is room for 200 people
in the club and 150 in the
53 restaurant.

The main focuses of this
project are the three green
steel structures that are
used to demarcate spaces
and create a modern and
sophisticated ambience.
The eclecticism of architecture
is renowned for achieving
54 a casual space.

There is a bar and DJ in
the first pavilion, with toilets
and bar on the ground floor.
The second hanging pavilion
is a cinema screen. The third
installation contains the
55 cloakroom and reception.

The exterior terrace was built
with a wooden floor. There is
continuity with the project's
interior, so that although clients
are inside the pavilion, they still
have the sensation of being
56 outdoors.

Both the interior and
exterior were created by
Jacob + MacFarlane and follow
a design line in wood and steel
that contrasts with the eclectic
and futuristic style of the large
green structure visible from
57 the exterior.

58 The intense green colour of the installations, along with the nocturnal lighting, provides an ambience that invites users to think that they are inside.

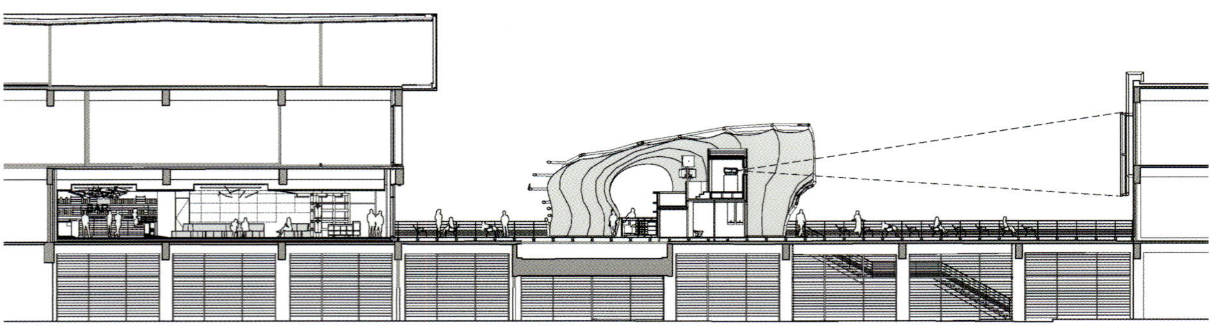

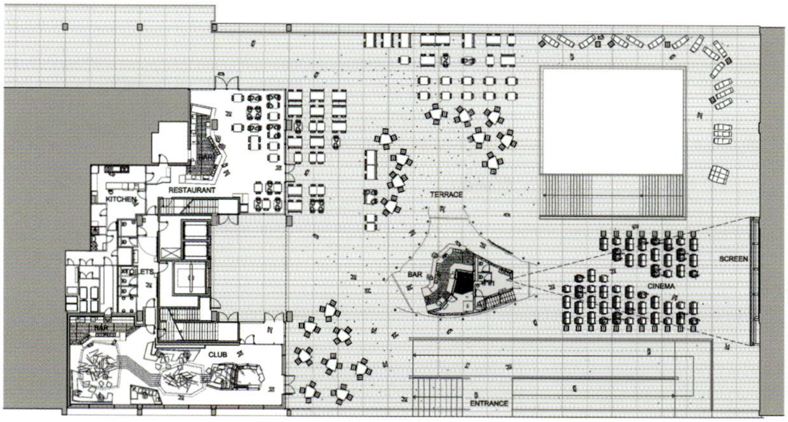

59 The purpose of this project is to create an urban space right in the heart of the city, where people can enjoy a film, lunch or a drink surrounded by the existing buildings.

60 The large outdoor cinema screen, next to the lunch area and the buildings that surround the area make this project an original and attractive space.

Table Cloth

BALL-NOGUES STUDIO

LOS ANGELES, CA, EEUU, 2010

AREA
N/A

CLIENT
UCLA HERB ALPERT SCHOOL OF MUSIC IN LOS ANGELES

PHOTO
© SCOTT MAYORAL

61 The result of the study of various reusable temporary installations on-site, this structure was created for the courtyard of Schoenberg Hall at the UCLA Herb Alpert School of Music in Los Angeles.

62 Hundreds of boards used as tables mimic the shape of a tablecloth, which functions as a side cover for part of the courtyard. The more than 200 wooden tables and stools are used as the background for performances held there.

63 The structure's main feature is to embellish the courtyard with basic furniture during performances, lectures, academic debates and other activities held in the outdoor space.

64 The project aims to follow sustainable architecture guidelines, stressing that temporary pavilions and structures can have the same, or even more impact than those that are permanent.

The chairs and tables used on
the front tablecloth as well as
in the rest zone were presented
to visitors when the exhibition
finished so they could be
65 reused.

Sustainability is the essential
basis of this project: using
existing materials and objects,
simple assembly and fast
dismantling allows you to reuse
the components without doing
any damage whatsoever to its
66 form or structure.

It's a versatile, economical
and sustainable project, as
it creates a construction
without the necessity of a
large investment and can be
removed quickly and simply.
Perfect for travelling exhibi-
tions, it boosts sustainability
67 and temporary architecture.

A simple structure created
from re-used tables and chairs
brings about a large scale
change to the place, as well
as serving as a sound proofing
screen when performances,
lectures or other activities
68 involving sound take place.

The curtain that covers one
of the courtyard walls is built
with hundreds of medium sized
tables and stools with three
legs. It needed to be small
and of a light material so that
69 it could be held vertically.

The project challenges our
perspective: it is common
to see tables and stools on the
floor; their sole function to
offer a rest place. The vertical
arrangement of the objects
completely transforms the
70 concept we have of furniture.

Kiosk m.poli

BEN BUSCHE + BRUT DELUXE

MADRID, SPAIN, 2008

AREA
2 x 3 x 2,4 m (HEIGHT)

CLIENT
MADRID CITY COUNCIL

PHOTO
© MIGUEL DE GUZMAN/ IMAGENSUBLIMINAL

71 The small construction is designed to be used for temporary street markets and craft fairs. It is not designed to be an individual object, but part of a whole existing in a small village.

72 The design is based on archetypal images such as city, house, fireplace, etc. When the prototype is closed, the kiosk is a volume covered with a pitched roof. In appearance, it is a house reduced to its minimum expression.

73 The success of these units lies in the design: a block with a square floorplan that does not require assembly or disassembly and that can be used to sell a wide range of products, with everything required for its correct use.

74 The kiosk is easy to install, transport and move thanks to the light weight of the steel and its original design. The construction also stands out for its use of recycled materials and once dismantled, it is fully reusable.

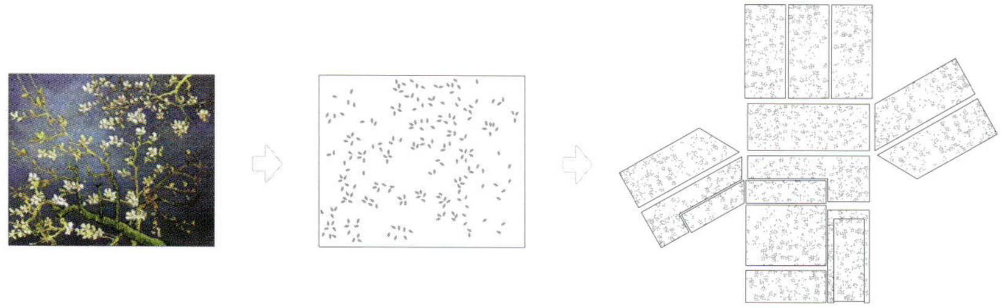

75 Four different types of steel façade were used for the construction: Corten natural rusted steel, polished stainless steel, matte stainless steel and steel with a black lacquered finish.

76 The base and structure of the kiosk are built using structural profiles and galvanised steel tubes, whereas the floor of the interior is slip-resistant sheet aluminium on MDF boarding.

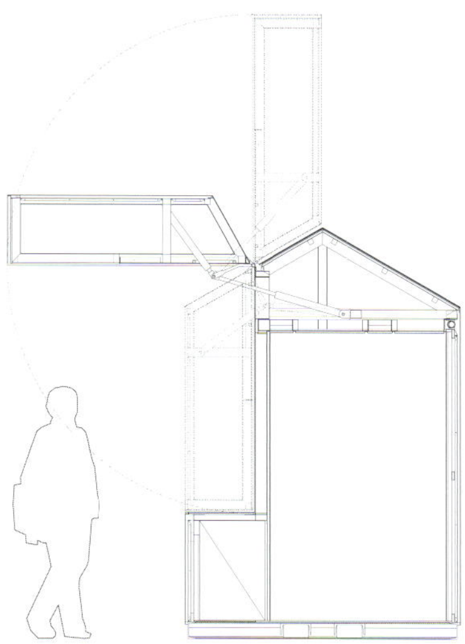

77 The opening hatch is opaque and has three changeable positions: at 0 degrees for closing the kiosk, at 90 degrees for shielding the counter from rain and sun, and at 180 degrees when the structure is completely open.

78 The interior can be accessed through a door in the front façade next to the serving hatch. The façades on both sides and the back do not have openings. Lacquered sheet steel plates and pre-galvanised and covers with Corten steel are used.

79 The structure that represents the fireplace is used as a large advertising board that is backlit at night. With this transformation, the kiosk reveals its interior when it is opened. The colour and contents can be changed.

80 When the design is opened, the kiosk changes radically. One part of its façade turns over the roof and the construction acquires a more upright and surprising ratio similar to a house with a large fireplace.

Mobile Craft Module

ADAM MARCUS + VARIABLE PROJECTS

SAN FRANCISCO, CA., USA, 2015

AREA
N/A

CLIENT
CALIFORNIA COLLEGE OF THE ARTS/CCA DIGITAL CRAFT LAB

PHOTO
© PROTOTYPING MOBILITY STUDIO, JOSEPH CHANG, JEFFREY MAESHIRO

The project consists of a series of deployable structures and is formed by individual modules that can be arranged so that they can be used for exhibitions, events and even as work spaces.

At night, the modules nest together and close completely, so that the exhibitions as well as their contents are properly guarded and safe from theft
82 or vandalism.

The structure is the pavilion for the *Prototyping Festival Market Street*, a three day event held in San Francisco for exhibiting new ideas for
85 public spaces.

Each module has a side opening that allows access to the shelves and interior work areas. The internal structure is reconfigurable and can be arranged in different ways by playing with lids that serve
83 as seats and work space.

The structure of the modules consists of welded steel tube with iron angles assembled at the corners that protect the lining of western red cedar
84 boards.

The fact that pavilions can
be handled and transported
easily allows them to be
exhibited in different places
without the need to spend
hours on assembly nor
to move tonnes of materials
86 and structures.

Using everyday materials such
as steel, and several red cedar
tables, a pavilion is created
that is perfect for exhibiting
works of art, working, resting
and contemplating the work
87 of the collaborating artists.

149 m² of PVC membrane
and 47.4 m² of air were used
to create this structure based
on simplicity and portability.
It shows that an impressive
structure can be achieved with
materials that are this simple
88 and easy to use.

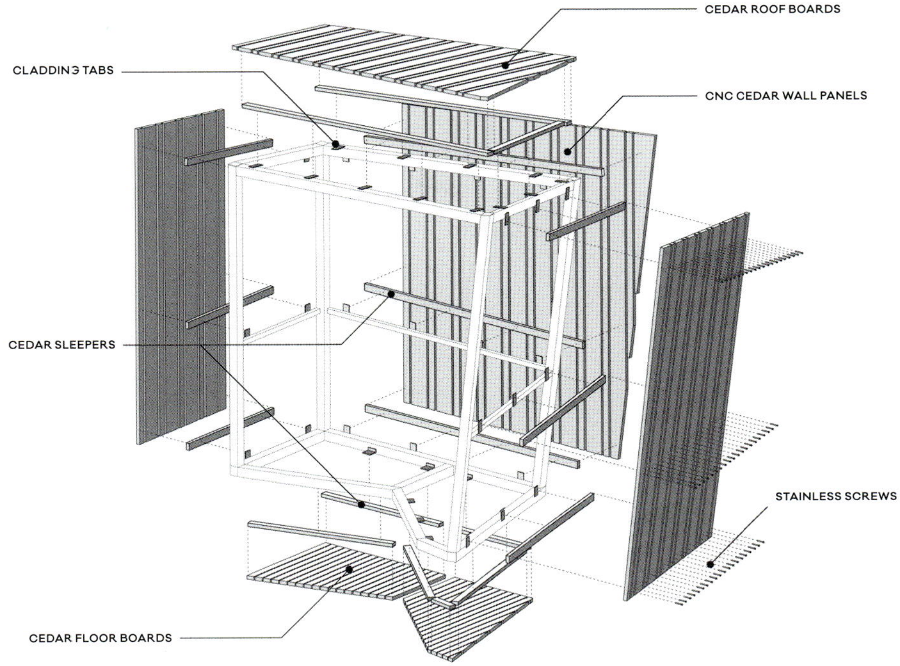

The cedar tables are carved
with abstract designs and
their fusion creates an effect
with the lines at the same
time as creating a drawing
where you can clearly see the
letters "CCA", the acronym of
89 California College of the Arts.

The project's main function is
to create a deployable structure
that optimises the use of the
space for many exhibition and
work activities. The interior
is versatile, comfortable and
safe as at the end of the day
90 it is completely closed.

Mobile POP-UP

HOLLWICH KUSHNER ARCHITECTURE + HWKN

NEW YORK, NY, USA, 2011

AREA
2 CUBES OF 6 m^2 EACH

CLIENT
UNIQLO USA

PHOTO
© MATTHEW HOFFMAN

This original project is to be
found in Area 2 of High Line
Park, in the same place as a
skating rink designed by the
91 same architects.

92 The two cubes were created in their entirety in Seattle to then be transported and installed at the entrance to the lot.

93 The cubes are pop-up shops created for UNIQLO.

94 When night falls, the shop cubes illuminate the gazes of the bystanders. This makes it a piece with double meaning: cultural and commercial.

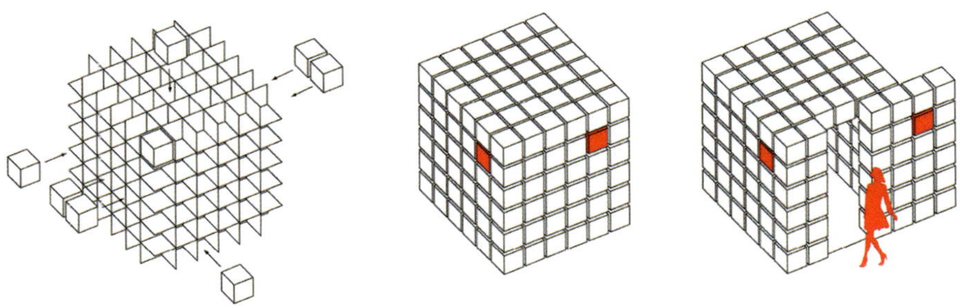

95 The grid lines, bright façades and simple structures create an attractive assembly that awakens the consumer's interest and invites visitors inside.

96 A pattern with a grid background is used to fix the cubes on the surface. The distorted grille creates an effect which imitates the vortex of skate blades that pass around it.

97 The message that UNIQLO want to communicate with these cubes is that architecture can enrich society, influencing culture, people and consumption.

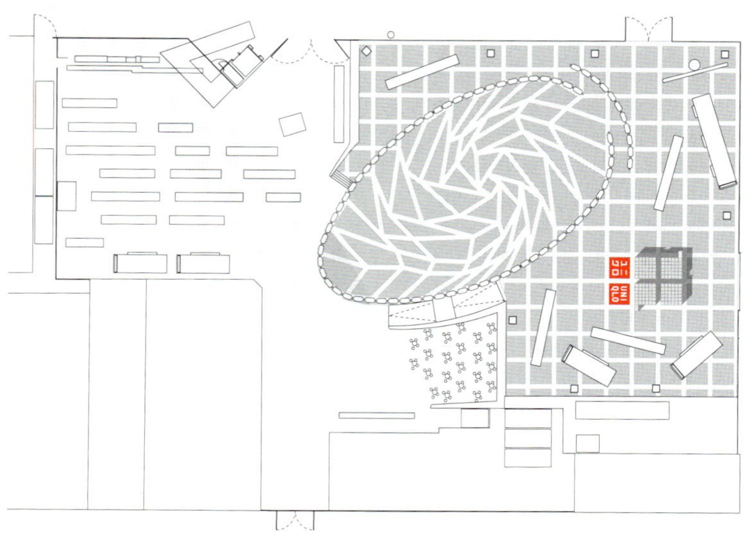

98 The porch section serves to invite the public to enter, try and buy the meticulously organised articles for sale.

99 As well as offering the brand's products, the purpose of this project is to provoke a stimulating visual reaction, which attracts the consumer's attention and makes them want to visit the interior.

100 During the day, one of the sides of the cube is open to show the interior. At the back, a large mirror is used to create the sensation of more space that perfectly combines with several lines of LED lights in the ceiling.

La Fabrique

BUREAU A

GENEVA, SWITZERLAND, 2013
AREA
N/A
CLIENT
N/A
PHOTO
© DAVID GAGNEBIN-DE BONS

101 The starting point for the creation of this original construction is Buster Keaton's short film *One Week* (1920). It describes how a recently married couple assemble their build-it-yourself house on a plot of land for seven days.

102 The short film explains how the couple's rival rearranges the components of the house to make assembly more difficult. This is the starting point for Bureau A's design.

103 With this project, the architects wanted to reflect that pleasure and the simple desire to build can become an integral part of the design.

104 Windows from demolition sites were used for the construction. The assembly process only took two days.

105 The project experiments with the fusion of the rigour of a construction company.

106 The architects question the difficulty of finding affordable construction spaces in western countries where the architectural process has lost its spontaneity.

107 The windows open onto an asymmetrical wooden frame to create the façade and roof, while the floors and walls are constructed from thick wooden tables joined together.

108 The construction process of the pavilion shows the simple pleasure of building in a natural environment but without altering it.

109 The nature of the pavilion resembles the emancipated architecture of the follies of garden culture. As Buster Keaton's short film was interpreted: La Fabrique is poetic and playful architecture in a serious context.

110 The idea of introducing spontaneity into the construction process resulted in a structure that looks a bit like an anarchic and eccentric garden.
A faithful reflection of Buster Keaton's short film: the couple ends up arguing about the disorganised components.

Viennese Guest Room

HERI&SALLI

VIENNA, AUSTRIA, 2015

AREA
N/A

CLIENT
ERWIN GEGENBAUER

PHOTO
© HANS SCHUBERT, MINNA LIEBHART

The architecture studio heri&salli designed this guest house for the Gegenbauer Vinegar Brewery in Vienna. The project consists of five small bedrooms with minimum intervention.

112 The entire wooden structure is treated with a natural finish. Wooden shutters were also designed for the large windows and can be used to block out natural light if required.

113 The main piece and practically the only piece of furniture inside is the *Viennese Guest Bed*. This is created using stacked wooden pallets to create a central area for sleeping.

114 This combination of wooden squares has multiple uses. Any additional furniture is redundant. The architects maintain that the centre of the home should be the bedroom, reduced to its minimum expression.

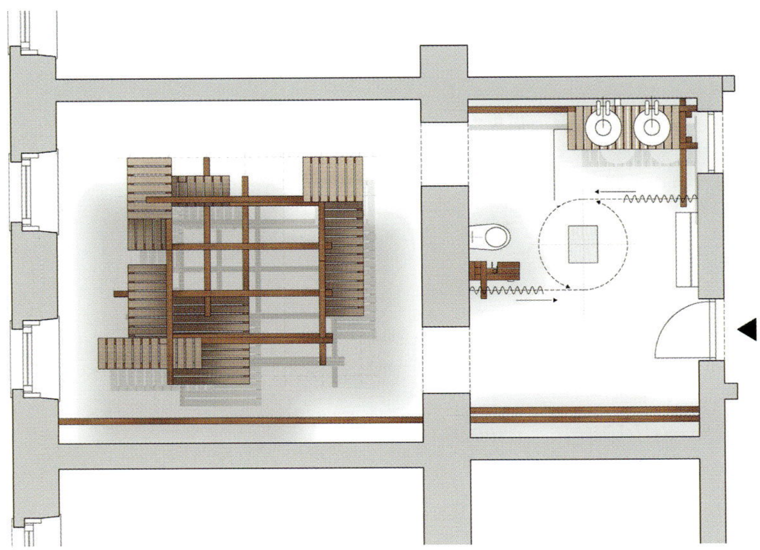

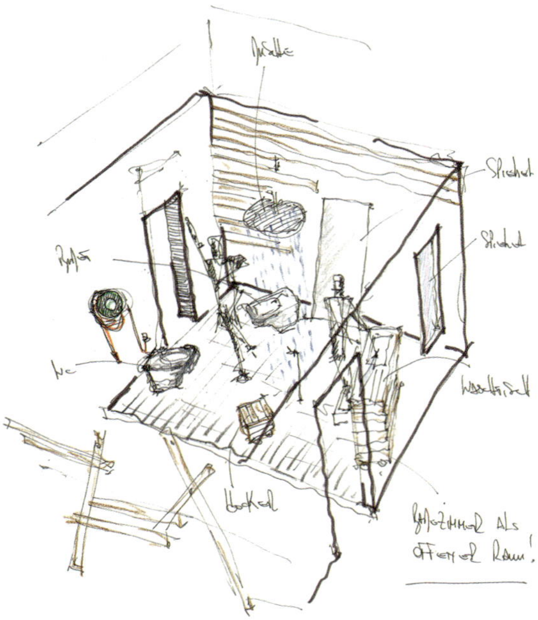

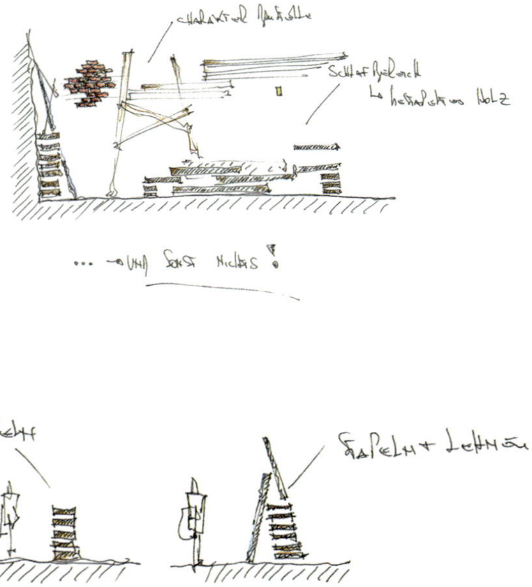

115 The room is really only its own framework, which delimits the space. The bathroom deserves a special mention for being the only space where privacy is maintained.

116 The main focus of the project is the bed built using a lattice of stacked wooden beams. Platforms were constructed around it that help to combine the functions of the room.

117 The architects deliberately left service lines and wiring on view. They also wanted their intervention to be minimal, leaving the original structure visible.

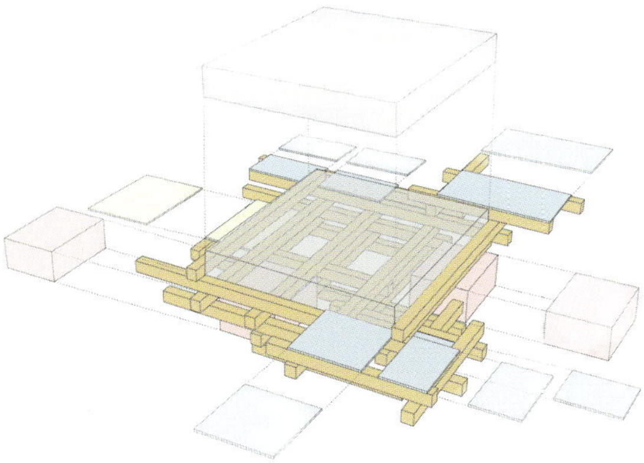

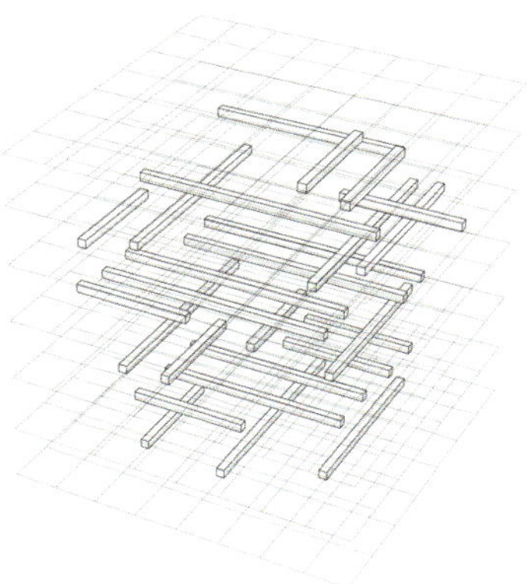

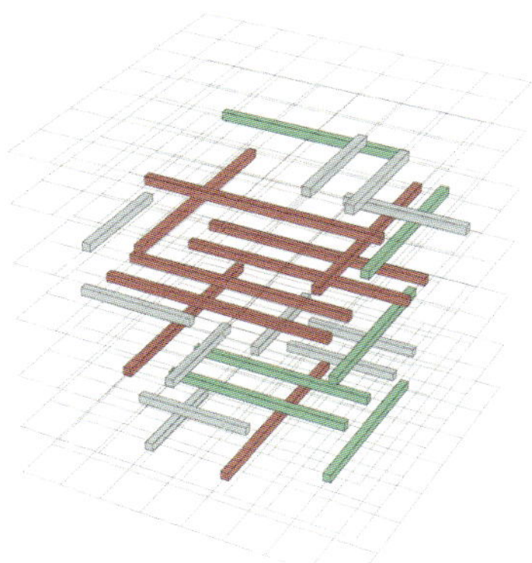

118 The ephemeral element of this intervention resides in the fact that here, all the accessories and functions are temporary frames, reflecting the stages of the guest's stay.

119 The existing extensions around the main bed are multifunctional and can be used as benches, tables or storage areas, depending on the users' needs and preferences.

120 Materials traditionally used for the construction of a conventional home, such as bricks, ceilings, floors, etc., became obstacles to demarcate the frames. In this sense, the visible details of the construction must be shown.

Flederhaus

HERI&SALLI

VIENNA, AUSTRIA, 2011

AREA
650 m^2

CLIENT
MQ – MUSEUMSQUARTIER WIEN

PHOTO
© HERI&SALLI, MISCHA ERBE

121 This ephemeral construction was designed as a physical tranquil shelter within the square in front of the MuseumsQuartier in the Austrian capital.

Fledershaus is a pun on the word
bat. It is a hanging structure
that provides entertainment.
Here, it is the human who is
122 hanging, seeking relaxation.

The Flederhaus was designed
to be a meeting point and
social centre for people
with curiosity and a vision
of the future. For this reason,
the user is free to use the
various hammocks arranged
to facilitate contact and
123 communication.

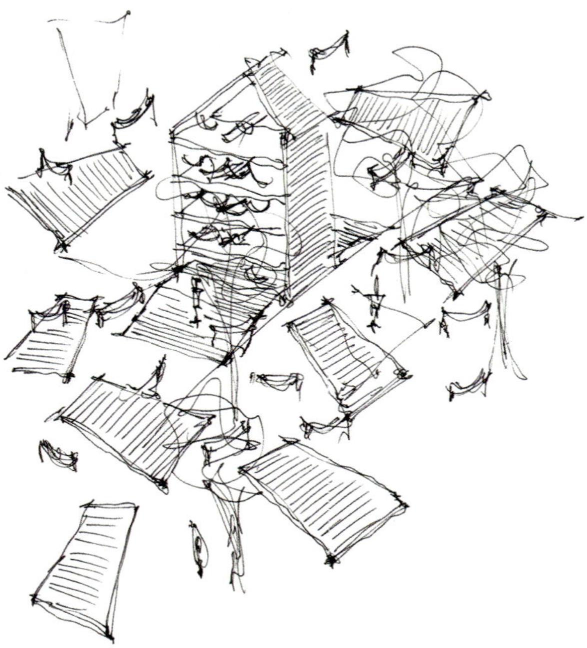

The abstract form of this
prototype departs from the
typical house as we know it.
It has a different use and
an unusual spatial opening.
It becomes a space open to
the public in an upright form
and without separations
124 between walls.

125—130

The construction is completely
open at the front and back.
The use of this ephemeral
installation was limited to
schedules and moved to a
new location: a developing
area that was in the process
125 of revitalisation.

The architects sought to
also make the structure a
monument to sustainability.
A large part of the construction
is wood, a resource with zero
126 CO_2 emissions.

This structure houses a series
of 28 hammocks installed for
visitors to use and enjoy. They
are distributed over five floors
and offer magnificent views
127 of the square on both sides.

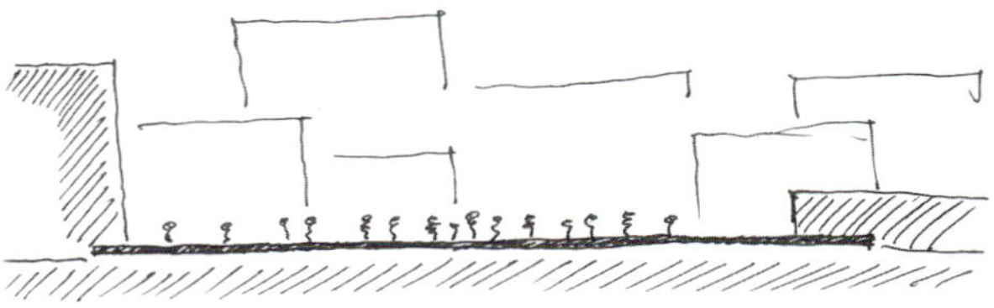

The profiles of typical Austrian
houses were the inspiration
for the heri&salli architecture
studio. Here, the shape
of the pitched roof is not
128 a coincidence.

To make assembly and disas-
sembly easy, this ephemeral
house is composed of prefab-
ricated elements and is not
structurally attached to the
ground. This means that the
project can be moved to
129 different areas of Vienna.

The architects received
instructions that the project
would be for public use.
Inside, a central stair case was
built to connect the building's
130 five floors.

OFF Office

HERI&SALLI

BURGENLAND, AUSTRIA, 2013

AREA
N/A

CLIENT
FOB – FACE OF BUILDINGS

PHOTO
© PAUL OTT

The project is an ephemeral office building built entirely from wood. Although this type of construction is normally solely dedicated to work, the concept of quality of life and leisure culture formed an integral part of the planning.

The project consists of a
structure in spatial grid, which
expands functionally. On the
outside it has a membrane that
breaks again and again, without
leaving the area indicated.
Light filters are installed in
132 existing cubes.

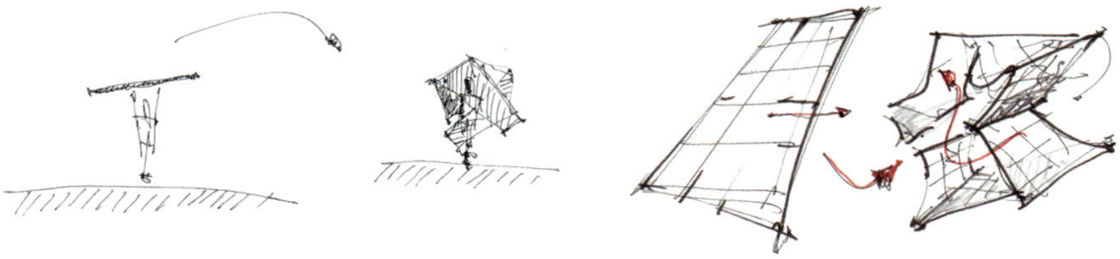

The horizontal axis for the
construction of beams and
support is erected in a 5 x 5 m
grid with a core in the shape
of an internal disk of solid
wooden panels. The outer layer
of the visible construction
defines the basic network of
133 the construction's extension.

134 During the summer months, the building is regulated by night time cooling. Using a ventilation system of sliding blinds, the cubes are opened and closed depending on the outside temperature.

135 Another example of energy efficiency created in this building is the pool, which is heated by excess heat from the cooling system. Rainwater is collected in a shaft and is distributed through pipelines.

136 Modern energy solutions and techniques were considered with the objective of achieving energy independence. In this sense, the building creates a sustainable and economical reference for its environment.

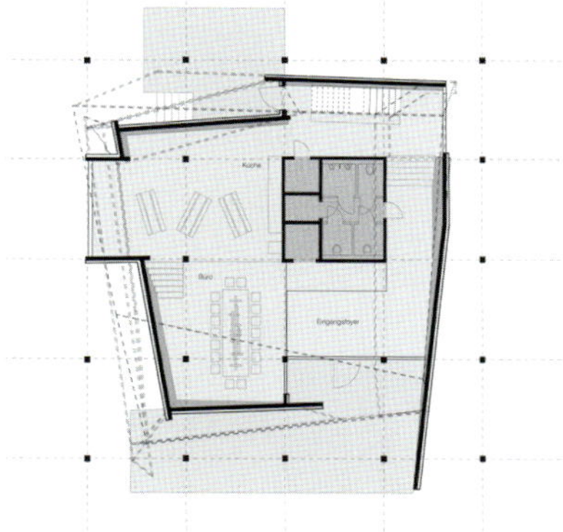

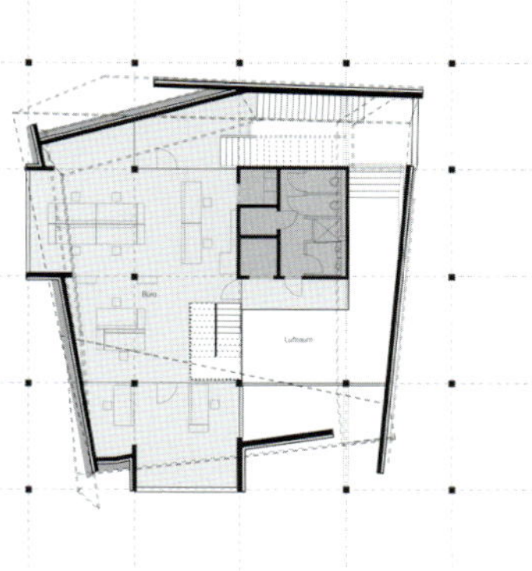

137 The entire interior and exterior structure is designed around energy saving. A very low heat transfer coefficient is achieved with 52 cm thick walls.

138 Following the minor consideration of the "go to work" concept, the meeting points were integrated with the lounges and relaxation areas, and a gym, pools, communal areas and a climbing wall were also installed.

139 The entire structure was created with wood: the interior with spruce and the exterior with larch. Canadian pine was the wood chosen for the roof.

Once again, the ephemeral element of this building is the constant change of use. The remaining 5,000 m^2 area can be used to create a garden or even places for keeping animals.

141—143

Tricentenari. Installations

BARCELONA, SPAIN, 2014

CLIENT
OFICINA TÈCNICA TRICENTENARI BCN AND FUNDACIÓ ENRIC MIRALLES

BCN RE.SET is a circuit of ephemeral architecture created in the street and was part of the Tricentenari commemorative activities, which commemorated the 300th anniversary of the events of 11th September 1714 in the city of Barcelona.

This collection of ephemeral interventions in a public space consists of seven installations that propose a reflection on concepts such as memory, identity, diversity, democracy and freedom, among others. They were designed by interna-
142 tionally renowned architects.

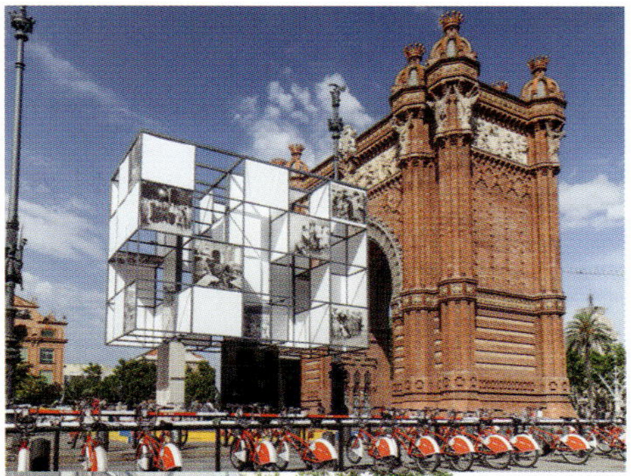

Architect Benedetta Tagliabue and sceneographer Àlex Ollé were the project curators and joint creators of the first installation. It was unveiled on May 29th at the Parc de la Ciutadella with the title
143 *Ciutadella Wall*

144 *Ciutadella Wall.* The first of the installations, consisting of a steel and concrete structure of 67 metres in length and a height that oscillates between four and seven metres. This wall reinterprets Barcelona's ancient historic wall and symbolises the current walls. It invites the visitor to reflect and play.

Tricentenari. Ciutadella Wall

BENEDETTA TAGLIABUE + EMBT,
ÀLEX OLLÉ + INSTITUT DEL TEATRE

AREA
N/A

PHOTO
© JAIME ROJAS, MARCELA GRASSI,
BENEDETTA TAGLIABUE + EMBT

Tricentenari. Memory

GRAFTON ARCHITECTS, ELISAVA / UPF

AREA
N/A
PHOTO
© JAIME ROJAS, MARCELA GRASSI, BENEDETTA TAGLIABUE + EMBT, RUNZE HU & JAIME FONT, EUGENI BACH & ALBERT CABRER

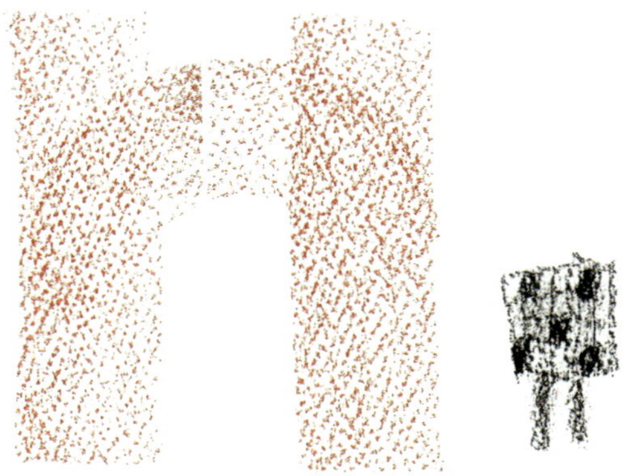

Memory. Erected over a painted wooden platform, the installation comprises a large nine-metre structure with images of the early 20th century taken by photographer Joan Branguli comprise the installation. There are also seven clay models representing different types of housing from pre-Roman times to the twentieth century.

Tricentenari. Identity

URBANUS, LA SALLE / URL

SURFACE
N.D.

PHOTO
© JAIME ROJAS, MARCELA GRASSI, BENEDETTA TAGLIABUE + EMBT, RUNZE HU & JAIME FONT, EUGENI BACH & ALBERT CABRER

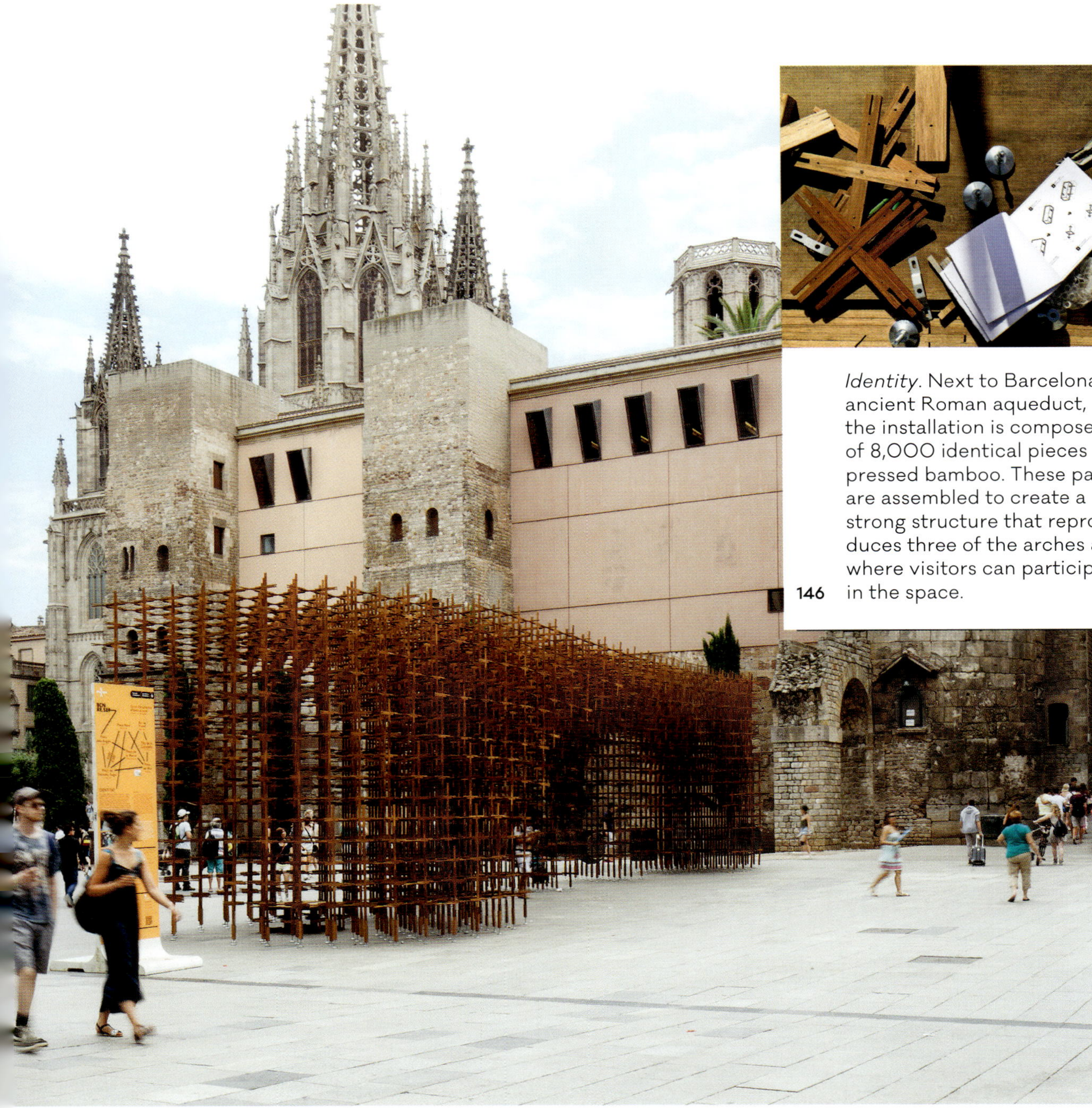

Identity. Next to Barcelona's ancient Roman aqueduct, the installation is composed of 8,000 identical pieces of pressed bamboo. These parts are assembled to create a strong structure that reproduces three of the arches and where visitors can participate in the space.

Tricentenari. Diversity

ODILE DECQ, RECETAS COLECTIVAS

AREA
N/A

PHOTO
© JAIME ROJAS, MARCELA GRASSI, BENEDETTA TAGLIABUE + EMBT

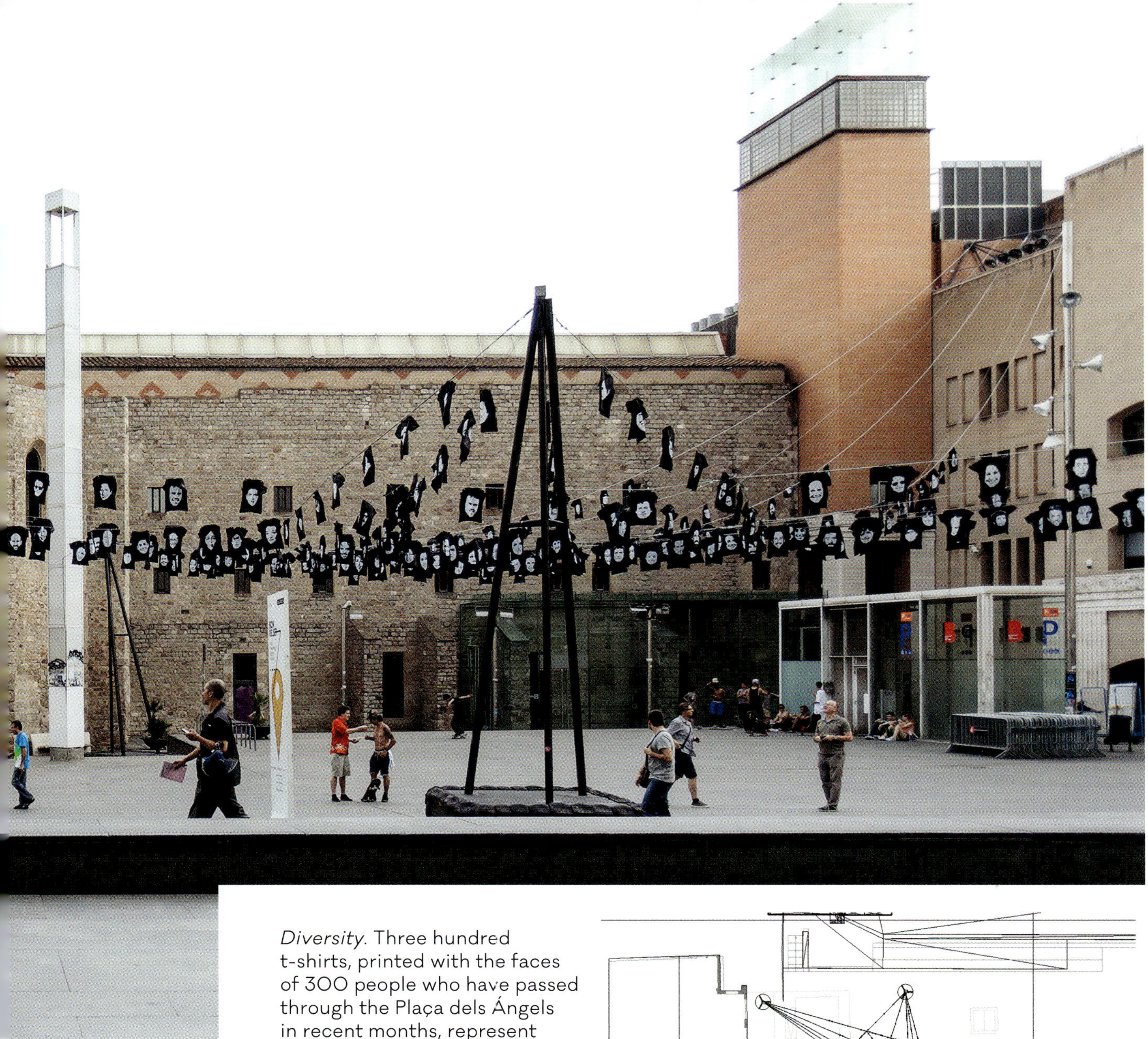

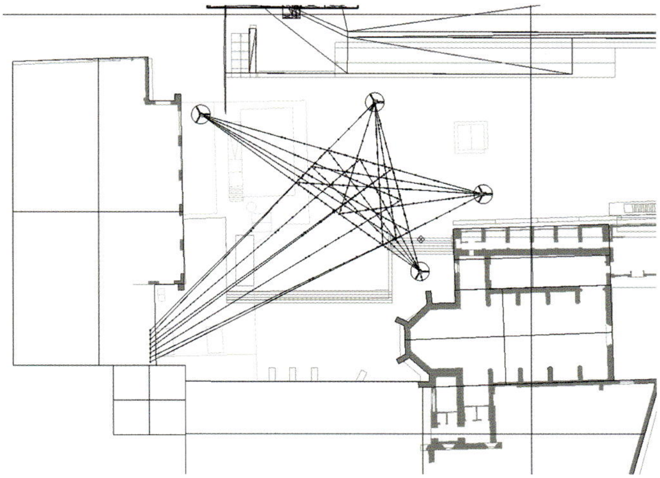

Diversity. Three hundred t-shirts, printed with the faces of 300 people who have passed through the Plaça dels Ángels in recent months, represent the diverse nature of the city of Barcelona. This installation provides shade and serves as a tribute to the Mediterranean tradition of hanging wet clothes to dry in courtyards and on rooftops.

Liberty. The power of liberty is expressed through reading. For this reason, the architects have created an installation that consists of three different trees situated in the Plaça de Salvador Seguí. The trunks and branches are made from steel and the ground from concrete. The leaves function as permeable shade so the
148 public can sit under them.

Tricentenari. Freedom

ANUPAMA KUNDOO ARCHITECTS, IAAC

AREA
400 m²

PHOTO
© ANUPAMA KUNDOO ARCHITECTS, JAIME ROJAS, JAVIER CALLEJAS, MARCELA GRASSI, BENEDETTA TAGLIABUE + EMBT

Democracy. "Walking down the aisle" is a traditional part of the wedding ceremony. At one end of the Plaça de la Mercè, there is a registry office and at the other, the Basílica de la Mercè. The installation is suspended in the centre and is composed of an enormous blue inflatable that symbolises human rights.

Tricentenari. Democracy

YAEL REISNER, PETER COOK, STRADDLE 3

AREA
N/A

PHOTO
© JAIME ROJAS, MARCELA GRASSI, BENEDETTA TAGLIABUE + EMBT

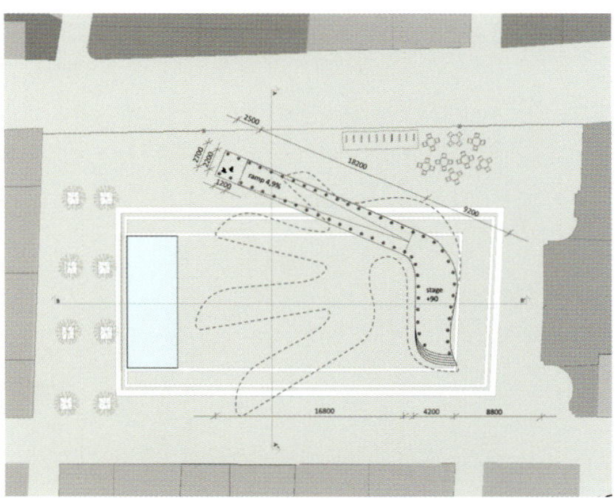

150

Tricentenari. Europe

ETH ZURICH, URBAN-THINK TANK, ESARQ / UIC

AREA
N/A

PHOTO
© JAIME ROJAS, MARCELA GRASSI, BENEDETTA TAGLIABUE + EMBT

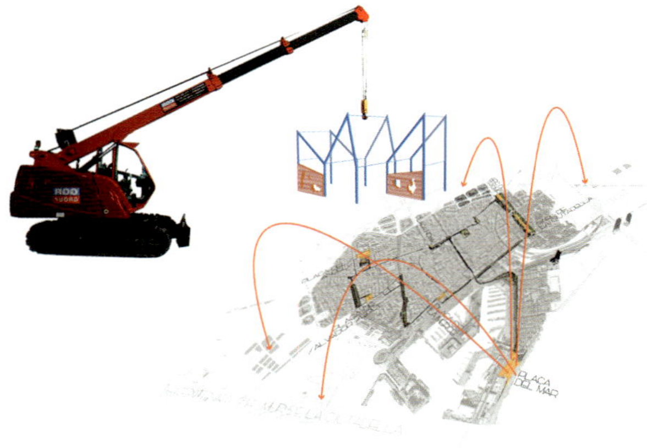

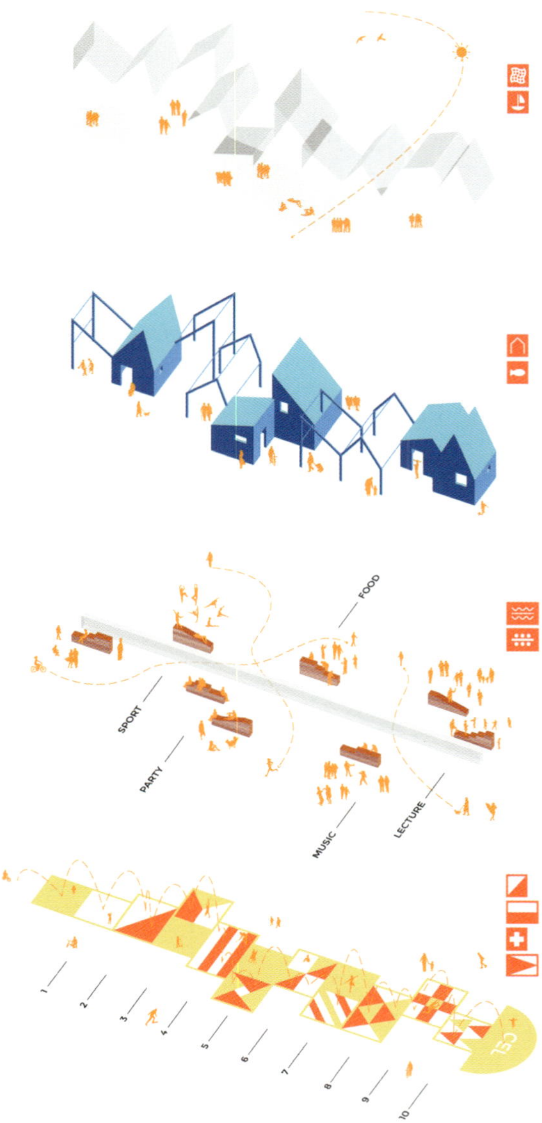

Europe. The concept of this installation is based on hopscotch, a children's game that is played in almost all European countries. A covered steel structure was constructed that recreated traditional beach huts. The giant hopscotch grid painted on the floor encouraged visitors to play.

Metropol Parasol

J. MAYER H. UND PARTNER ARCHITEKTEN

SEVILLE, SPAIN, 2011
AREA
5,000 m^2
CLIENT
SEVILLE CITY COUNCIL, SACYR
PHOTO
© NIKKOL ROT FOTOGRAFIE

151 The project is a multifunctional structure inside which there are places for leisure and relaxation, markets, various shops and an area that plays the primary role of the construction: being a great viewpoint.

152 Its large structure and original shapes are the main attraction for tourists and architecture lovers. The height of the construction is 28.50 metres and it has a total of four floors.

153 Known as "Mushrooms of the incarnation", it is the world's largest wooden structure. It has four large wooden columns that accommodate the access lifts for its four floors.

154 It has become a cultural and tourist landmark in Seville's Plaza de la Encarnación, described by many visitors and admirers as the Andalusian capital's new contemporary city centre.

155 It measures approximately 150 x 70 metres and was the winning project of a public competition organised by the Seville city council. The objective of the winning project was to completely change the appearance of the square.

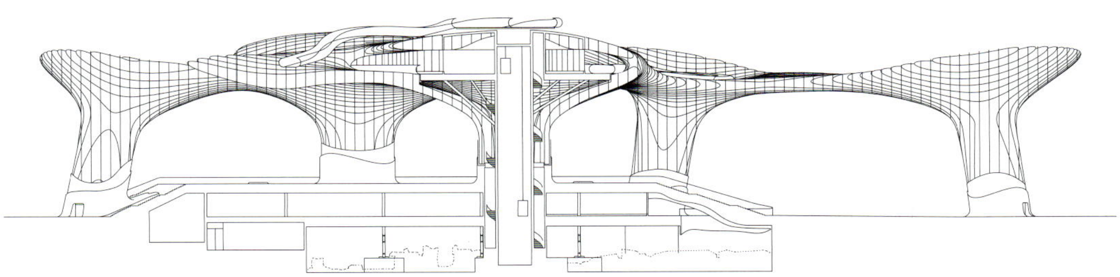

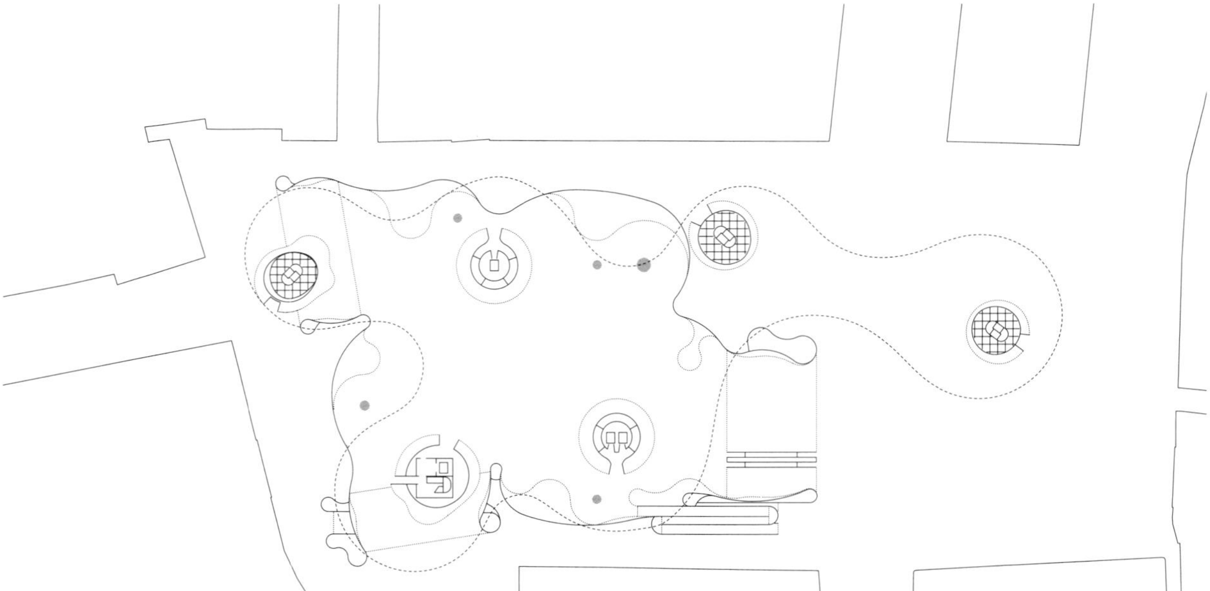

The result of the project was somewhat different to the original idea: during its construction they opted to replace metal with wood to optimise the development and construction of the structure.

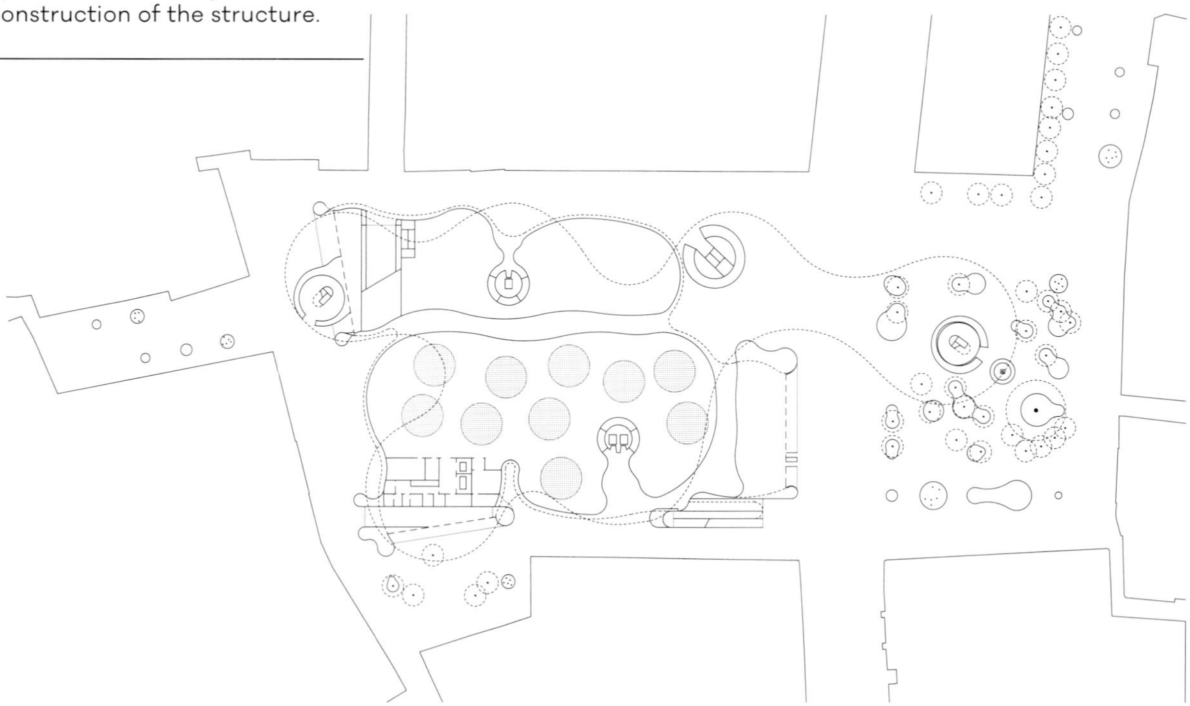

The large wooden structure that gives form to this project is covered by a polyurethane cover that provides a perfect finish. This, in conjunction with the outstanding parasols and curved forms, creates a stunning visual effect.

158—160

This is a highly active infra-
structure that, on one hand,
promotes the premises that
are inside and, on the other,
attracts foreign tourism to
158 the square.

The fusion between the lines
that are reminiscent of a cluster
of mushrooms, has led to the
structure becoming a recog-
nisable international landmark
159 as well as a visitor attraction.

In January 2013, the project
was selected as one of the
five finalists from a total of
420 projects for the European
Union Prize for Contemporary
Architecture – Mies van der
160 Rohe Award.

There Were Once Two Villages...

CRISTINA BESTRATÉN, AINA BIGORRA,
ERIK HERRERA + DONDECABENTRES

RIVAS-VACIAMADRID, SPAIN, 2008

AREA
N/A

CLIENT
CULTURA EN LA CALLE FESTIVAL, RIVAS-VACIAMADRID CITY COUNCIL

PHOTO
© DONDECABENTRES

161 Through the sculptural array of pieces of wood, a relationship of identity is created between the historical memory of the place and the visitor.

162 A construction with pieces that are different but equal at the same time: different forms but identical materials. The structure is characterised by being deep but not thick, open but intimate.

163 Interaction with the past and reuniting generations are the main functions of the project.

164 The scenography for this installation is constructed using a common pattern with variations. Each piece of wood is unique and represents the profile of a home.

165 The aim of the installation is to become a landmark with a distinctive social character that represents the location and its memory.

166 Inviting imagination and play, the installation makes it easy for visitors to convert each one of the parts into their own home. All of them together will be a village.

167 A series of more suggestive and active pieces invite the user to interact. The location becomes an action, attraction and play space for young and old.

169 One of the main pieces of the structure is "El cuenta-cuentos" (The storyteller). Inside, the visitor is invited to share stories and create a collective space full of magic, recollection and happy memories.

168 A place where children make memories and adults recall trips to their relatives' villages, connecting different generations.

170 It seeks to create a physical space capable of accommodating each inhabitant's small emotional spaces. A place of reflection, distraction and journeying to the fondest memories.

Shell.ter

LIKEARCHITECTS

VILA NOVA DE CERVEIRA, PORTUGAL, 2012

AREA
23 m^2

CLIENT
CANAL 180, VILA NOVA DE CERVEIRA CITY COUNCIL

PHOTO
© JOÃO MARQUES, EVA VIEIRA, JOSÉ CALISTO

171 Rather than using them for their normal purpose, chairs are used to create pavilion-style arches, providing rest, shade and a new decorative feature in the place where they are installed.

172 Throughout June, the Lazer do Castelinho park is displaying this structure of 168 chairs that occupies an area of 23 m^2 and serves as a decorative feature during the LIKEarchitects summer workshop held in the park.

173 In the gardens of a national park in the north of Portugal, this original pavilion was installed, constructed exclusively from organised and stacked blocks of plastic chairs.

174 As if it were a tunnel, it invites observers to walk through it and contemplate how the chairs act as pergola-style roof and walls, creating a place to rest, sheltered from the sun.

175 Because of the sun's rays a shadow is cast upon the structure itself, creating an even more sophisticated effect. This attracts visitors who approach the pavilion to view it.

176 A simple framework formed by white plastic chairs is enough to create a space that arouses the curiosity of the public without creating any environmental impact. Its simple structure allows it to be moved quickly and easily.

177 On the banks of the river that crosses the park, children can run through the structure as if it were a play area, protected from the sun by the canopy created.

178 From a distance, the shape of the pavilion appears complex, when in reality it is no more than a set of arches created with chairs arranged so that rather than act as seating, they become a decorative feature.

179 An arrangement of white plastic chairs is enough to create a temporary and economical decorative feature. In this sense, the cost of production and transport has been minimal.

180 Once the month of June was over, the white plastic tunnel was disassembled and can be used as a sun shelter, relaxation space and play area in other parks or public spaces that would offer this type of exhibition.

The Peace Pavilion

ATELIER ZÜNDEL CRISTEA

LONDON, UNITED KINGDOM, 2013

AREA
62 m²

CLIENT
ARCH TRIUMPH

PHOTO
© SERGIO GRACIA/
ATELIER ZÜNDEL CRISTEA

181 The inflatable pavilion was installed in Bethnal Green Gardens during the summer of 2013 with the idea of providing a space for resting, socialising, conversing, escaping and enjoying the surrounding natural space.

182 The creators wanted to convey a message of peace and harmony. They sought to symbolise silence, purity, tranquillity and casualness through a piece that can be freely observed.

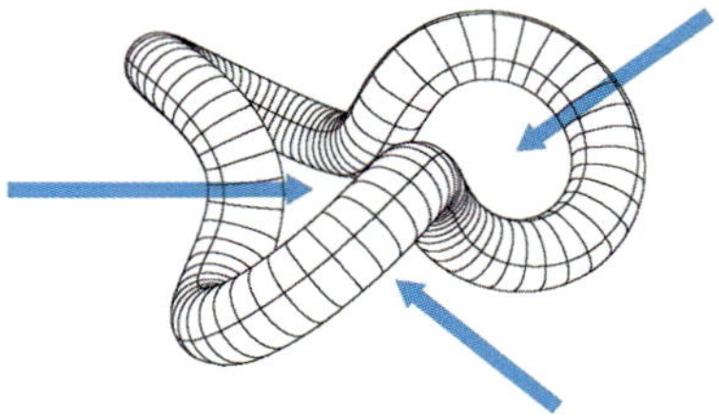

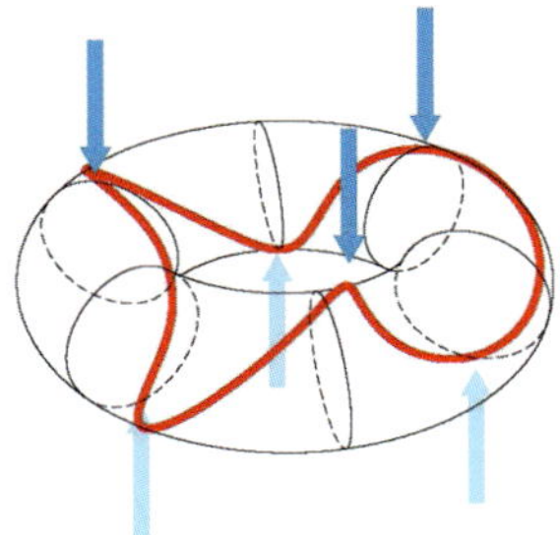

185 Based on precise geometric research, a perfect symmetrical PVC structure was created. With a height of 4 metres and area of 62 m², the installation can be assembled, disassembled and transported easily.

186 149 m² of PVC membrane and 47.4 m² of air were needed to create this structure based on simplicity and portability. It shows that an impressive structure can be achieved with materials that are this simple and easy to use.

183 A polished aluminium and wood base, united with air and PVC treated membrane resulted in this structure that pays homage to the ancient pyramids.

184 After it has been removed from the gardens, the pavilion will be sold to a collectors or museums so that it can travel through different countries and can be viewed by people from all cultures and social conditions.

187 Inside the pavilion, chairs invite rest and contemplation of the installation from inside.

188 The PVC membrane was protected by security guards to prevent graffiti on the walls or other actions that might endanger the structure.

189 The architects' main idea was to design a structure that would convey peace and become an interactive space for its visitors where they could walk, relax and take interest in the represented cause.

190 The large size of the structure, together with the white colour contrasting against the green of the gardens, produces a striking visual effect and transforms a simple garden into a place that must be visited.

TorÚs

ENRIQUE SORIANO, PEP TORNABELL + CODA-OFFICE

BARCELONA, SPAIN, 2013
AREA
N/A
PHOTO
© ANDRES FLAJSZER
CLIENT
ÚSBARCELONA

191 The installation was commissioned by the ÚSBarcelona festival organisers with very clear conditions: a very limited budget and very little time to complete assembly and disassembly.

192 The project sought to create the lowest ecological impact, using lightweight technology that could be applied to transformable kinetic structures. Instead of hinges or anchors, it was decided to use elements that were elastic and flexible to enable manipulation.

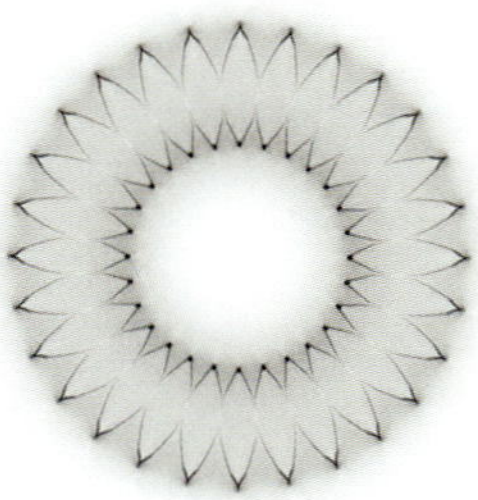

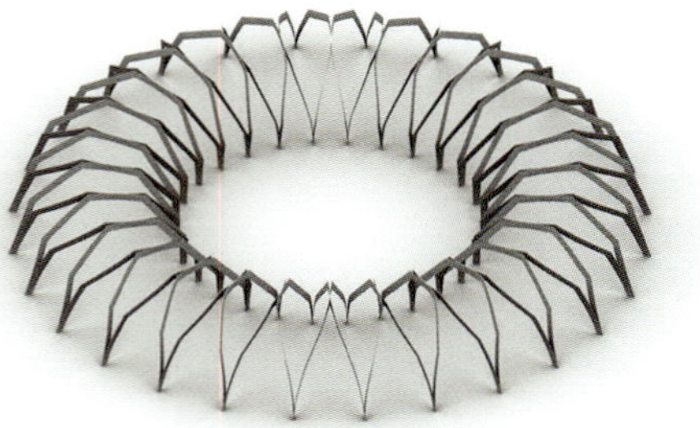

193 The structure is based on an independent arch-shaped section, which allows the installation's own weight to be discharged. A toroid was also constructed by closing one of the curves.

194 Flexible wood was used to give the installation a curved form and circular trajectory. The interior is simple and spacious, sufficient for the task for it was made for.

195 Each arch is deployed until it meets the next one where it is fixed. The structure's flexibility means that it can be folded away in just twenty minutes with the help of four people.

196 The material used, in this case flexible wood, as well as the dry construction procedure, contributed to the project's completion within the established deadlines.

199 The arch was designed to fit into a plywood board. This minimised the amount of material required for the structure and simplified the logistical processes involved.

197 Using the play that the wood used can give, and exploiting its potential to the maximum, a structure was successfully created that could easily be installed, disassembled and transported.

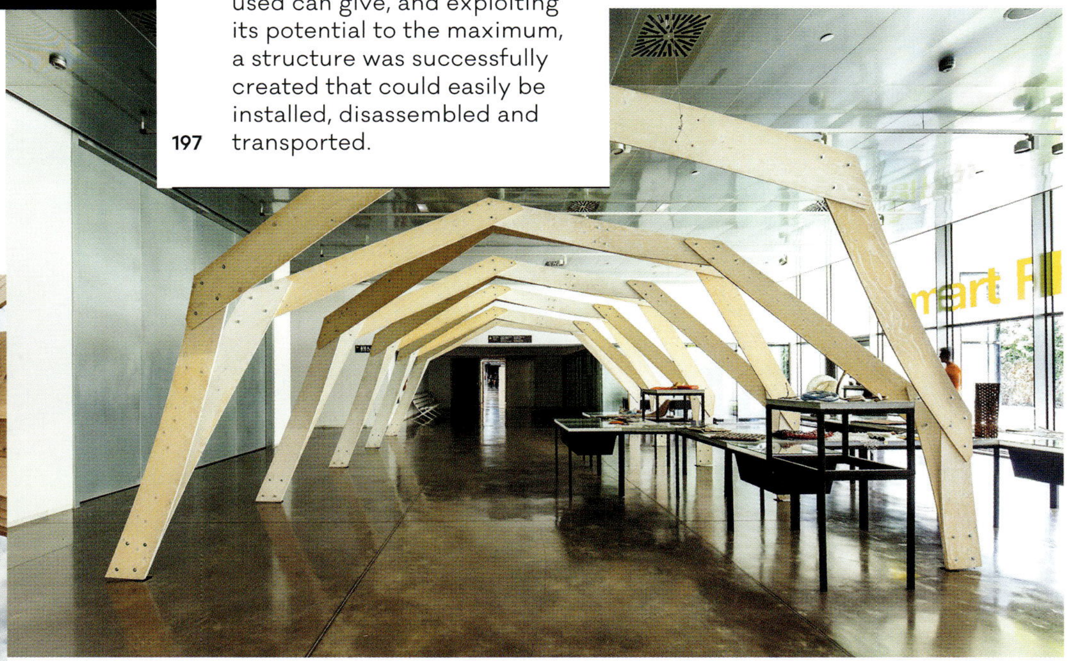

198 It is a deployable experimental structure. Its most unusual aspect is that it has no hinges; its transformation is based on the elastic deformation of the material used.

200 The project remained installed during the festival and accommodated various activities. One of its uses after being disassembled was as a linear community greenhouse.

playLAND

LIKEARCHITECTS

PAREDES DE COURA, PORTUGAL, 2014

AREA
TUNNEL 15 m^2; SILO 10 m^2; STAGE 36 m^2

CLIENT
O MUNDO AO CONTRÁRIO, PAREDES DE COURA CITY COUNCIL

PHOTO
© DINIS SOTTOMAYOR PHOTOGRAPHY

The artistic installation
is composed entirely of a
collection of inflatable swim
rings of different colours that
are organised and arranged
to create a fun tunnel of 15 m
201 in length with an area of 36 m^2.

The simplicity of the design
and the versatility of the
rings allow all sorts of designs
and forms to be created for
the installation in very little
time. Due to this special
characteristic, the visual result
is different on each day
202 that passes.

playLAND was created with
the intention of changing a
quiet village in the north of
Portugal into a children's play
area for the duration of one
week. Performances, games
and entertainment were the
203 highlights of the week.

The installation has three
notable spaces and moments:
the more informal zone where
children's shows are performed,
the circular tower where
children can play and jump,
and the tunnel-shaped pavilion
204 that they can run through.

205 Vivid colours such as orange, green and pink create a world of light and fun using a simple swim ring.

206 Swim rings that inflate and deflate are used to create a sense of space and volume, as well as the opportunity to design different installations every day for a daily change of the project's aesthetics.

207 Organising the swim rings in a circular manner creates a rest area that protects visitors from the sun. It is also a place to rest whilst attending a concert or a story telling.

208 For a few days, Paredes de Coura was transformed into a recreational space which recreated a Lego structure to human scale and could rapidly and simply be transformed and disassembled.

209 Ease of transport and the fact that the swim rings could be inflated and deflated meant that ephemeral and fun forms could be constructed on a large scale in a very short space of time and without the need for a large financial investment.

210 The three spatial interventions were created for *O Mundo ao Contrário*, which means "the world in reverse". It was a week-long event where a playground was created with a street theatre, concerts, circus and installations.

Bus Stop Symbiosys

LIKEARCHITECTS

PORTO, PORTUGAL, 2010

AREA
10 m^2

CLIENT
ADDICT - AGÊNCIA PARA O DESENVOLVIMENTO DAS INDÚSTRIAS CRIATIVAS

PHOTO
© DINIS SOTTOMAYOR PHOTOGRAPHY, DIOGO AGUIAR, MANUEL MAGALHÃES

211 In 2010, ADDICT- Agência para o Desenvolvimento das Indústrias Criativas, suggested a temporary structures competition to improve the daily lives of the citizens of this tourist city.

214 Bus Stop Symbiosys is a structure attached to the canopy of the bus stop that insinuates, but does not explain, its function, leaving the citizen to interpret its use.

212 Aside from the small budget, innovation was especially important, as well as the integration of the proposed item into the urban landscape and its easy assembly and disassembly.

213 The site chosen for this project was Largo dos Lóios, an important communications hub in the city's historical quarter where there were three anodyne bus stops.

215 It resembles a worm or a new Loch Ness monster resting on one of the sides of the bus stop and provides extra seating for users.

216 This urban happening creates a new spatial relationship with a pre-existing element – the canopy – and revalues it to gain visibility for the two structures in a relationship that is certainly symbiotic.

219 The structure not only increases the seating area, it also invites people to amuse themselves, reconsider and rethink the urban space.

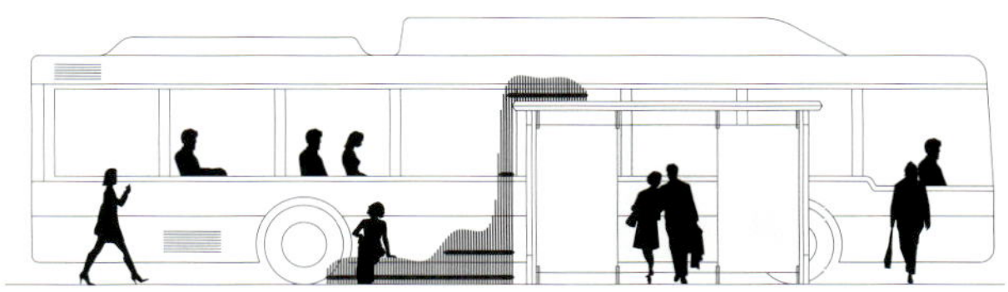

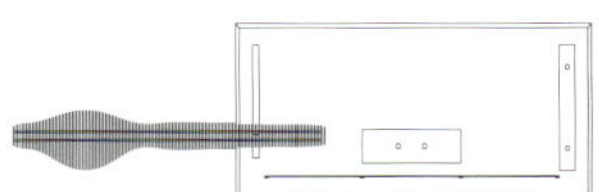

217 Taking advantage of the dichotomy between new and old, the installation is designed as a *plug-in* for the historic quarter, clearly claiming and reclaiming that it is situated in a contemporary city.

218 The ninety seven 16 mm panels that form this colourful serpent were digitally designed and cut. They were designed, produced and installed in a few days.

220 **The LIKEarchitects installation certainly created expectations during the time it was on show: Is it a bench? A sculpture? A piece of urban art? It is a design open to exploration.**

Frozen Trees II

LIKEARCHITECTS

LONDON, UNITED KINGDOM, 2014

AREA
250 m^2

CLIENT
GET LIVING LONDON

PHOTO
© ANDREIA GARCIA PHOTOGRAPHY

221 A collection of plastic bag dispensers gave rise to the Christmas installation. Like frozen trees, they decorate an outer surface of 250 m^2.

222 The translucent plastic of the Ikea dispensers is perfect to use with illumination for the installation. The light can pass through the holes and illuminate the space.

223 Each tree contained monochrome white LED bulbs. These have a low energy consumption and allow the light to be adjusted in order to control its impact.

224 The pre-fabricated structure is light and easy to assemble. It is easy and fast to transport and install, meaning that it can easily be installed anywhere.

Hundreds of dispensers are used to create a total of thirty trees. When night falls, these are softly illuminated and create an atmosphere full of fantasy and Christmas spirit.
225

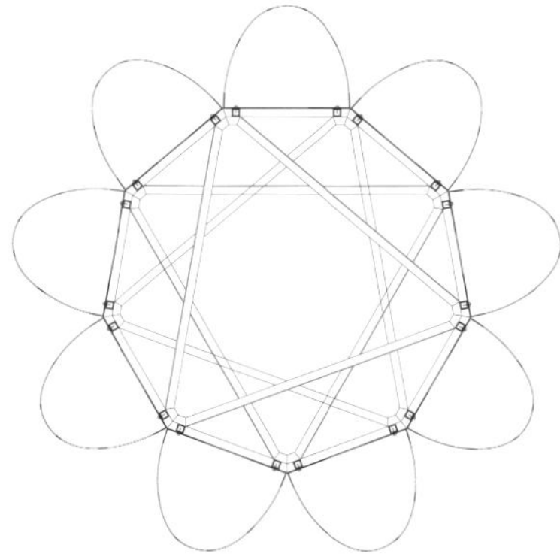

All the cylinders, or Christmas trees, have a height of 3.6 metres. The form and size of each structure are the characteristic features that attract those who pass through
229 the surrounding area.

There are three different shapes: the bases of five, ten or fifteen boxes define the width of the towers. On the other hand, the height of the
230 30 structures is the same.

The energy for lighting each tree is provided by a car battery. This ensures that the installation is low-cost and lasts throughout the festive
226 Christmas period.

The pieces of polypropylene are reusable and recyclable. This also allows the installation to be transported and enjoyed
227 in other locations.

The illumination is provided by forty five 12 volt car batteries, ten chargers and 330 metres
228 of white LED tape.

Tripod

LIKEARCHITECTS

PORTO, PORTUGAL, 2013

AREA
2 m^2

CLIENT
LOCOMOTIVA-PORTO LAZER

PHOTO
© JOSÉ CAMPOS PHOTOGRAPHY

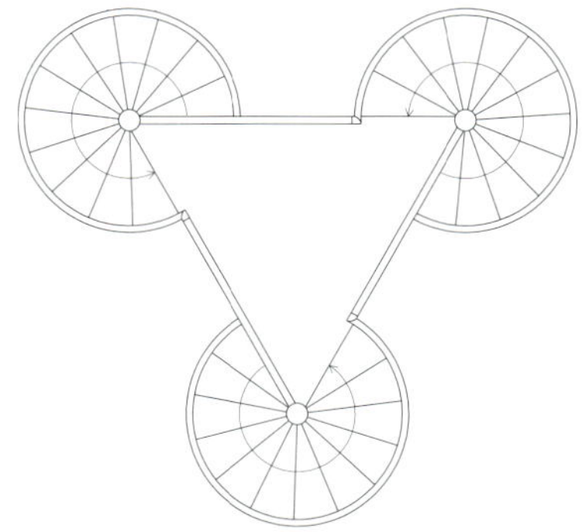

231 The structure is a small tribute that the architects wanted to make to two of Porto's most characteristic features: steps and balconies. It is a steel construction with a surface area of 2 m^2.

232 It is composed of six purple steel parts attached to a concrete base. The arrangement of these creates three spiral staircases whose interiors connect, and a balcony at the top.

233 The design is based on the shape of an equilateral triangle so that a staircase can be created on each side of the structure. At the top, there is a small completely open balcony.

234 The purpose of Tripod is to cause amazement and admiration when visitors climb it to discover the city. At the same time, they are also being observed by the people around the structure.

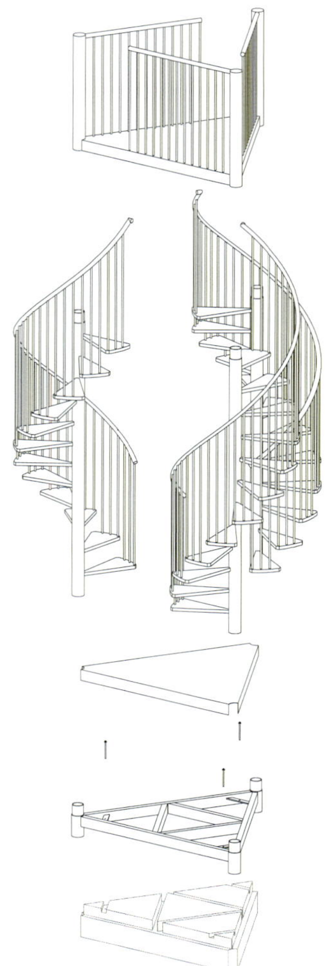

235 With this structure, the architects are paying homage to the city's famous steps, such as those at the entrance to the Casa da Música, and to the traditional balconies that can be seen in the 19th century historical quarter.

236 The assembly was exhibited for the first time in Porto's Largo de São Domingos during the month of March. In June 2015, it reappeared in Largo da Rua Chã, this time painted a different colour.

237 The route established when we climb the installation is always the same: climb up, contemplate the landscape from the balcony and go back down. The reference to the endless clover leaf knot is achieved with the three staircases.

238 Once it has been installed, Tripod has two functions: to decorate the square and to serve as a children's play area.

239 The simple structure allows it to be assembled in various places quickly and without complications. The design of its base fits seamlessly with the surrounding area.

240 The Tripod design team was inspired by the work of the Dutch artist M.C. Escher. There were also outstanding references when it came to designing the structure: the Möbius strip and the clover leaf knot.

Mur

ANNA PRATS, JOAN VALLS

BARCELONA, SPAIN, 2014
AREA
140 m^2
CLIENT
FIRA DEL COMERÇ DE SANT ANTONI
PHOTO
© ANNA PRATS, JOAN VALLS

241 The wall or partition is composed of a total of 728 Moritz beer crates which the brand offered to the market for holding the trade fair in Barcelona's famous Mercat de Sant Antoni.

242 The objective was to create a single decorative separating element. The objective was that it should have volume and presence, be seen from a distance and help to identify the fair as a special event for the neighbourhood.

243 From a distance, the wall looks almost opaque. However, if directly observed, it becomes almost transparent since the free spaces between the crates provide a view of what is happening on the other side.

244 Based on the set of crates that the sponsor offered to the traders, the idea arose to create a large wall of stacked crates that would serve as partitions and also as shelving.

245 The crates are arranged so that the spaces between them spell the word FIRANTONI The spaces that serve as letters are perfect for seeing what is happening on the other side of the wall.

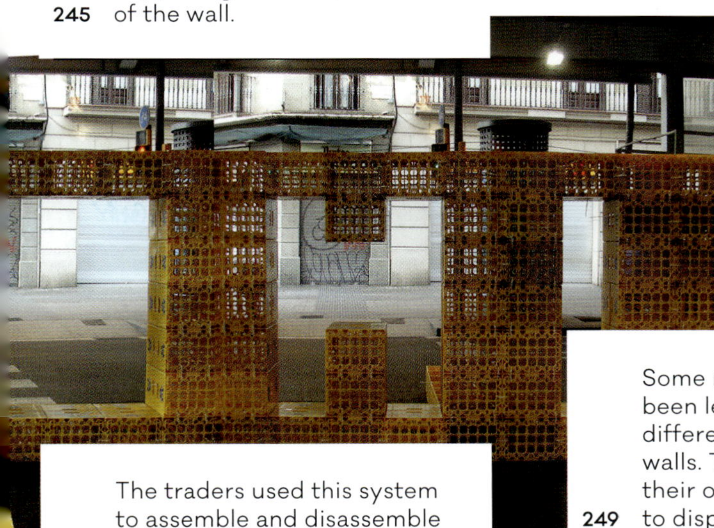

246 The traders used this system to assemble and disassemble the walls in very little time. Once dismantled, the crates could be piled up and kept in a corner, occupying hardly any space.

247 This fair is where the neighbourhood traders display their products in a festive atmosphere. Throughout the fair, all kinds of activities take place with the aim of revitalising the neighbourhood's trading.

248 The aim of the competition was to design and install spacers between the fair stalls. The designs were carried out in two hours by the members of the winning teams and they were installed during the fair.

249 Some rows of crates have been left out, separating and differentiating neighbouring walls. This way, each trader has their own demarcated space to display their products.

250 The beer crates demarcate a total of 20 points of sale and 6,000 plastic cable ties were needed to anchor them. The assembly and disassembly of the partition was carried out with volunteers.

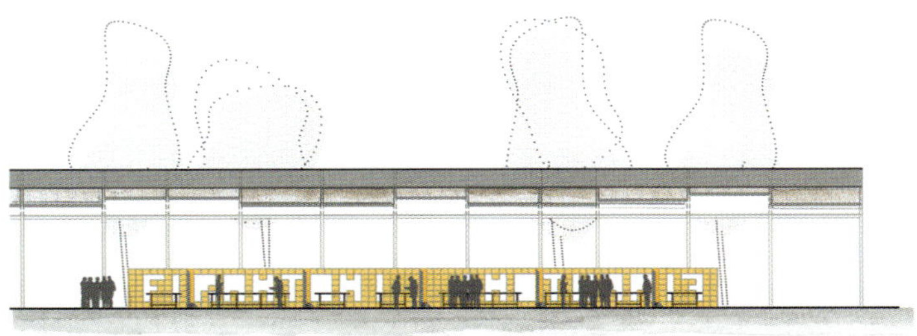

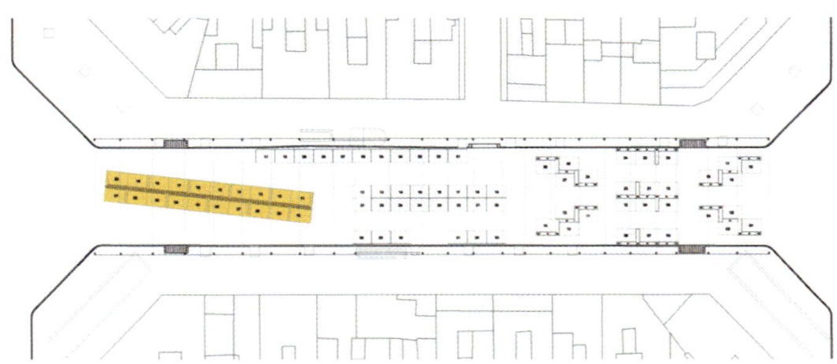

Wireframe Tower

LIKEARCHITECTS

VILA NOVA DE CERVEIRA, PORTUGAL, 2012

AREA
10 m^2

CLIENT
CANAL 180, VILA NOVA DE CERVEIRA CITY COUNCIL

PHOTO
© JOANA DOMINGUES

251 The idea to construct the Wireframe tower arose during one of the summer workshops organised by LIKEarchitects. The original shape of the clothes horses was used and gave rise to the 10 m^2 installation.

252 During the course of the day, taking advantage of the natural light, the project was fused with the urban context of the location. This creates a dense, linear and geometric shadow on the pavement.

253 The assembly of the Wireframe tower is quick and simple. This allows the installation to be transported to different locations and assembled in squares and human transit zones, with hardly any effort.

254 During the day, the installation does not go unnoticed but may be less attractive in the eyes of those who view it. When night falls, its illumination completely transforms it into a visually spectacular piece.

255 An item as ordinary as a rack for drying clothes, with its traditional colours, is converted into a work of art viewed by hundreds of people.

257 The ends of the clothes horses can be opened and closed so the extendible flaps are converted into the structure's mutable skin, introducing diversity to its contours.

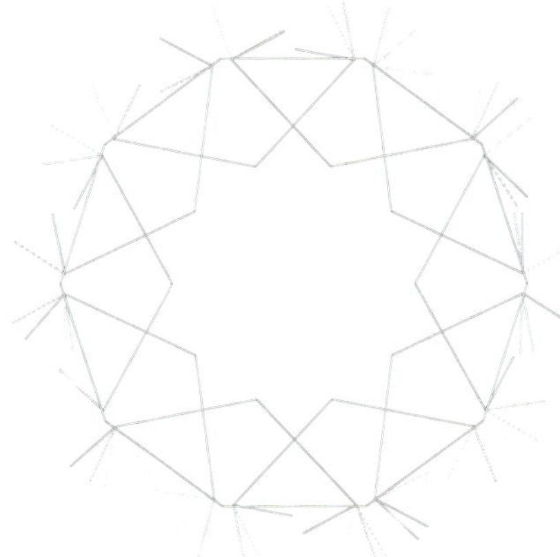

259 The use of the drying rack as a metric module for the assembly provides a series of vertical associations that benefit the structure. The extendible flaps are revealed before the compact lines of the piece's contours.

260 The installation is arranged around a decagonal prism and is located in the main square of the historical quarter so it can be viewed by citizens as well as tourists visiting the city.

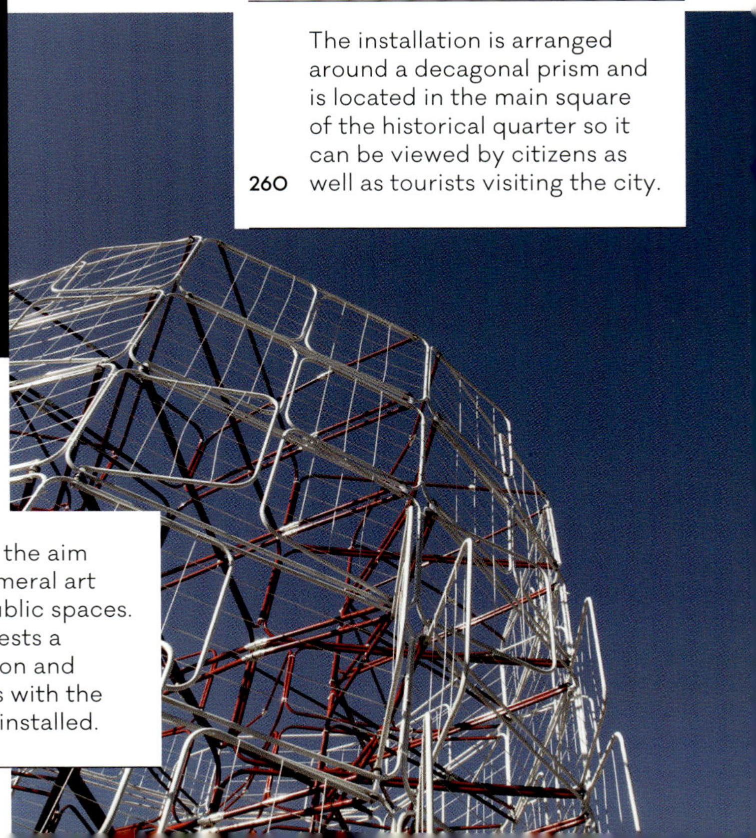

256 When the night falls, the structure is illuminated and the view is transformed: the white colour enhances the external aspects while the red shows the details of the interior.

258 It was created with the aim of promoting ephemeral art and creativity in public spaces. The structure suggests a defence construction and creates strong links with the place in which it is installed.

Water Out to Dry

CRISTINA BESTRATÉN, AINA BIGORRA, ERIK HERRERA + DONDECABENTRES

CALDES DE MONTBUI, SPAIN, 2012

AREA
N/A

CLIENT
MIAU (INDEPENDENT FESTIVAL OF URBAN ART)

PHOTO
© DONDECABENTRES

261 Clothes hanging on roofs and balconies are a familiar sight in Mediterranean villages and towns. An everyday activity that has inspired this project with great visual impact.

262 Changing appearance, attracting glances, transforming a laundry into a visual attraction using poetry and metaphor. A projected loaded with colours, simplicity and originality.

263 The project concept is simple. It reverses the order and function of the elements: washing water in warm clothes and storing it in little bags as a decorative showcase. Water is the main feature of the project.

264 Based on the idea of "hanging clothes", the project seeks to transform the concept to achieve an effect in which colours and water are the main features. Poetic play and a change of look that transforms a neutral scenario such as a clothesline.

265 This is an artistic attraction that attracts the eye of all those who pass around it. A simple clothesline is transformed into an improvised museum open to the public, an original multicoloured poetic play.

268 This intervention is based on poetry and the metaphor of distorting the ordinary and transforming it into an ephemeral installation, resulting in the space appearing to be totally renovated.

266 A collection of plastic bags filled with coloured liquids is all that is needed to transform an area dedicated to hanging clothes into an artistic space, which attracts the gaze of passers-by.

267 This project is aimed at emphasising this symbol from an artistic perspective and at converting an ordinary space into a small open-air museum where the main attraction is simple bags full of coloured water.

269 The project proves the aspect of a place can be changed without large sizes or costly materials, and proposes a reflection on culture and tradition.

270 The installation could be seen in October 2012 in Caldes de Montbui and was erected by MIAU (Independent Festival of Urban Art). The result was an artistic ephemeral art action: transforming a simple façade into a colourful showcase.

Tourne*Around*

CRISTINA BESTRATÉN, AINA BIGORRA,
ERIK HERRERA + DONDECABENTRES

MONTPELLIER, FRANCE, 2012

AREA
93.7 m^2

CLIENT
HOTEL AUDESSAN

PHOTO
© DONDECABENTRES,
PAUL KOZLOWSKI

271 The aim of the project is to transform a courtyard using mirrors to achieve the effect of multiplying its details, forms and spaces. This completely modifies its appearance and main function.

272 The aim isn't for the installation to become a prominent feature, instead it works to change the reality of its environment.

273 The project is created using elements as simple, economical and easy to acquire as cleaning wipes, mirrors that act as telescopes, metal buckets, small pieces of wood, screws and soil.

274 As if it were a flowerpot with sunflowers, a structure is created with a metal bucket for the base, and the wipes surround the mirror representing the sunflower's petals.

275 Telescopic mirrors are used to function like sunflowers, adapting to the place and reflecting the ground, the entrance door, the sky and the façades in the courtyard.

276 A different outline can be created every day thanks to the use of individual buckets as project components. The same occurs with the mirrors, which can be set at different heights and arrangements as desired.

277 Throughout the day, the appearance of the installation changes, showing different lines and outlines at the beginning of the day, at noon, in the afternoon and at the end of the day, taking advantage of the sun to create the desired effect.

280 The everyday items that constitute the project invite visitors to reproduce it in their homes.

278 The role played by the mirrors is paramount to the installation as they help to play with the perspective of its surroundings; they create distinct reflections and angles that make better use of the space where they are installed.

279 It is a temporary project, perfect for transporting and using in different spaces and environments. Being composed of individual items, it is ideal for all kinds of surfaces, both interior and exterior.

Built to Wear

BALL-NOGUES STUDIO

SHENZHEN, CHINA, 2010

AREA
N/A

CLIENT
SHENZHEN HONG KONG BIENNALE OF URBANISM

PHOTO
© BALL NOGUES STUDIO

Constructed in 2009 for
the Biennale of Urbanism
in Hong Kong, *Built to Wear*
was constructed in the under-
ground space of the Shenzen
281 civic square.

It is a large architectural
scale structure hung from the
ceiling and was created using
hundreds of items of clothing
manufactured by the largest
clothing company in the United
282 States, American Apparel.

This project comprises a
suggestive and original mixture
of G-strings, bathing suits,
t-shirts, vests, dresses, baby
clothes and other types of
garments. As the installation
was dismantled, the garments
283 were given to visitors.

The structure has a double
function: to demonstrate
that green architecture is
achievable as only clothing
was needed to create this
structure, and to provoke
the discreet and almost silent
consumerism of the visitors
284 that view it.

285 The visual concept of the piece is basic: a structure can be created with cheap and sustainable materials, in this case items of clothing, and it does not need to kept stationary for years in the same place. The architecture is ephemeral and it will become more so.

286 A simple hanging structure, items of clothing and pegs to hang them are the only materials needed to create this original and economical piece. It has attracted the attention of all the visitors who have seen it.

287 Temporary structures are gaining space from permanent structures and recycled, cheap and everyday materials are winning the battle with expensive and difficult to use materials.

288 The location of the installation is perfect for viewing. Being hung from the ceiling, in the centre of the room and having a base of water underneath it, which reflects and increases its size, makes it perfect for achieving the desired impact.

289 The installation shows that recycling materials as simple as clothing can create a social impact, without the need for extravagant, costly or large designs.

290 Temporary structures are having an increasing impact on society. It is continuously moving and there is no longer room for permanent installations that occupy space and leave no room for new creations.

291—295

Yarn Bombing

MARINA FERNÁNDEZ RAMOS, ASOCIACIÓN CULTURAL Y JUVENIL LA CHORRERA

VALVERDE DE LA VERA, SPAIN, 2013

AREA
N/A

CLIENT
CITY COUNCIL OF VALVERDE DE LA VERA

PHOTO
© LUIS RAGEL, MARINA FERNÁNDEZ RAMOS

291 This artistic intervention was created with materials as simple as re-used plastic bags, yarn, *hula-hoops* and tights. Together with crochet and embroidery, a unique project with great visual impact has been achieved.

292 One of the unusual things about this project is that the inhabitants of the town were able to contribute to its creation by creating mosaics and decorations based on those that typically adorn its streets, using crochet and embroidery.

293 This textile project functions as a sunshade during the day and as a guide towards the town square when night falls, thanks to its integral lights. They also create the effect of traditional summer party decorations.

295 This is a clear example of ephemeral and sustainable architecture as all the materials are re-used and, once they have been removed from the exhibition, they can be re-used for their social, decorative or architectural function.

294 Re-using rubbish bags is perfect for creating long strips that can cover the entire structure as they are light and easy to work with, as well as being economical and sustainable.

Yarn Bombing demonstrates that traditional techniques such as embroidery and crochet can be used to create decorative features for contemporary architecture, and that anyone who knows the processes involved can take part in the creation.

297 The installation emphasises the identity of the place and creates a festive, colourful and co-operative atmosphere in the town since the town's inhabitants have taken part in its creation.

299 The project's main participants are the women and, to a lesser extent, the men of the town who volunteered to assist in its creation. Crochet and embroidery are the only techniques used to create this spectacle of colour.

300 The production of the structure was carried out in open workshops where crochet and embroidery techniques were taught so that everyone could participate and contribute to the project.

298 All everyday materials and items can be perfect for creating architectural work with great visual impact.

Loom-Hyperbolic

BARKOW LEIBINGER ARCHITECTS

MARRAKECH, MOROCCO, 2012

AREA
N/A

CLIENT
MARRAKECH BIENNALE

PHOTO
© BARKOW LEIBINGER, JOHANNES FOERSTER

301 For the Marrakech Biennale, held between 29th February and 3rd June 2012, the architects conceived an undulating canopy opposite the Koutoubia Mosque an historical place that is emblematic of the city.

302 The irregular slightly bent forms of the wooden posts soften the hard geometry of the digital computer drawings. The lines of the yarn generate a ruled geometry which forms the hyperbolic surfaces.

303 The built structure permits the creation of a 5 x 5 m grid with a height of 2.5 m which is repeated 18 times. This height permits viewers to walk around and through it.

304 The installation creates a feeling of transparency and transience in contrast with the solid opaque masonry surfaces around it. All materials and manufacturing were locally sourced.

305 In addition to cotton, simple hand-peeled pine lamp posts were used by joining them to steel plates and tubes to establish and secure the desired geometry. Then, the yarn was pulled over the frames whose positions were alternated.

306 Based on Moroccan handcraft tradition, the architects found other uses for soft cellulose fibres. Their lightness and resistance to traction permit the creation of sculptural installations.

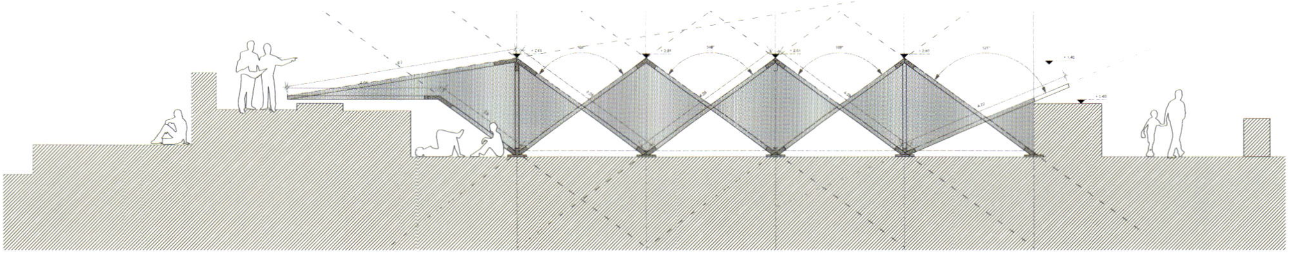

307 The truly public nature of the place ensured that the project could be seen by day or night and it was designed for a local family audience, as well as for foreign visitors.

308 The main fabric used in this intervention was cotton. Between huge trunks of pine, cotton yarn was stretched to form a structure of hyperbolic curves.

309 The installation can be seen from the top of the Mosque and can also be moved around or through, thanks to the versatility of the series of tents.

310 This is another example of how in ephemeral architecture, the use of software programming and local craft techniques can create a spectacular visual result.

Corol·la

XEVI BAYONA

OLOT, SPAIN, 2014
AREA
N/A
CLIENT
OLOT CITY COUNCIL
PHOTO
© XEVI BAYONA

311 Situated in one of Olot's main squares in 2014, the project was the winner of the Emporia d'Or National Prize for Ephemeral Architecture in the category of best event covering.

312 It is a temporary installation constructed with eight thousand metres of cellophane plastic in different colours. It acts as a cover to shelter various cultural activities held during a weekend.

313 The *Corolla* is a flower's inner covering. The plastic and the colours are used in such a way that they mimic the shape of petals to create an effect similar to a collection of flowers.

314 In the centre of the perimeter, there is an opening that allows natural light to enter. When the sun's rays come into contact with the colours of the plastic, they create a fun effect on the floor of the covered square.

315 The installation is used to decorate the square and to provide a canopy over the various activities that take place there. It also acts as an urban experiment that aims to recreate a different atmosphere in the place where it is installed.

Orange, pink and purple are
the colours used for the canopy.
With the light of the sun, the
tones are transformed and
adopt different nuances, such
316 as ranges of blues and reds.

A sphere-effect surrounded
by colours is created on the
floor of the plaza. The use of
a material as light as cellophane
allows it to be moved by a slight
breeze, which changes the
317 appearance of the sphere.

The buildings that surround
the square serve as an anchor
for the cellophane canopy.
It creates an atmosphere where
the colours are the main focus
318 as if it were festive decoration.

The plastic cover does not create
a large area of shade or shelter
but it does act as a filter for the
breeze. The slightest movement
creates the sensation of a better
319 ventilated and shady place.

Once the weekend's activities
are over, the cellophane instal-
lation will be dismantled. Storing
the material will require hardly
any space and it can be used as
an artistic installation for another
320 event.

Pulp Pavilion

BALL-NOGUES STUDIO

INDIO, CA, USA, 2015

AREA
N/A

CLIENT
COACHELLA VALLEY
MUSIC AND ARTS FESTIVAL

PHOTO

321 Installed on the site of the *Coachella Valley Music and Arts Festival* held in the Californian desert, this project, constructed using a paper pulp mixture, aims to offer a restful space for visitors.

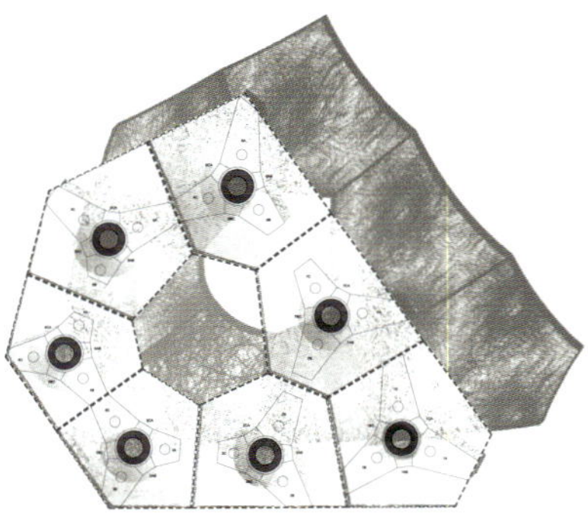

322 The idea was simple: a pulp made of paper with water and pigment over an organic string blind were enough to create an installation that would be a decorative feature and a place for visitors to rest.

323 When the sun set and night fell, a set of light sources embedded in the project's seating and columns illuminated the whole area. This created an optical effect that illuminated the area and allowed visitors to carry on enjoying the festival.

324 This structure proves that paper is perfect for architectural projects, as its pulp plays a leading role in its construction. Once the work is removed, this paper can be used again for new projects as it has not been chemically treated.

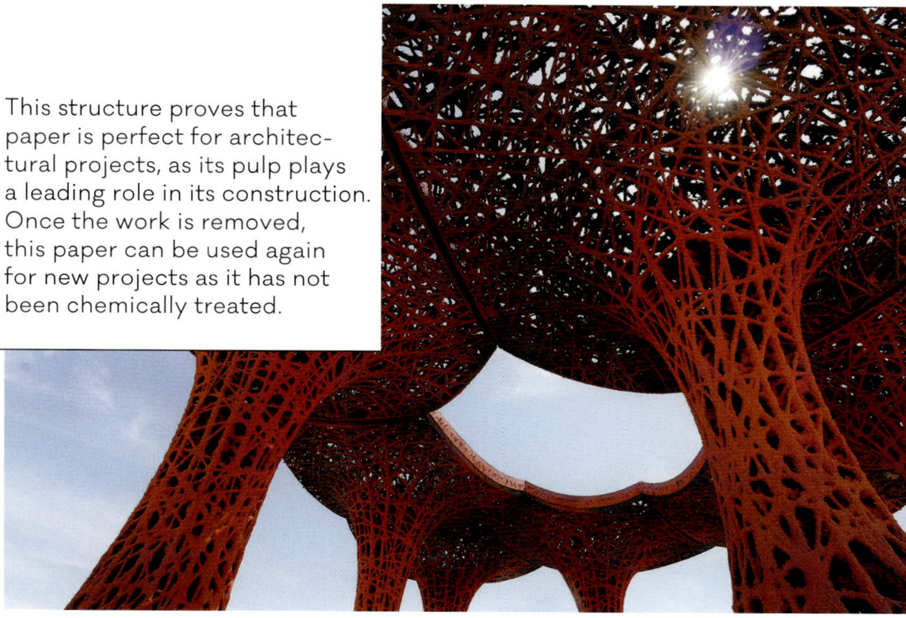

327 The mixture of water, paper and pigment attached to a tight network, has given rise to this original structure, which aims to create a visual impact in a festival where all elements have a unique feature.

325 The pavilion was the perfect place for a rest, as it protected visitors from the sun and offered a place where they could chat and enjoy the festival while the gentle breeze filtered through the gaps.

326 The arid climate and the wind blowing through the pavilion structure enabled it to dry out more quickly and naturally so its splendour was preserved for much longer.

328 The construction materials contained no toxic materials, so they could be recycled or composted after the two weeks of the festival.

329 Inside this large-scale structure, a blind protected visitors from the heat and sun and invited them to rest on benches and seats arranged around the supporting bases.

330 The majestic pavilion was created using more than 2,000 metres of twine and more than a tonne of orange paper pulp. The result was a spectacular structure because of its great size.

Liquid Sky

BALL-NOGUES STUDIO

NEW YORK, NY, USA, 2008

AREA
N/A

CLIENT
MoMA, P.S.1 CONTEMPORARY ART CENTER

PHOTO
© BENJAMIN BALL, MARK LENTZ, PAUL JOHNSON, STEPH GORALNICK

331 The project was installed in the courtyard of the P.S.1 Contemporary Art Center in Queens, New York and was the result of a competition where young architects gave free rein to their creativity to design a piece of ephemeral architecture.

332 The designers define this structure as a kind of circus tent where, instead of a canvas covering the surface, an array of fluorescent scales overlap, creating a psychedelic colour effect.

333 The project is a combination of a space dedicated to events and a structure where materials and the digital world interact to create a different, modern atmosphere where simplicity plays with modernity.

334 The six towers constructed from untreated utility poles act as a support for a large framework of shades of pink. At the same time, it functions as a rest area for visitors in the museum courtyard.

The tensioned structure changes the profile of the courtyard as it is higher than the museum walls. Six utility pole towers support this structure and offer the visitors a space to rest thanks to the hammocks and seats at
335 their bases.

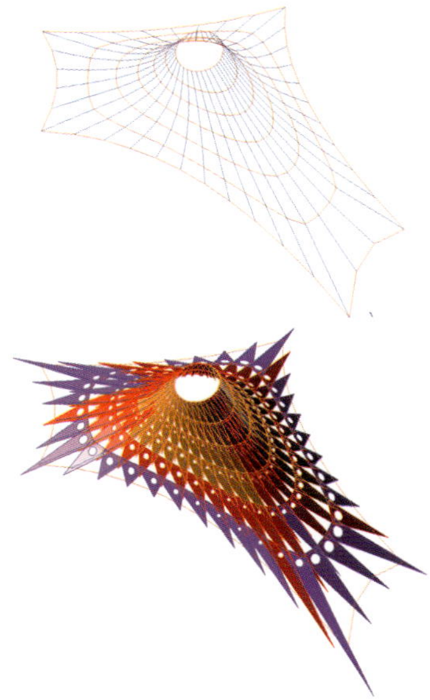

The Mylar fabric is one of the main features of the project, it covers the top of the structure and instils a feeling of euphoria, thanks to its
336 intense colours and floral prints.

An array of translucent petals in shades of pink provide shade and shelter to the visitors, leaving the sun to filter through, although without it disturbing those who decide to go under
338 the structure.

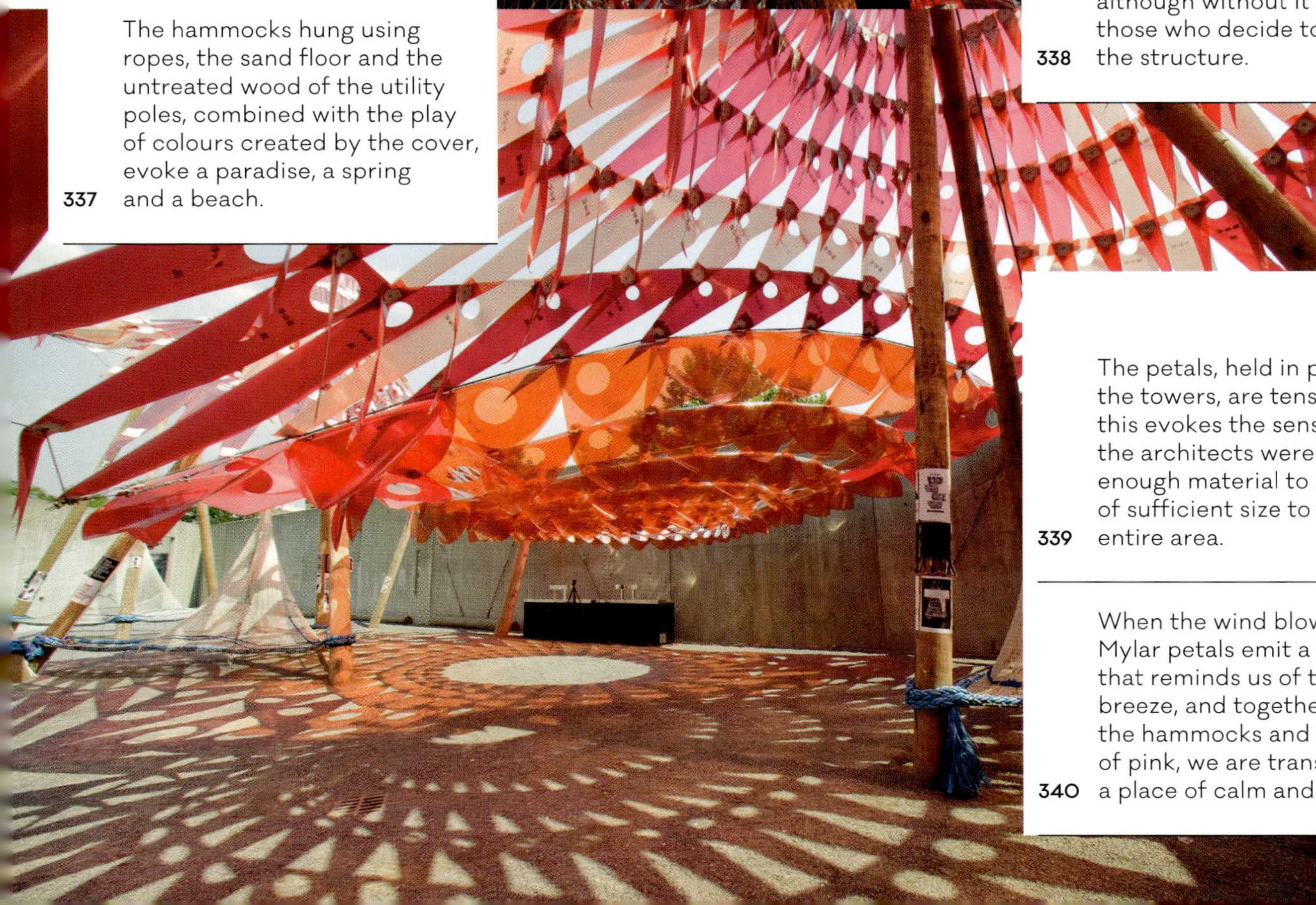

The hammocks hung using ropes, the sand floor and the untreated wood of the utility poles, combined with the play of colours created by the cover, evoke a paradise, a spring
337 and a beach.

The petals, held in place by the towers, are tensioned and this evokes the sensation that the architects were left without enough material to make a tent of sufficient size to cover the
339 entire area.

When the wind blows, the Mylar petals emit a murmur that reminds us of the sea breeze, and together with the hammocks and the shades of pink, we are transported to
340 a place of calm and relaxation.

341—346

Wendy

HOLLWICH KUSHNER ARCHITECTURE+ HWKN

NEW YORK, NY, USA, 2013

AREA
465 m^2

CLIENT
MoMA, P.S.1 CONTEMPORARY ART CENTER

PHOTO
© HWKN, MICHAEL MORAN PHOTOGRAPHY

341 Wendy was the winning project of the Young Architects Program (YAP) held by the Museum of Modern Art and the MoMA PS1 in New York. It was exhibited in the outdoor area of MoMA PS1, Long Island on 1st July 2012.

342 During the summer that it was exhibited, Wendy was responsible for cleaning the air of the area creating an effect equivalent to reducing the area's traffic by 260 cars.

343 Wendy is composed of a nylon fabric treated with a modern and innovative spray containing titanium oxide nanoparticles which neutralise particulate pollutants. It is therefore a structure that is as functional as it is decorative.

344 The construction of Wendy was simple, economical and fast. A scaffold was used to create the structure and gives rise to a volume of 21.5 x 21.5 x 14 m, optimising the use of the space provided.

345 Thanks to the scaffolding, it was possible to create a structure where the design was as simple as a star shape, whose large tips and nylon fabric are the most important parts. It is a simple but powerful installation.

346 The original structure can be found at one end of the museum where visitors can enjoy its original shape. The work is positioned in such a way that it won't disturb the transit of people or the other activities and spaces.

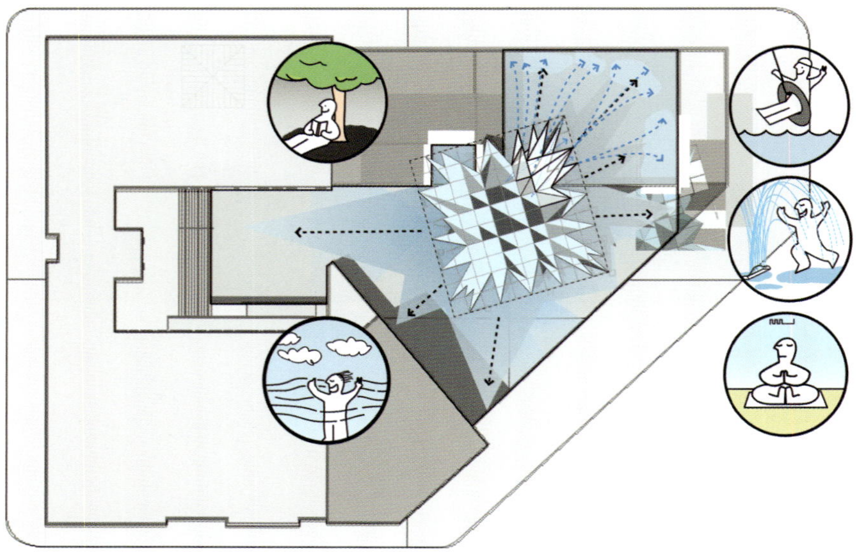

The objective of this intervention is twofold: to surprise visitors who walk around it and to clean the air with the titanium nanoparticles and elastic fabric that covers it, using a technology known
347 as *catalytic clothing*.

The more tips, size and fabric this original structure has, the greater impact it will have on the area in which it stands: it will be more visible and will help clean the area's air more quickly, covering a much larger
348 radius.

Wendy demonstrates that physical boundaries can be crossed with a simple structure by using elements such as shade, music rain and wind. The nylon fabric is used to
349 improve air quality.

The project demonstrates that ephemeral architecture has an impact on both social
350 and ecological issues.

MoMA PS1

Bab al Bahrain Pavilion

NOURA AL SAYEH, LEOPOLD BANCHINI + BUREAU A

BAHRAIN, KINGDOM OF BAHRAIN, 2009

AREA
N/A

CLIENT
MANAMA CAPITAL OF ARAB CULTURE 2012, MINISTRY OF CULTURE, KINGDOM OF BAHRAIN

PHOTO
© EMAN ALI, CAMILLE ZAKHARIA

351 The Bab al Bahrain pavilion is a temporary ephemeral project created to open a civil debate on the great public space issue.

352 As well as functioning as an interactive space for all audiences, the project housed an exhibition of finalist's samples that had been entered into an open competition about the future of Bahrain.

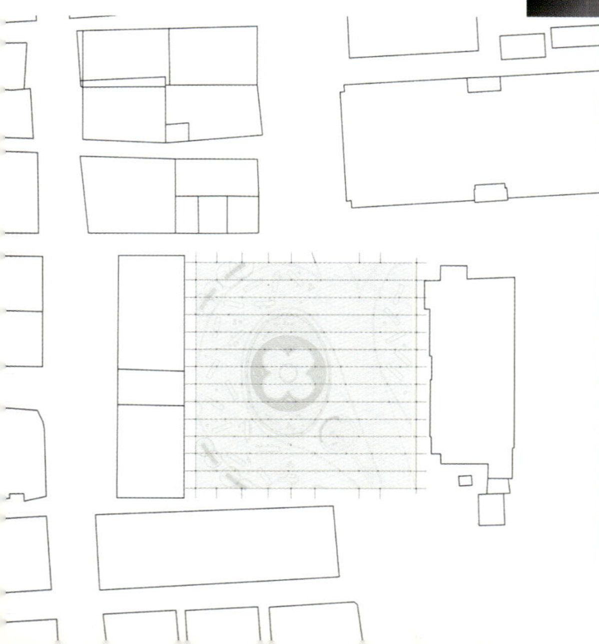

353 The square in which the temporary pavilion is located is a place that has become a roundabout almost exclusively dedicated to traffic. However, due to its historical importance and central location, there is a desire to convert it into a lively public square.

354 The architects' design seeks to question the use of contemporary urban spaces in the Arab world, taking recent political events into account

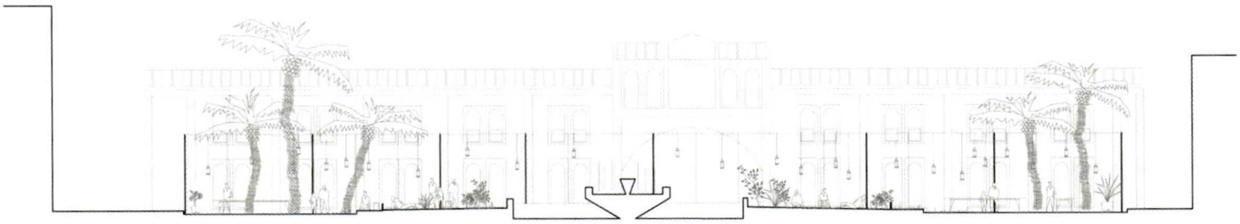

355 A fabric that provides translucent shadow to the entire area and modifies the perception of the user. Now the space is closed and changes according to climatic conditions.

356 The only urban furniture that was constructed for the occasion and that was available in the existing square were large tables made by a local workshop.

357 Under this fabric canopy, the traffic was considerably reduced, which allowed the public to reclaim the streets and interact to carry out all kinds of activities.

358 The temporary pavilion was constructed over a couple of weeks with the aim of reinstating a strong sense of place and to redefine the square as a representative space in Bahrain.

359 The use of the reflective heat shield made with silver fabric, low technology used for greenhouses, and the process of evaporation produced by a spring, produces a micro-climate around the installation.

360 The pavilion aims to transform the existing square into a new shared space, acting as a 1/1 scale model for encouraging the debate over the future use of the square.

Schaustelle

J. MAYER H. UND PARTNER ARCHITEKTEN

MUNICH, GERMANY, 2013

AREA
615 m²

CLIENT
FREISTAAT BAYERN, MINISTERIUM FÜR WISSENSCHAFT, FORSCHUNG UND KUNST, STIFTUNG PINAKOTHEK DER MODERNE

PHOTO
© J. MAYER H., DENNIS BANGERT, HILDE STROBL ARCHITEKTURMUSEUM TUM

361 The temporary pavilion is located in the Pinakothek der Moderne, a modern art gallery in the centre of Munich. It has an area of 615 m^2 and is designed to perform and display various experiments.

362 The project is being used as a temporary exhibition space for the four Pinakothek collections. It provides a space for holding conferences, exhibitions, workshops, performances, video and audio performances as well as other artistic performances.

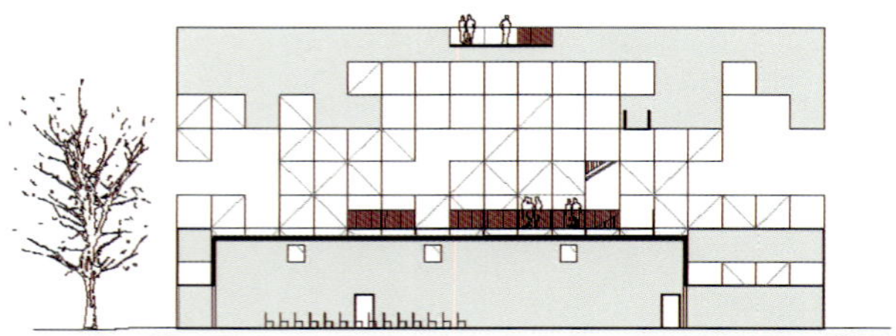

363 Its structure is created from reusable scaffolding that creates a flexible space, closing at the base, and opening in the upper part where events are held and more artistic installations are exhibited.

364 The broad structure of the scaffolding allows visitors to pass through it while they contemplate the works on show or enjoy various events, such as projections or performances by day or by night.

365 Being a pavilion constructed with scaffolding, an atmosphere of freedom is created where people can interact with the museum, pieces, achieving the creation of a work that surpasses a typical classical exhibition.

A three-dimensional mesh of prismatic elements was created on a base of orthogonal and diagonal metal bars. The scaffolding structure is approximately 20 m high,
366 15 m wide and 40 m long.

Between the scaffolding and the stairs, hanging seats have been installed where visitors can rest and contemplate the site's various zones to the rhythm of a gentle rocking
367 between poles and platforms.

368 The different artistic representations on display are distributed over the scaffolding structure's three floors.

369 A series of translucent panels are arranged on the ground floor and show the name of the space in upper-case letters. This floor houses the two-floor hall for multiple uses and has a surface area of approximately 280 m^2.

370 This temporary project has been carried out using materials destined for construction sites and this is because part of its purpose is to share details of the renovation work taking place in the museum.

Swiss Pavilion for ARCO

2B ARCHITECTES

MADRID, SPAIN, 2008

AREA
N/A

CLIENT
PRO HELVETIA; SPANISH MINISTRY OF DEVELOPMENT

PHOTO
© 2B ARCHITECTES, DRACE, LUIS ASÍN LAPIC

371 For Madrid's ARCO fair, the 2b architectes studio presented a highly symbolic pavilion that fits perfectly into the spatial context.

372 The semi-transparent pavilion was built in the shape of a pure white Swiss cross, evoking the Swiss flag.

373 The project seeks to create a dialogue between the empty space and the dense development and connects its own ephemeral character to the existing building to create a comprehensive project.

374 The installation is a variation on the classic *Swiss Box* theme. It is composed of two 31 metre boxes with overlapping sides, turned at an angle of 90 degrees.

375 The main construction material is wooden planks. Its low weight permitted the original layout of the boxes. This material is also very characteristic of Swiss architecture.

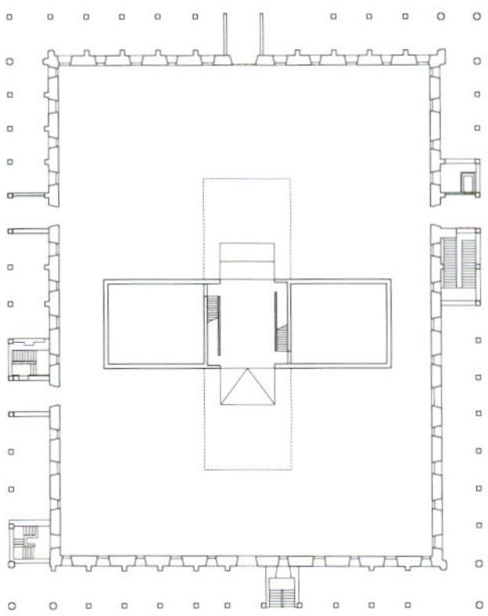

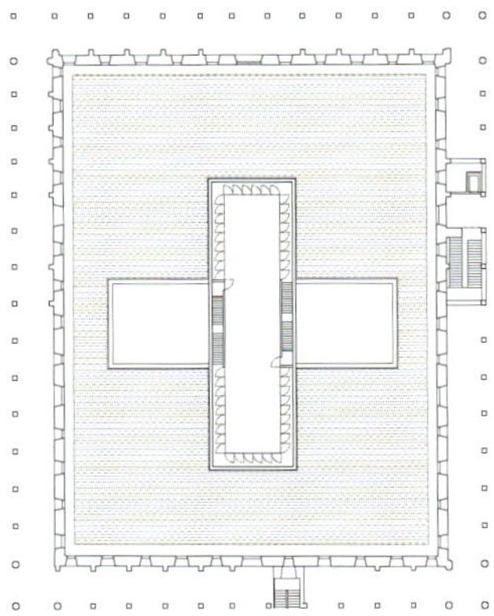

376 The same translucent polycarbonates were used for the walls and woodwork as well as for the façades. OSB and DM panels painted white were chosen for the interiors.

377 Access to the area through this space invites visitors to immerse themselves in the festive atmosphere.

378 Inside the pavilion, the radiant white stands out unifying the space and playing with its inherent neutrality.

379 By night, the illuminated box becomes a giant lantern, thanks to its polycarbonate membrane and the red textile strips.

380 The courtyard of the Conde Duque Cultural Centre was transformed into a silent Swiss landscape in the heart of Madrid.

Brick-Topia

MARTA DOMÈNECH, DAVID LÓPEZ, MARIANA PALUMBO + MAP13

BARCELONA, SPAIN, 2014-2015

AREA
253 m²

CLIENT
EME3 INTERNATIONAL FESTIVAL OF ARCHITECTURE

PHOTO
© MANUEL DE LÓZAR, PAULA LÓPEZ BARBA, ÁLVARO VALDECANTOS, MAP13

381 The Brick-Topia pavilion is the winning project in the "Build-it" category of the EME3 International Festival of Architecture, held in Barcelona in June 2014.

382 The purpose of the festival is to discover and share new forms of architecture and town planning through innovative and daring works.

383 The architects used the potential of computer aided design to design a traditional partitioned vault construction system.

384 The pavilion was constructed in the courtyard of the former Fabra i Coats spinning mill; it added structure to the location and organised the flow of visitors.

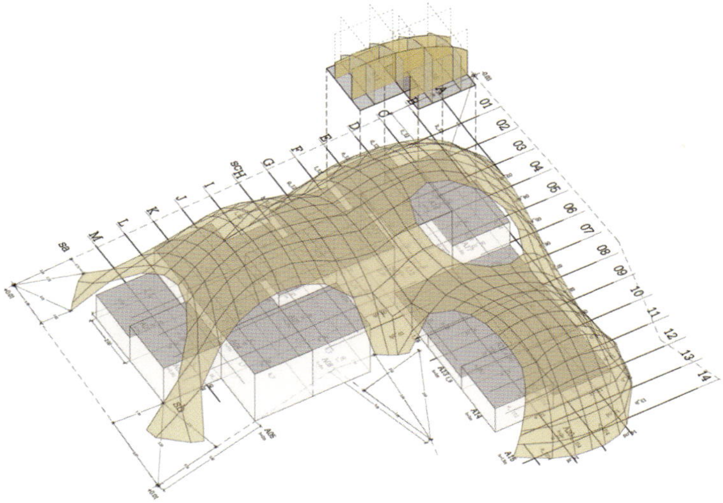

385 This intervention configures a new space with new forms and textures, where various activities can be carried out under the pavilion as well as around it.

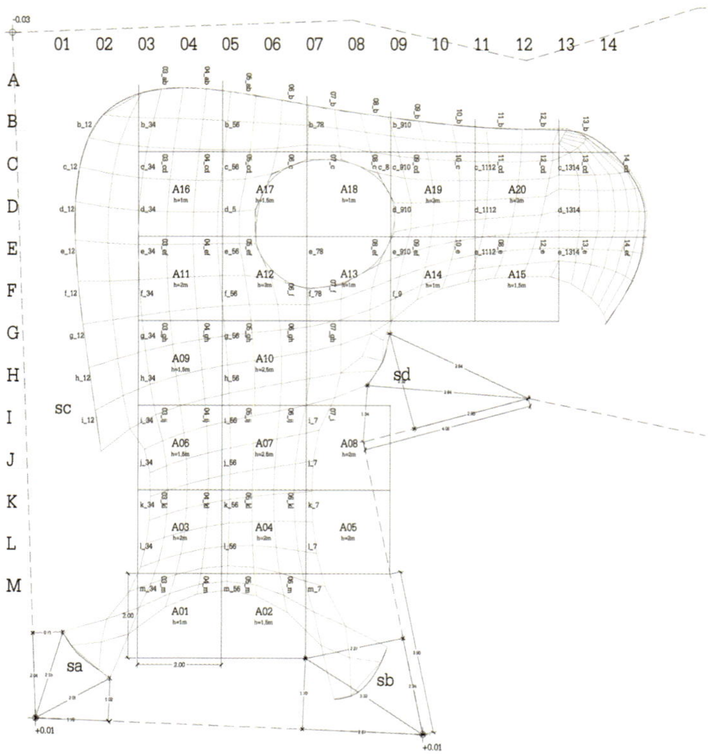

388 The outcome of this lengthy academic research is a collection of traditional materials and procedures combined with the latest *form-finding* and structural calculation tools.

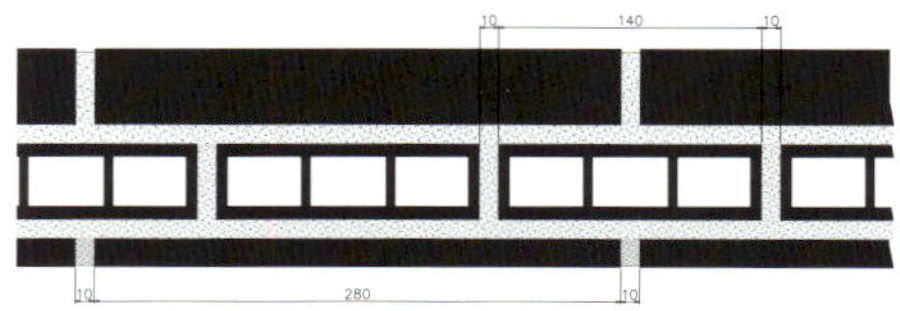

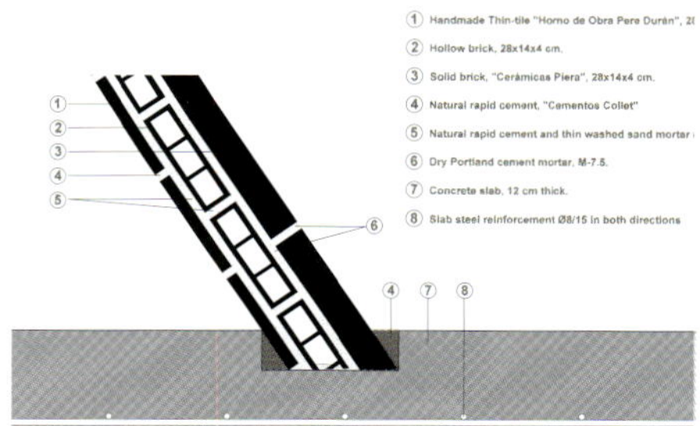

386 The material used to create the vault is the same as that of the former factory, raising a new topography that counters industrial construction and provides a concave and sheltered space.

387 The domed pavilion raises the contemporary validity of this traditional construction system that is widely used in various parts of the world. It is an economical, sustainable and very versatile system.

389 Slender and inclined supports, arches, different dome heights, different degrees of curvature and a large hole in the shell are some of the features that were incorporated into the design.

390 This project aims to restore the expertise and imagination of the hands that built it. Brick-Topia was constructed by builders who have created a work of excellent craftmanship.

Jukbuin Pavilion

ENRIQUE SORIANO, PEP TORNABELL + CODA-OFFICE

BARCELONA, SPAIN, 2013

AREA
N/A

CLIENT
EME3

PHOTO
© ANDRES FLAJSZER

391 The aim was to create an efficient structure that only needed energy. To do this, traditional techniques such as basketry were fused with engineering techniques using materials such as plywood to create the project.

392 The interwoven planks are highly adaptable and are supported by flexible wood. This combines rigidity with forms that are flexible and light.

393 The structure is built with WISA birch slats cut into 5 centimetre strips. The rest of the pieces are presented in a combination of three different sizes.

394 The interior space of the ephemeral structure occupies a total of 90 m^2.

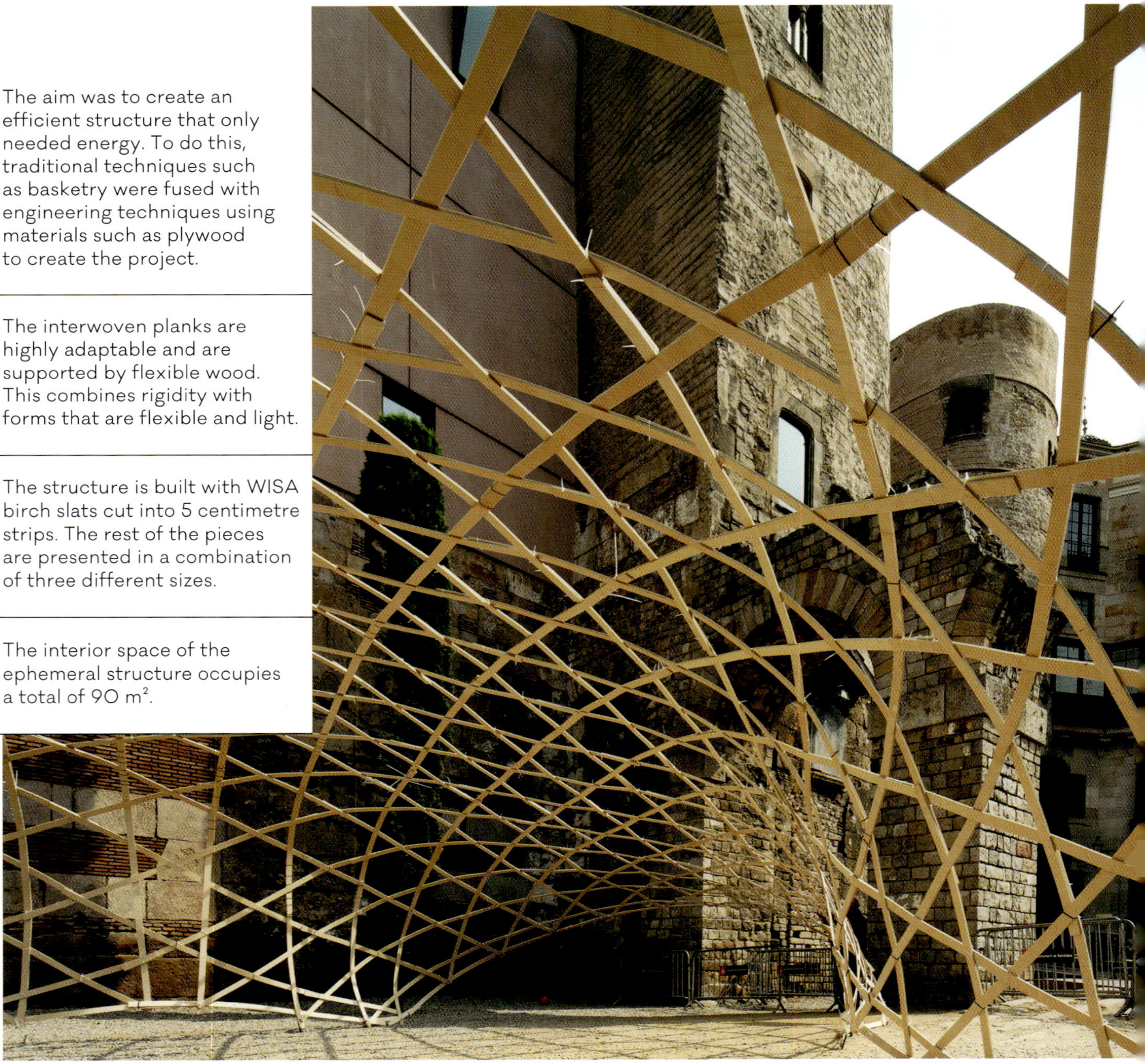

395 The wood of the marquee contrasts with the stone of the floor and the façade of the cathedral behind it.

396 The proposal seeks to demonstrate alternatives to current construction systems. In the pavilion, only fifteen standardised panels were used that do not generate any waste.

397 The installation is situated in a historical area of the city, and transforms the public space without generating visual obstacles.

399 The pavilion was constructed in record time and with a very limited budget. The use of renewable material and a public site were essential to achieving this objective.

400 The installation was included in the EME3 festival of architecture held in Barcelona, where various exhibitions took place as well as debates organised by ETSAV students.

398 A triaxial construction technique was used, which helped to simplify the manufacturing process. The absence of bolts also allowed space and time to be optimally used.

Stack n' Build

LIKEARCHITECTS

PORTO, PORTUGAL, 2012
AREA
44 m^2
CLIENT
UNICER / SUPERBOCK, CREATIVE INDUSTRIES AWARD
PHOTO
© DAMNWORKS-CREATIVE MOTION STUDIO

401 The temporary Stack n' Build pavilion was created with a combination of a total of 620 beer crates. The installation was located in the gardens of the Serralves.

402 The design used in the construction of the pavilion is perfect for assembly and disassembly, which can be done in a short time without any harm at all being done to the appearance of the beer crates.

403 It is a non-intrusive construction system combined with very strong materials, which allows the project to be installed in other locations with the option of whether to use the same structural design.

404 The intense red colour that is characteristic of this brand of beer and therefore of the plastic crates that form the structure, contrasts with the green of the gardens where it is located, creating a colourful visual impact.

Imitating the Lego building
system and with the help
of small metal anchors,
a temporary structure was
successfully created in a way
that even if it is damaged by
visitors, there is no danger
405 of it breaking.

The installation's design is
based on the combination
of a vertical alignment and
horizontal curvature, which
is achieved by using small
metal links installed between
the crates to help sustain
407 the structure.

The connection between the
different beer crates is
achieved using the grids on
their sides. This connection
allows interweaving and
creating forms that go beyond
408 a straight and boring structure.

As well as serving as a
decorative project in the
garden where it is installed,
children can play with the
structure, connecting and
decorating the different
409 crates with coloured tubes.

Imitating the Lego building
system and with the help
of small metal anchors, a
temporary structure was
successfully created in a way
that even if it is damaged
by visitors, there is no danger
406 of it breaking.

The project design occupies an
area of 44 m^2 and is a versatile
structure, with which different
forms, sizes and shapes can
be created. It can be adapted
for each location according
410 to needs and environment.

The Andy Warhol Temporary Museum

LIKEARCHITECTS

LISBON, PORTUGAL, 2013

AREA
75 m²

CLIENT
SONAE SIERRA

PHOTO
© FERNANDO GUERRA / FG+SG ARCHITECTURAL PHOTOGRAPHY

411 Located in Lisbon's Colombo shopping centre, the exhibition occupies a surface of 75 m² and displays a total of 32 original works of art by the North American artist Andy Warhol, for whom the exhibition is named: *Andy Warhol – Icons*.

412 The use of paint cans as the exhibition structure, combined with the works displayed inside, recreates the artist's philosophy, which played with mixing different styles, in this case industrial and pop art.

413 The exhibition is located in the central square of the shopping centre, a perfect location as it is the nucleus that most people pass through when they visit to do their shopping or have a drink.

414 The paint tins allow an attractive abstract-style exterior to be created, assuming the identity that so characterises the pop art icon created by Andy Warhol.

415 The inscrutable design that can be contemplated from the exterior contrasts with the total openness of the structure at the top so that from the top floor, the interior can be seen without the tins used in its construction acting as a visual obstacle.

416 For four months, the original showcase converted the main square of the shopping centre into a small museum, a walk-through artistic zone where the famous artist's original works could be viewed.

417 The temporary exhibition received more than 100,000 visitors during the four months when it was installed in the shopping centre, enabling a free and accessible display of the works of Warhol.

418 To provide stability to the structure so that the works could be safely displayed, it was decided to fill the first three rows of tins with sand.

419 The interior was designed as an enclosed space where the walls define the path to be followed. A transparent roof allows light to enter and ensures there is a visual connection between the interior and the exterior.

420 Four exhibition rooms flow in succession between the paint tins. Organised thematically, an organic route is created that defies the rationality and the symmetry of the main square in the shopping centre.

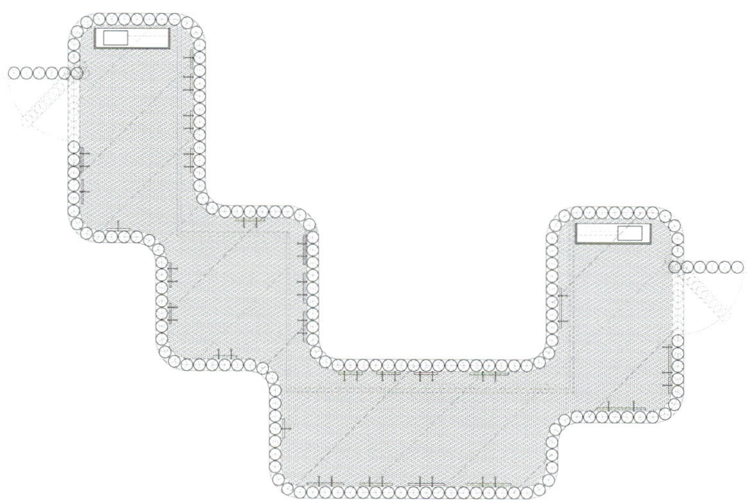

WonderWALL

LIKEARCHITECTS

LISBON, PORTUGAL, 2014

AREA
150 m^2

CLIENT
SONAE SIERRA

PHOTO
© FERNANDO GUERRA / FG+SG ARCHITECTURAL PHOTOGRAPHY

421 The installation provides a temporary exhibition space under the large dome of the Colombo shopping centre. The curtain between the interior and exterior consists of 20,000 strips of fabric.

422 The structure is based on two main pieces formed by assembling sixteen triangular frames. The frames of the first structural part are disguised with black and white fabric strips.

423 The second part of the structure combines coloured fabrics with steel cables. Together, these strips are connected to a membrane and create the frame required to complete the installation.

424 The floor of the structure is composed of a series of round platforms so that the visitor does not step on the shopping centre floor at any point, but instead floats in a kind of pool.

425 The roof of the installation is a large dome that shelters it from the strong lighting of the shopping centre. Inside, the play between lights and chromatic shades creates an ambience that is different to the exterior.

426 Visitors can go through the walls created using strips of fabric The airflow causes these to move randomly and creates an airy atmosphere that is different with every moment that passes.

427 The strips of black and white fabric and the stepping platforms change colour frequently thanks to lighting effects in a colour play that transforms the space.

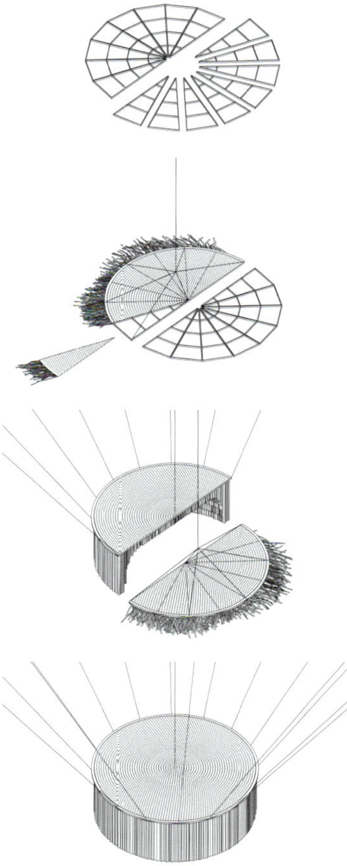

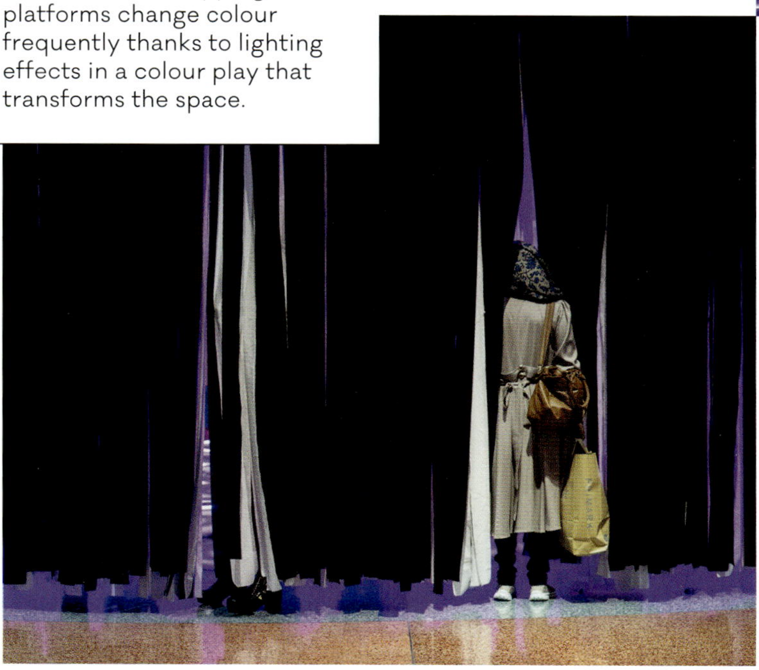

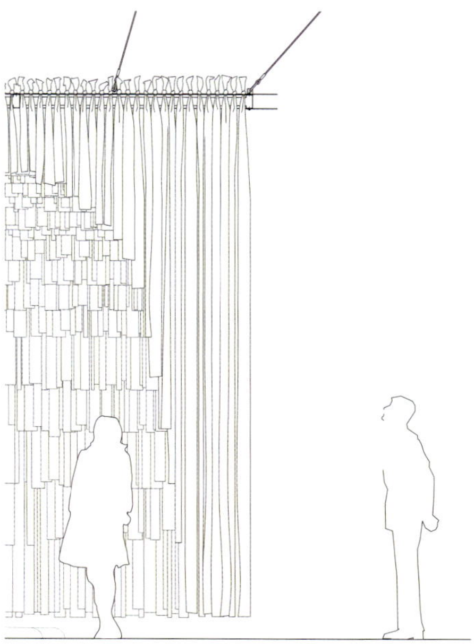

428 Visitors interact with the *pool* created in the interior. They play in it, running and jumping across the stepping stones that change and act as a base. When they change colour, they modify the appearance of the installation.

429 The powerful light emitted from inside can be seen from the exterior, attracting and arousing the curiosity of people in the shopping centre.

The installation occupies a space of about fourteen metres in diameter and four metres in height. It is in the main square of the shopping centre. It allows the visitor to escape from the commercial and consumerist atmosphere for a while.

Three Kings Factory

XEVI BAYONA

OLOT, SPAIN, 2011

AREA
N/A

CLIENT
OLOT CITY COUNCIL

PHOTOS
© XEVI BAYONA

431 The Christmas structure has been installed in the Olot children's home and has become a space for reflection on the spirit of Christmas.

432 It was decided to use the children's home to store Christmas presents. Hundreds of cardboard boxes represent the excitement of children and adults.

433 For one year, gold, frankincense and myrrh hand over the leading role to these cardboard boxes. Inside them are hundreds of people's wishes for the whole year.

434 The installation was designed to be assembled by simply stacking a series of boxes. In a short while, a traditional cloister was transformed into a place of excitement.

435 The installation was designed to be assembled by simply stacking a series of boxes. In a short while, a traditional cloister was transformed into a place of excitement.

436 The installation is intended for all audiences. Its neutrality allows visitors of all ages to project their hopes and dreams onto it.

437 The combination of cardboard boxes from anywhere, a simple set of lights and spectacular staging gave resulted in a magical installation.

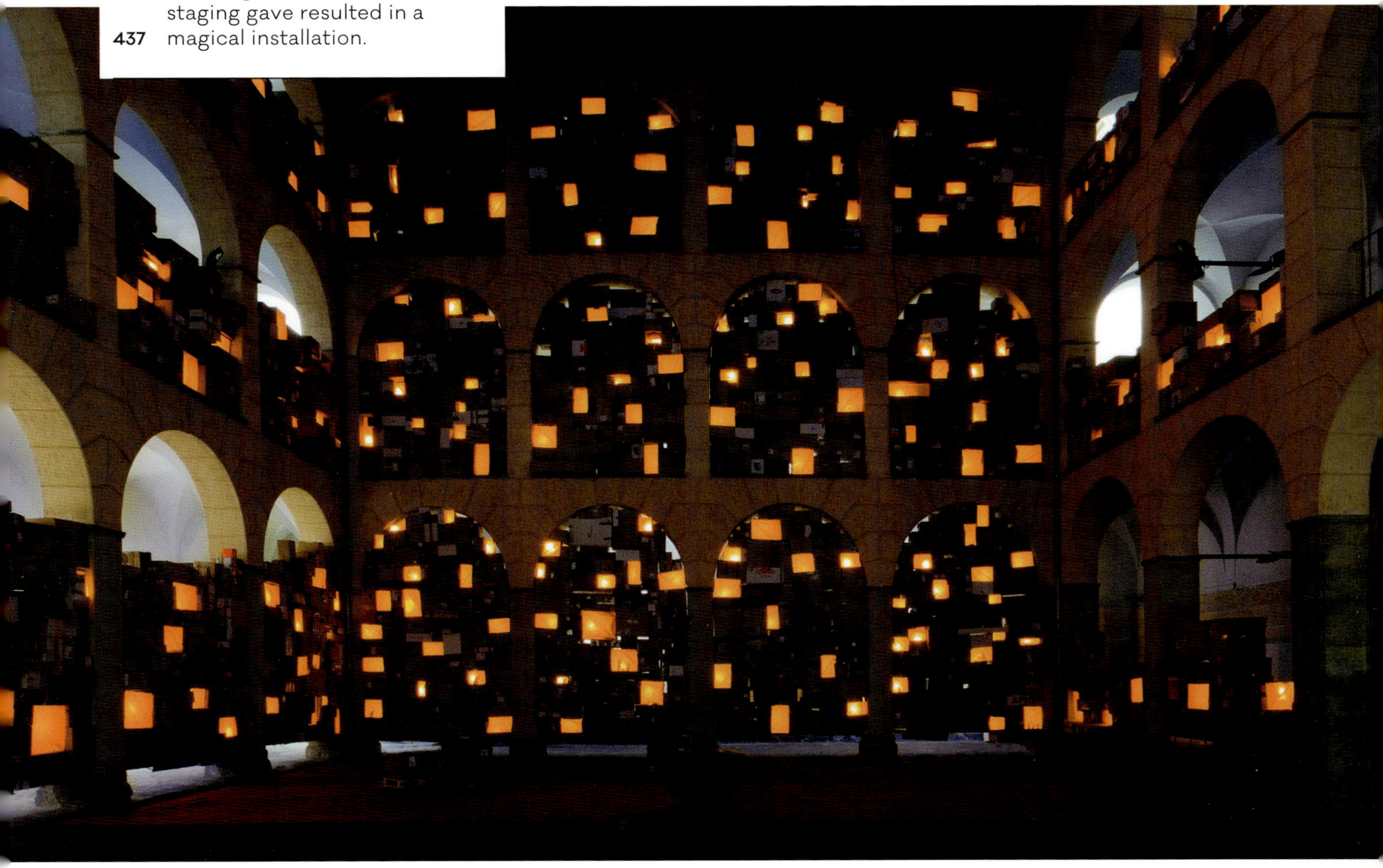

438 A perfect symbiosis is formed by the play created between the lights, the cardboard boxes and the figures between them. A three-in-one that provides something new to Christmas imagery.

439 The only work needed to carry out this project was to stack the cardboard boxes. No design or structure needed to be made, the spaces of the cloister, just had to be filled.

440 It made it to the finals of the FAD Awards for Architecture and Interior Design 2012 in the ephemeral interventions category thanks to the design and staging of the project.

441—445

El Ranchito

NEREA CALVILLO, MARINA FERNÁNDEZ, LAURA MIGUELÁÑEZ, FRANCISCO TRIVIÑO + C + ARQUITECTOS

MADRID, SPAIN, 2012

AREA
3,400 m^2

CLIENT
EL MATADERO

PHOTO
© MIGUEL DE GUZMÁN

441 *El Ranchito* is an exhibition project that shows the process of creating works of art rather than the works themselves. A total of 34 local artists and collectives participated in this large exhibition of diverse styles.

442 The project houses various kinds of installations which visitors can learn about in the library or documentation areas. It also includes a bar and a socialising area where the different processes can be studied at leisure.

443 All of the project's strategies have been carried out with reusable materials such as recycled wooden pallets, plastic curtains and adhesive tape: materials that are simple, economical and promote sustainability.

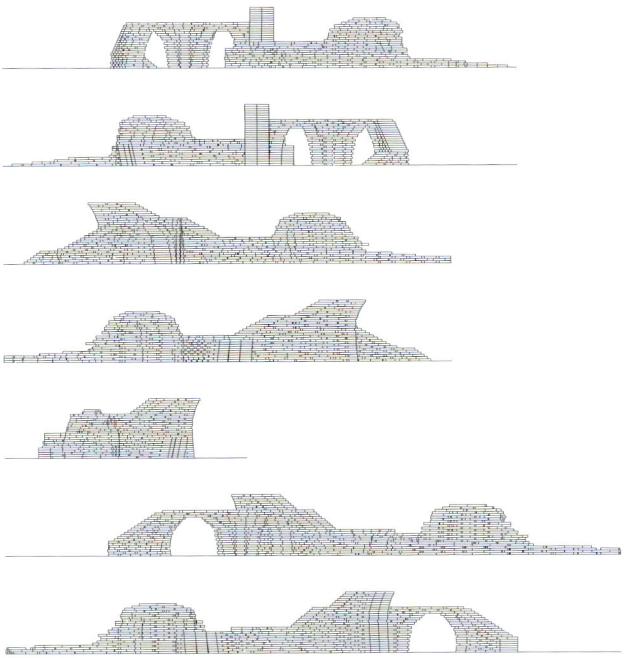

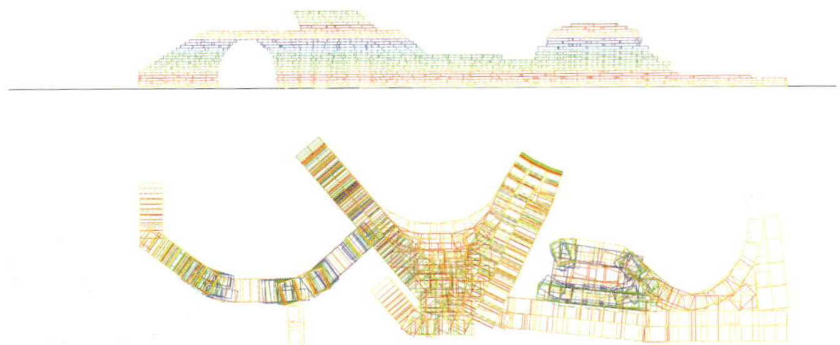

444 A walkway-viewpoint was made from wooden packing pallets, allowing the visitor to enjoy the projects from different angles and viewpoints.

445 The appearance and functionality of Warehouse 16 at the Matadero were transformed with simple materials such as wood, plastic and insulation tape. This allows anyone to go in and view the interior.

446 Walls are unnecessary: plastic curtains are used to separate the different exhibitions. This means that better use can be made of the space and saves money on materials and construction.

447 The goal of *El Ranchito* is to create links between the artistic communities of Spain and to exchange items with the country invited to the event, in this case Argentina. This creates a link between Matadero Madrid and Panal 361.

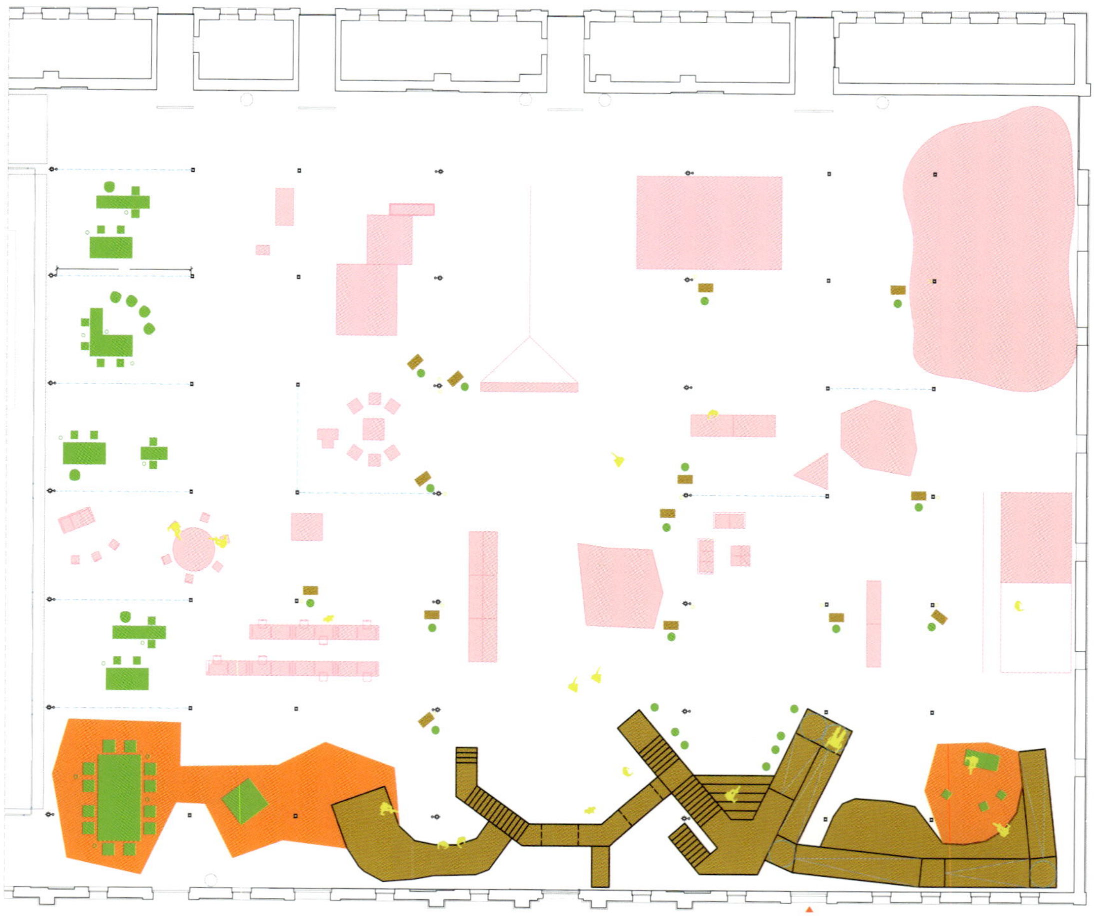

As if it were a guided visit,
the insulating tape on the floor
shows us the route for viewing
the different structures and
exhibitions, demonstrating
that the most basic of things
448 can be the most useful.

The selection of exhibitors was
made via a public call for entries
and allows all kinds of projects
to be displayed, demonstrating
that temporary pieces have
as much weight and impact as
449 those that are permanent.

It is a project where the leading
role is played by art, investigation,
identity design and free publi-
cations. Matadero Madrid has
successfully created an exhibition
where every type of art has its
place and where sustainability
450 plays the leading role.

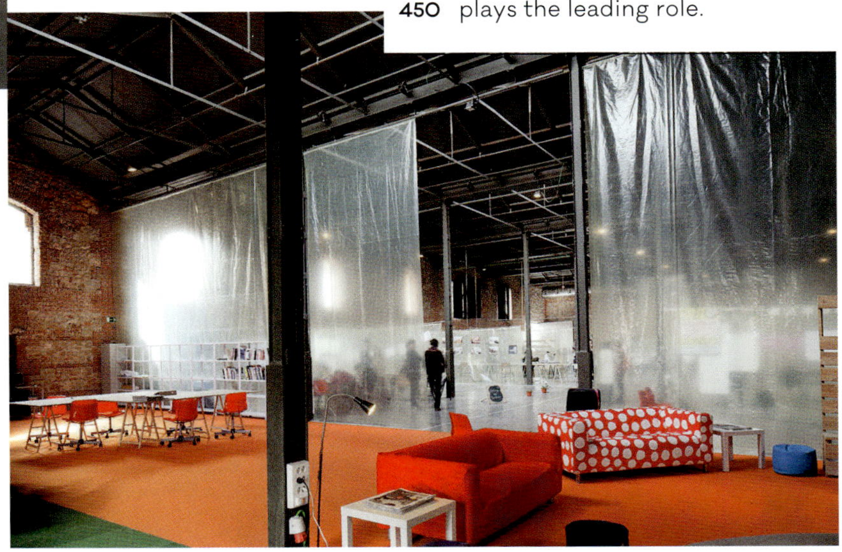

Capturing a Moment

CRISTINA MASFERRER, GUSTAVO TORRES, ÈLIA CLEMENTE

GIRONA, SPAIN, 2014

AREA
N/A

CLIENT
GIRONA CITY COUNCIL

PHOTO
© CRISTINA MASFERRER, GUSTAVO TORRES, ÈLIA CLEMENTE

451 *Capturing a Moment* is an ephemeral intervention that forms part of the floral display *Girona Temps de Flors* which takes place every May.

452 This show, which fills streets, squares and unique spaces with floral and ephemeral installations, has been taking place for 60 years and enjoys well-deserved international recognition.

453 The space used is inside the Santa Llúcia chapel, with its remarkable beautifully-proportioned serene interior.

454 Formally, the instalment reproduces the precise moment in which a field of cotton is caught by the wind, freeing multiple cotton flakes, leaving them suspended in the air.

455 The careful choice and layout of the material have created an gravity-defying optical effect. The static and precise capture of a moment in time, which portrays a dynamic and invasive floral explosion.

456 Le carillon lointain de bols tibétains et un arome intense amplifient l'expérience sensorielle du projet.

457 Cotton flakes remain suspended and immobile, defying the laws of physics and surprising the visitor. It represents the ephemeral paradigm.

458 Six hundred 70 cm high units of natural cotton, 8,000 cotton balls and 5,000 m of transparent polyamide thread were used in its creation.

459 The *Capturing a Moment* installation, with its self-contained beauty, is intended to move the viewer through a perceptive experience, which alludes to memories and senses.

460 These days, architects perceive that the effectiveness of the most diverse and innovative proposals can be tested with installations that are ephemeral and sometimes high-impact.

Sonalls

CRISTINA BESTRATÉN, AINA BIGORRA, ERIK HERRERA + DONDECABENTRES

SANT CARLES DE LA RÀPITA, SPAIN, 2014

AREA
N/A

CLIENT
EUROS, TERRES DE L'EBRE FESTIVAL OF SOUND AND VISUAL ARTS

PHOTO
© DONDECABENTRES

461 In the old Santa Maria de la Ràpita convent, the project aims to create a visual and playful experience in an emblematic environment that has continuity for a period of time.

462 A total of 185 large balls are arranged over three levels where you can play like children. These create a space that attracts, excites, and invites you to enter and forget what is outside.

463 An ambience has been created that is bright, dreamlike and warm, where you can enjoy the delicate and light touch of the balls accompanied by a fun sound effect created by the bells hidden inside.

464 The use of basic and primary elements, such as light, form and sound, create a magical space that plays with visitors' perceptions, awaking within them the desire to play, interact and be surprised.

465 The project successfully creates a relaxing sensation, a sensitive climate that cares for and pampers visitors, immersing them in a magical place. It is a vibrant space where you can lose and transform yourself.

466 The 185 balls are arranged on three levels and form a 1.20 m high structure. As visitors spend time lying between the balls, the height doesn't detract from the fun.

467 It is an ephemeral piece, quick to construct, dismantle and transport; a space without function can be completely transformed into a place of entertainment for young and old.

468 The contrast between the white of the balls, the lights installed on the floor and the courtyard's thick stone walls creates a different ambience. The bells round off the climax by providing sound and expectation.

469 Basic materials, neutral colours and existing walls are all that is needed to create an installation that, far from decorating the space, transports the visitor to a place of dreams, freedom and games.

470 Unlike other projects and installations, *Sonalls* seeks to create an experience of sound and vision, not a work of art. Its position, between stone walls, is perfect for creating the desired impact.

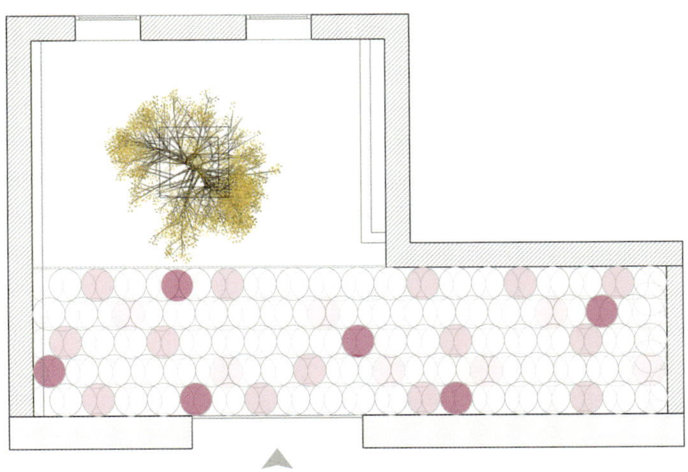

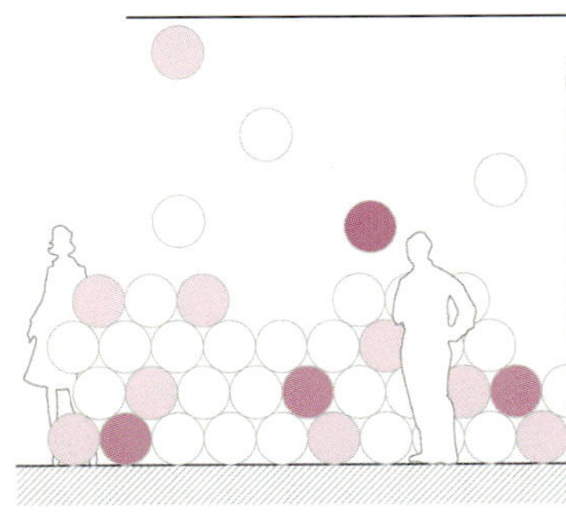

Concordança

CRISTINA BESTRATÉN, AINA BIGORRA, ERIK HERRERA + DONDECABENTRES

BARCELONA, SPAIN, 2008

AREA
N/A

CLIENT
TUDANZAS FESTIVAL

PHOTOS
© DONDECABENTRES, VÍCTOR MARTÍNEZ LÓPEZ

An area of the Sant Agustí
convent in Barcelona is trans
formed by this installation:
subtle dances through the
coloured tapes create a new
471 perception of the space.

The project is part of the
TUDANZAS Festival held in
Barcelona in April 2013 to
celebrate the international
472 day of dance.

The project was installed in
a room with stone walls and
a slightly ruined look. This
enabled a contrast to be
created with red tapes and
473 the arrangement of chairs.

Just several chairs and metres
of fabric were needed to create
this project. Red was chosen as
the colour for the wood as well
474 as the tapes.

The transformation of the
cloister was carried out with
a minimal budget. The various
acts performed in the space
created a different atmosphere
475 every time.

476 The lighting is created from the interaction between natural light entering through the large windows and light generated by the bulbs in the room. The stone of the wall creates a fainter tone.

477 The designers, Dondecabentres are known for designing moments, rather than objects. They wanted to choreograph the space with this project: ephemeral architecture at the service of emotions.

478 The architects want to seek out new experiences for the public and for experimentation with new stage formats. This ephemeral performance is created with very little material and the help of the dancers.

479 As is characteristic of this architects' and designers' studio, this is a clear example of the tangentiality between disciplines: ephemeral architecture project, installation and scenography.

480 The architects used the slogan "choose your tape, dance and leave your mark" to create an ephemeral, light and simple structure. The dancers delicately and softly move between the tapes.

Indexical{Space}

CRISTINA BESTRATÉN, AINA BIGORRA, ERIK HERRERA + DONDECABENTRES

BARCELONA, SPAIN, 2013

AREA
N/A

CLIENT
HAND MADE DANCE

PHOTOS
© DONDECABENTRES, MARTINA ALCOBENDAS

481 The project demonstrates that a fusion between dance and photography can be used to create a distinctive installation. The aim is to create a stage experience that is different to the rest.

482 The scenography of the installation combines the photography exhibition with dance. The effect of the fusion between movement and staging was sought.

483 Transparent film is used to help define the desired scenery. The tapes mark the route of the choreography.

484 Three central elements act as the background scenery. The dancers interact with them and reinforce their purpose.

485 Three contemporary dancers participate in the show, moving through space and generating independent concepts.

486 The combination of cling film, frames with images and white paper figures interacts to create the scenery. The dancer is responsible for completing the scenography.

487 The arrangement of the elements is not random. Each one of the central elements achieves a defined function that varies with the light and the dancer's movement.

488 The scenography of the installation combines the photography exhibition with dance. The effect of the fusion between movement and staging was sought.

490 The lighting used is essential to highlight the fundamental features of the installation.

489 A mesh in the ceiling supports part of the scenery. The lighting effect together with the choreography completes the artistic project.

Centennial Chromagraph

ADAM MARCUS, DANIEL RAZNICH + VARIABLE PROJECTS

MINNEAPOLIS, MN, USA, 2014

AREA
N/A

CLIENT
UNIVERSITY OF MINNESOTA
SCHOOL OF ARCHITECTURE

PHOTO
© ADAM MARKUS, DANIEL RAZNICK,
JORDAN BARLOW

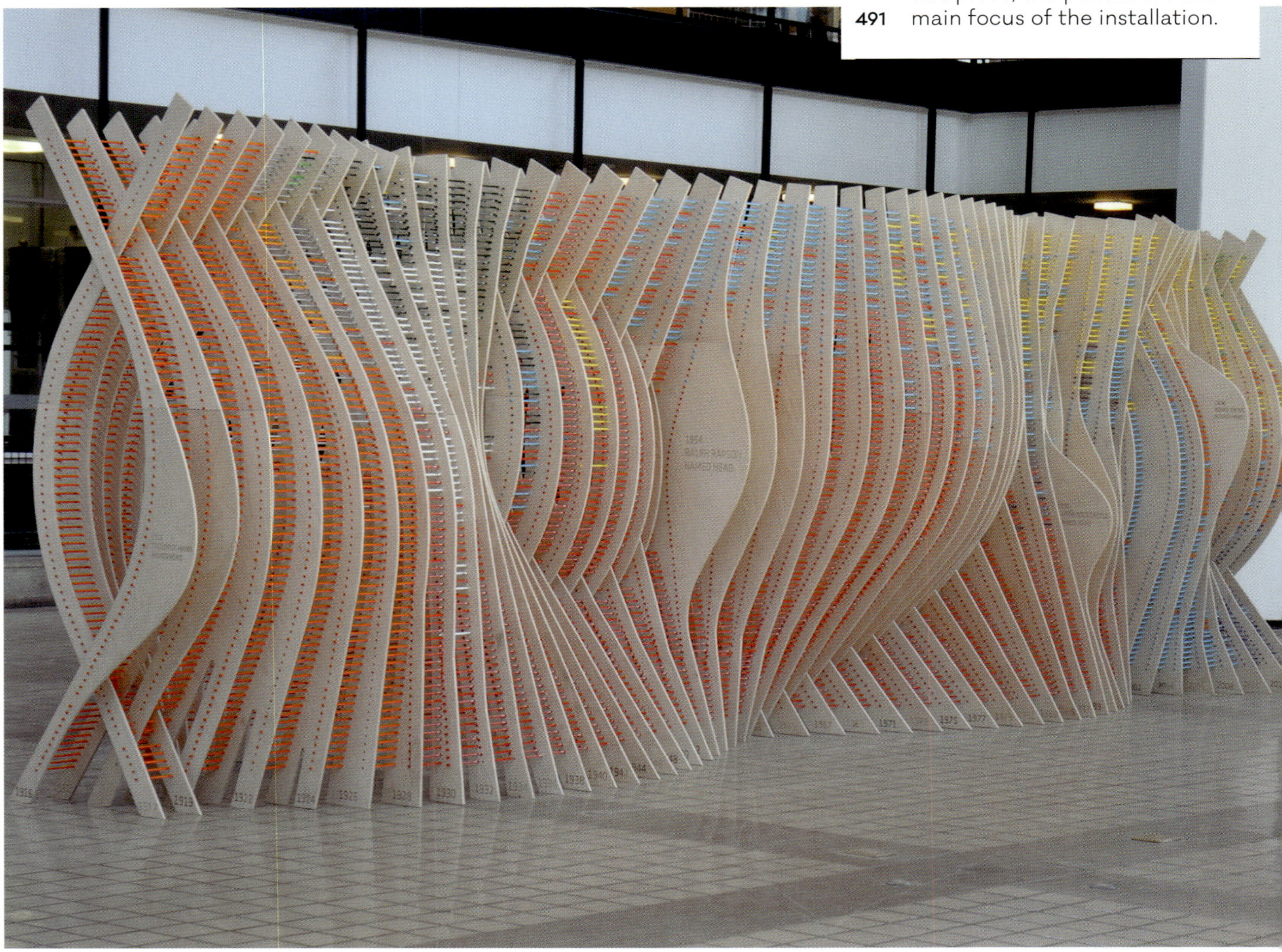

491 The *Centennial Chromagraph* project is a life-size representation of the University of Minnesota School of Architecture. Fundamental to this piece, the pencils are the main focus of the installation.

492 The project was constructed in the central courtyard of Ralph Rapson Hall. It also functions as a centrepiece for the school's centenary celebrations and is admired by all passing visitors.

493 The nucleus consists of 100 plywood ribs joined to 8,080 coloured pencils which colour the structure in an original and attractive way. As well as providing decorative interest, the structure represents the school's history.

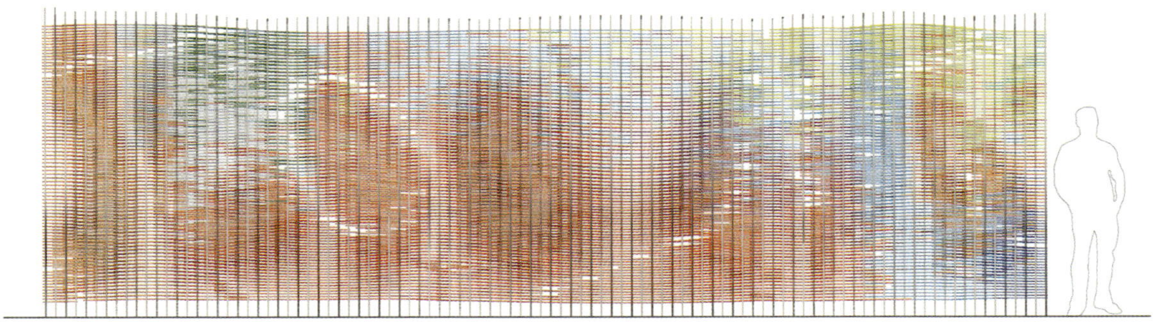

494 The different colours of the pencils represent the different courses taught in the school during its one hundred years, whilst the wooden ribs represent its different historical eras.

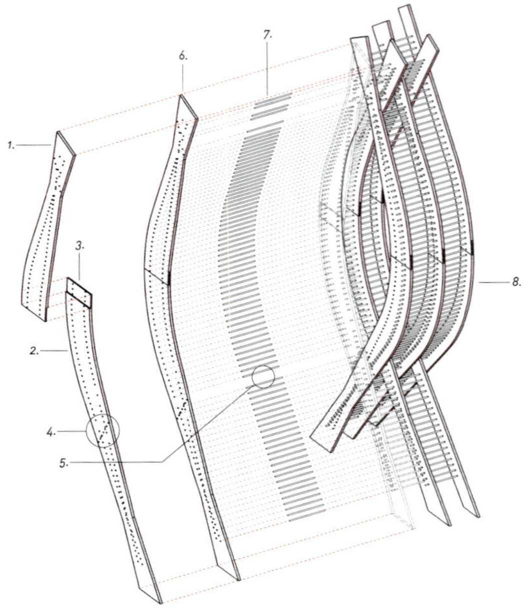

497 Data analysis resulted in two design strategies: chromatic strategy and spatial strategy. Firstly, a curved structure represents the different eras of the school's history. Secondly, a coloured set of data represents the titles obtained.

495 **Different events at the school are represented in each of the structure's curves. The wooden ribs and coloured pencils have a double function: to decorate and teach.**

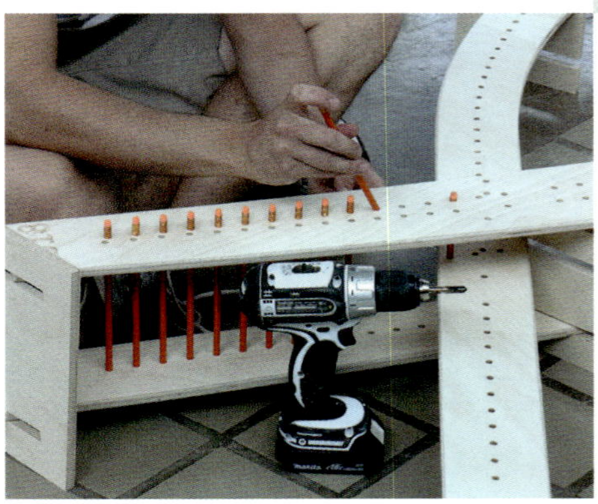

496 The structure's 100 ribs take us on a journey through time and show us the school's different eras. The main materials used in the installation were the pencils and the plywood for the ribs.

498 It only took ten days to create this project. The students' contribution of using historical data to create forms and making use of different materials to represent the project has been fundamental to the project.

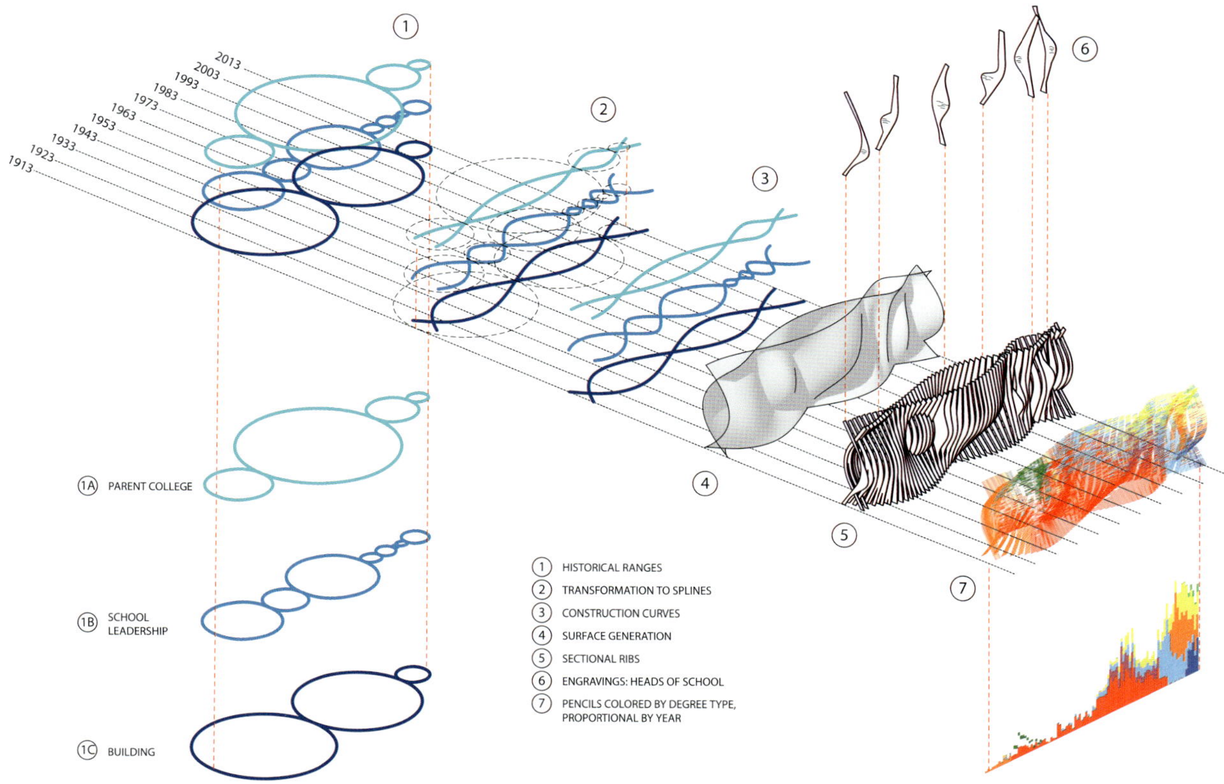

499 The project was designed by software that performed an analysis of archives created by ex-students, encompassing the size of the classes, grades and geographical locations of the graduates.

500 All the information is presented chronologically and schematically through the superimposed curves. These control the general shape of the installation. Spatiality and chromaticity are the two main distinguishing features.

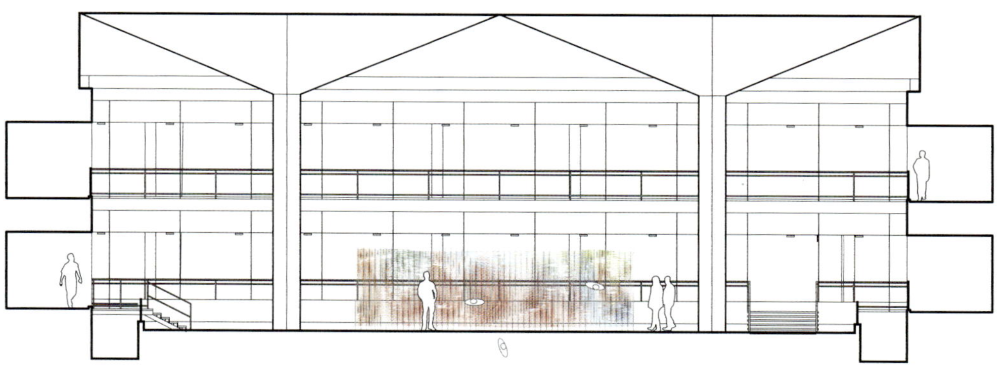

Chromatic Screen

LIKEARCHITECTS

PORTO, PORTUGAL, 2012
SURFACE
1 m^2
CLIENT
RAR IMOBILIÁRIA
PHOTO
© DINIS SOTTOMAYOR PHOTOGRAPHY

501 Designed for *Porto Design Week* 2012, *Chromatic Screen* is a piece that explores the limits between art, design, architecture and urban installation.

502 Defining itself as an intervention feature, Porto Design Week transcends the space of the fair, projecting the city as a landmark in the world of design and architecture.

503 The reinterpretation of an everyday object, a coloured plastic children's clothes hanger, has served to define a new space, a protected area in a room without visual barriers.

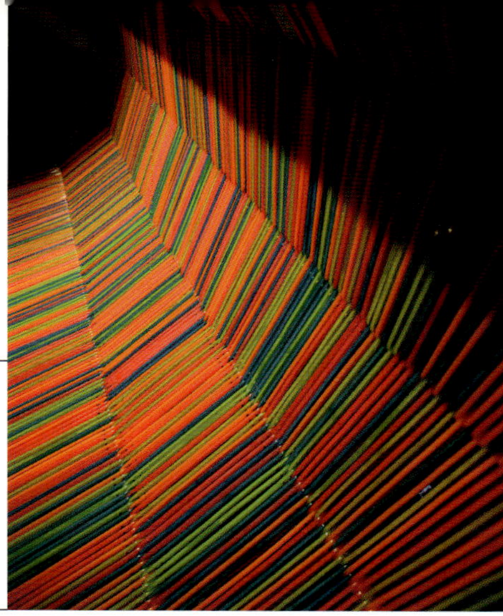

504 The *Chromatic Screen* constitutes a spatial organiser that immerses the visitor in a polychromatic kinetic experience that alternates moments of opacity with others of transparency.

505 LIKEarchitects studio specialises in ephemeral interventions based on the combination of fundamental architectural knowledge and more radical experiences.

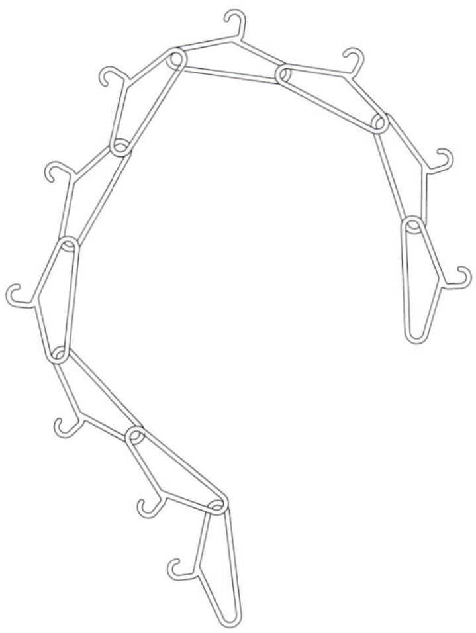

506 **When a light source is introduced from the inside, the viewer sees the effect of a giant two metre high multicoloured polypropylene lamp.**

507 Just over 2,000 Ikea Bagis clothes hangers of four different colours were used to create this two metre high multicolour polypropylene space organiser.

508 The creation of a space that is simultaneously concave and convex due to the shape of the hangers and their arrangement, leaves the possible uses for this installation to the viewer's imagination: room divider, curtain, lamp, den, etc.

509 One year later, *Chromatic Screen II* was created, a twin project made with 4,000 black and white hangers, but this time in a landscaped exterior that radically contrasted with the installation.

510 This young collective's proposals aim to initiate a critical dialogue around architecture and urban performances.

DAM Pavilion

BARKOW LEIBINGER ARCHITECTS

FRANKFURT, GERMANY, 2009

AREA
N/A

CLIENT
DEUTSCHES ARCHITEKTURMUSEUM

PHOTO
© UWE DETTMAR,
BARKOW LEIBINGER ARCHITECTS

511 Structural engineer Werner Sobek created a temporary pavilion for Frankfurt's Deutches Architekturmuseum (DAM) on the occasion of its twenty-fifth anniversary. The exhibition showed the history of the architecture of temporary structures.

This architectural pavilion
was not designed as a building
in itself. It is a prototype to use
as a model to test the limits
and capacities of a speculative
installation for construction
in areas with warm climates
512 and temperate seasons.

The pavilion's final destination
should have been the garden
of the Museum für Angewandte
Kunst but the construction
remained at the prototype
stage. Sponsors such as Bayer
Makrolon, Bretor Kemmlit,
MBM Construction and 3M
were essential for obtaining
513 materials and production.

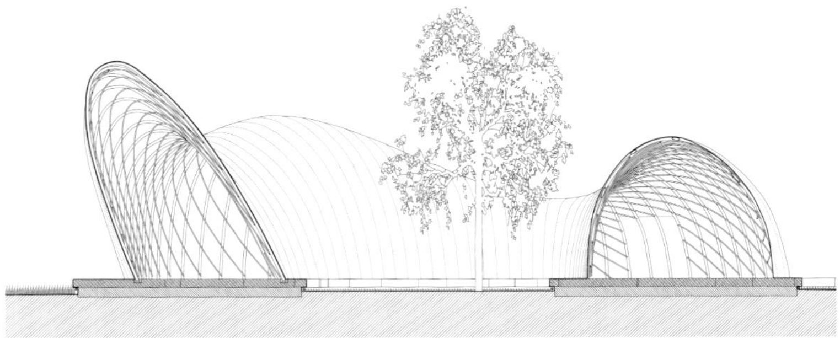

514 The project consists of a light structure constructed with steel tubes bent in three directions and with a transparent exterior skin. A 30 mm tube stabilises the structure, which is joined to a foundation of pre-cast concrete.

515 Multiple overlapping tiles were used to provide protection against inclement weather and, above all, it offers natural ventilation during the summer exhibition season.

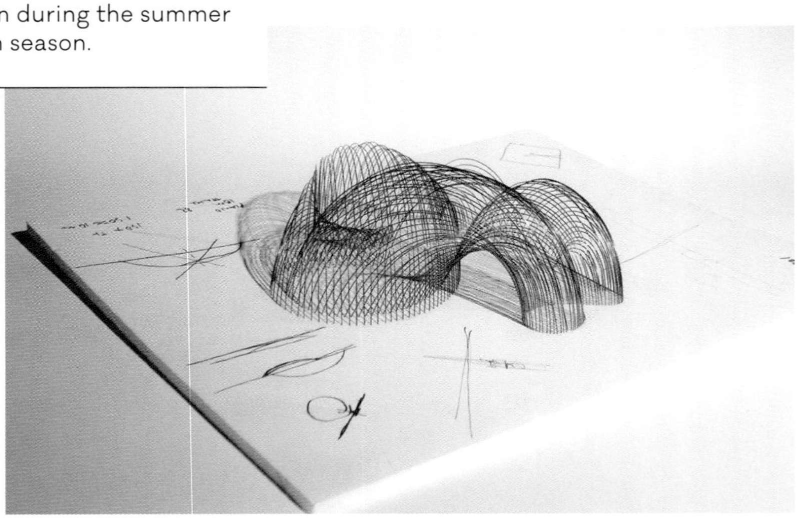

516 With the help of a computer program designed for the occasion, different sized circles were projected onto a vaulted area. First, a model of one of the five arches was created with a coating that would form part of a section of the pavilion.

517 A Velcro closure was created to attach the tiles to the structure. This enabled rapid construction and easy adjustments. The tiles were attached to photovoltaic panels that were positioned parametrically to allow solar gain.

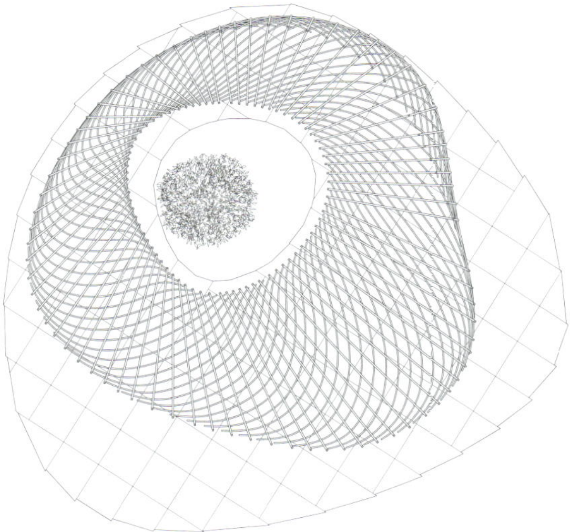

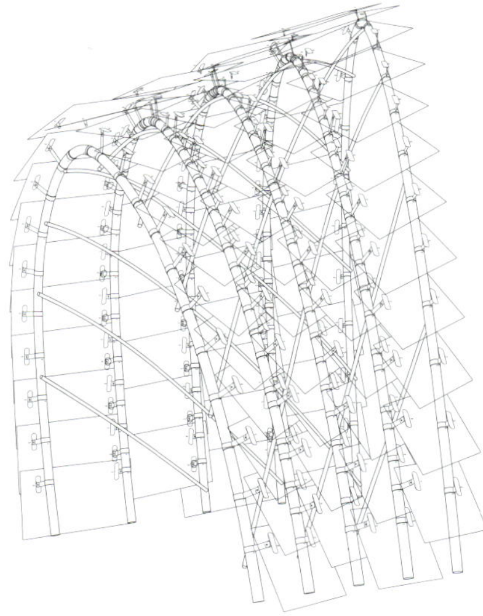

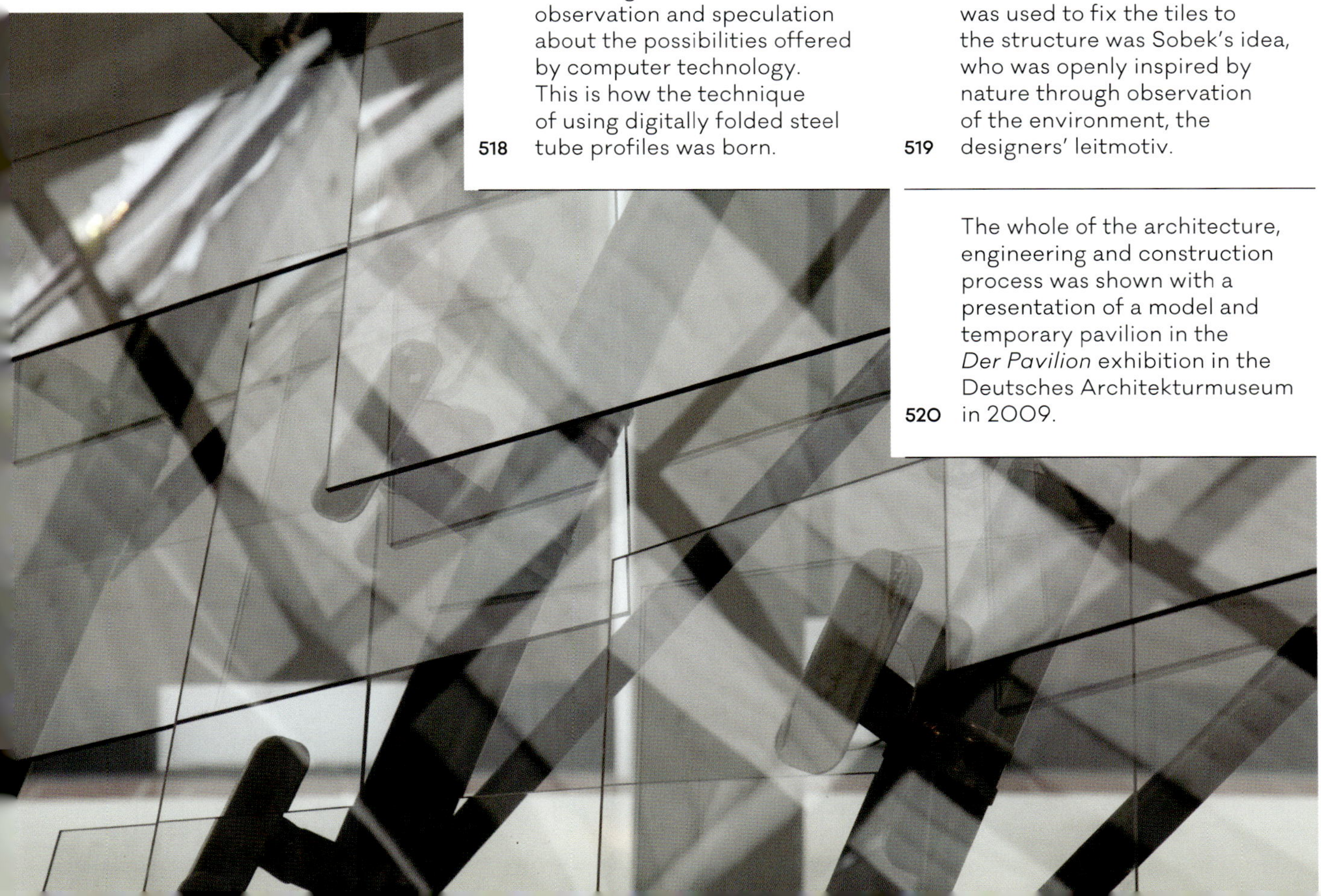

The designers advocate
observation and speculation
about the possibilities offered
by computer technology.
This is how the technique
of using digitally folded steel
518 tube profiles was born.

The invention and development
of the Velcro closure that
was used to fix the tiles to
the structure was Sobek's idea,
who was openly inspired by
nature through observation
of the environment, the
519 designers' leitmotiv.

The whole of the architecture,
engineering and construction
process was shown with a
presentation of a model and
temporary pavilion in the
Der Pavilion exhibition in the
Deutsches Architekturmuseum
520 in 2009.

Spiral Space

XEVI BAYONA

OLOT, SPAIN, 2008

AREA
N/A

CLIENT
GARROTXA-RIPOLLÉS BRANCH OF THE COAC

PHOTO
© XEVI MOLINER, XEVI BAYONA

521 The project stems from a request from the delegation of the Garrotxa-Ripollés branch of the COAC. The aim was to make an exhibition for the finalist entries in the FAD awards 2008.

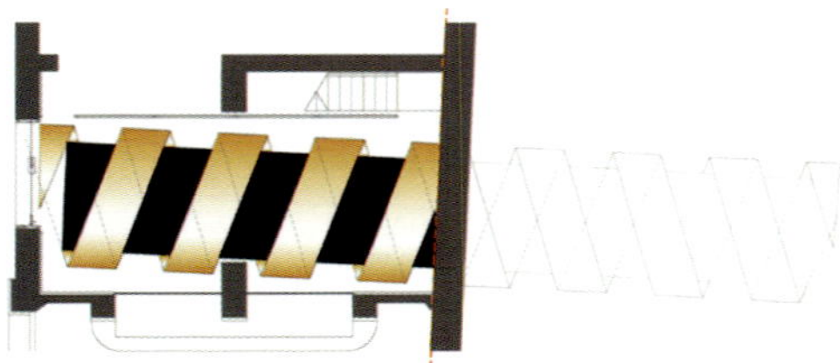

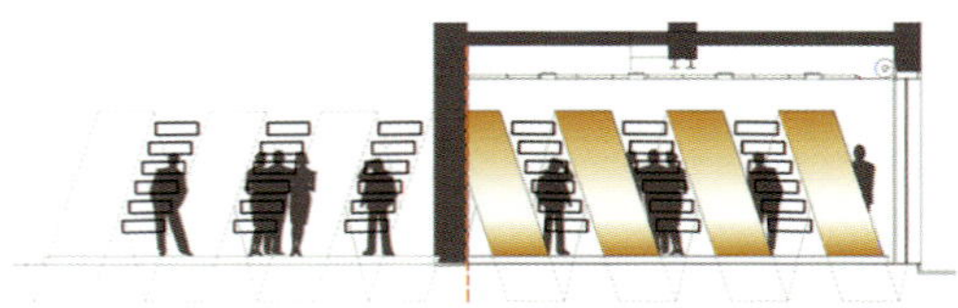

522 The selected proposal should comply with two existing conditions: it must fit both a very small budget and spatial limitations.

523 The mirror at the end of the room duplicates the image and creates a double perception of the space. The perpendicular spiral-shaped installation is in the background.

524 A new limit is generated, changing the spatial perception of the room and breaking away from the rigidity of its walls. This is achieved with a spiral which, in combination with a mirror, generates the illusion of increased depth.

525 The arrangement and organisation of the panels generated an angle of vision that made reading easier and enabled more panels to be installed along the length of the spiral.

526 A walkway separates the black carpet from the floor. Along with white lines on the floor, an optical illusion is created as it generates an illusion of the spiral continuing.

527 To achieve a low-budget installation, materials such as a platform, lights and wiring were used from former exhibitions. Drums that were no longer used were also recovered and used to help create an embracing ambience.

528 The ends of each drum were removed with a circular saw. A cut was made lengthwise in the cylindrical surface to make a rectangular sheet.

529 The ambience created by the installation invites escape from the daily routine. It could be defined as a kind of urban refuge that provokes contemplation and reflection.

530 Recycling the drums for the installation enhances its chromatic richness. These show their rusted insides, while on the outside the original colours are still preserved.

531—540

Nativity Book

XEVI BAYONA

OLOT, SPAIN, 2009

AREA
N/A

CLIENT
OLOT CITY COUNCIL

PHOTO
© XEVI MOLINER

The purpose of the *Nativity*
Scene Book installation is
to provide the library with
531 a unique space.

The forms of the assembly
is one single material: a large
sheet of foldable cardboard.
The unusual aspect is that one
of the pages of the book is
extended, creating an original
532 design.

The figures of the nativity
scene are just silhouettes cut
from the same corrugated
cardboard. These decorate
and show the route for the
533 user to view.

The ribbon, created from
a page of the book, is foldable
and rises towards the roof.
In the different stages, there
are figures that simulate
534 those of a nativity scene.

535 The route of the nativity scene begins at the top of the sheet, where the sky is represented, and descends until it arrives at the birth scene at the base.

536 The lighting in the space generates shadows on the pop-up scenes. This creates perspective and distorts the perception of the figures.

537 Being a vertical nativity scene, the viewer can look at it from all the floors in the library. From each floor, a different stage can be seen.

538 The installation allows visitors to create an abstract reading of the nativity scene tradition. A cardboard sheet easily represents this custom.

539 The choice to represent the nativity on the page of a book is perfect for a library. This creates a fusion between tradition and the function of the space.

540 The use of foldable cardboard allows the installation to be assembled and disassembled in very little time. It doesn't take much space to store and can be easily transported.

Porte des Savoirs

EPFL+ECAL LAB + ALICE STUDIO EPFL

LAUSANNE, SWITZERLAND, 2014

AREA
N/A

CLIENT
VAUDOISE INSURANCE

PHOTOS

541 The project is an interactive, innovative and stimulating design that interacts with the space. It transports travellers to another dimension to immerse them in a spiral of knowledge. It makes them forget that they are really in the entrance to a metro station and not in a large interactive room.

542 *Porte des Savoirs* creates a game of scale between the movement of the text and the body of the visitor through space. The visitor's visual contact, along with the speed, movement and different sizes of the representation, creates a direct relationship between individual and information.

543 A collection of interactive tables allow the user to connect and get directly involved with the project, which creates a social link between the exhibition organisers and the visitors.

544 The main idea of the project was to submerge visitors in a rather intellectual environment through the installation of panels and representations arranged in the entrance to the metro station.

545 A system comprising mirrors that amplify the space and screens that display the main news, allows passengers to break the monotony of the daily commute.

546 The structure consists of more than 18 000 LED bulbs that are used to create a visual effect. It also makes optimum use of information displays and creates a spectacular effect with the mirrors and the ceiling.

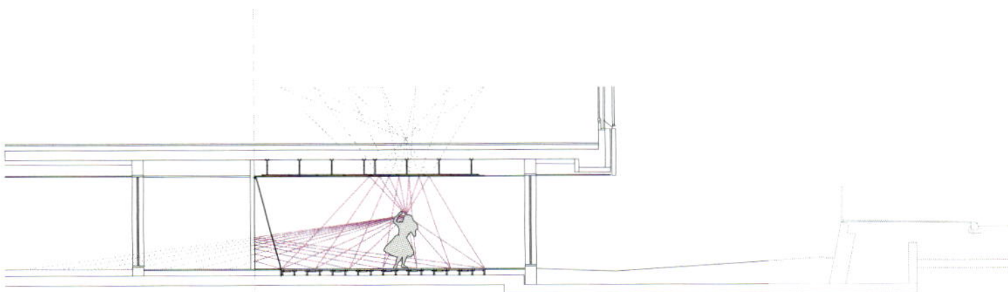

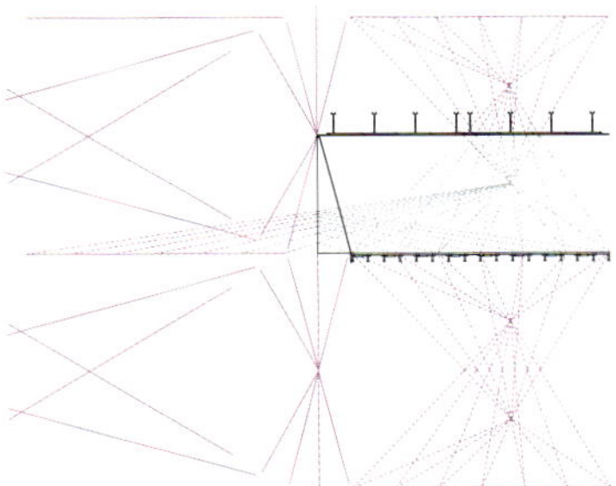

547 Text appears reflected on ceilings, floors and walls, enveloping visitors in a bubble of information.

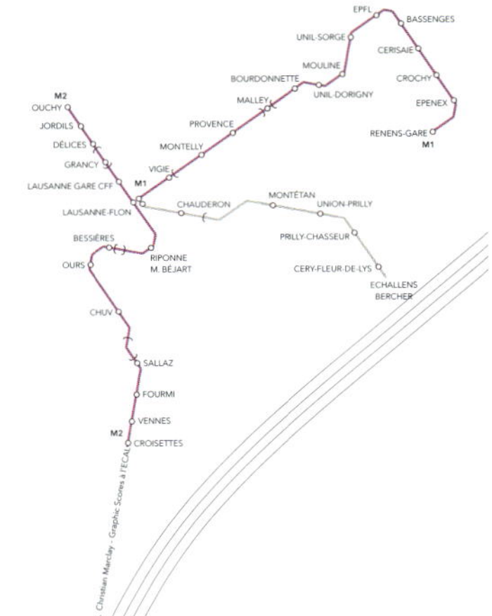

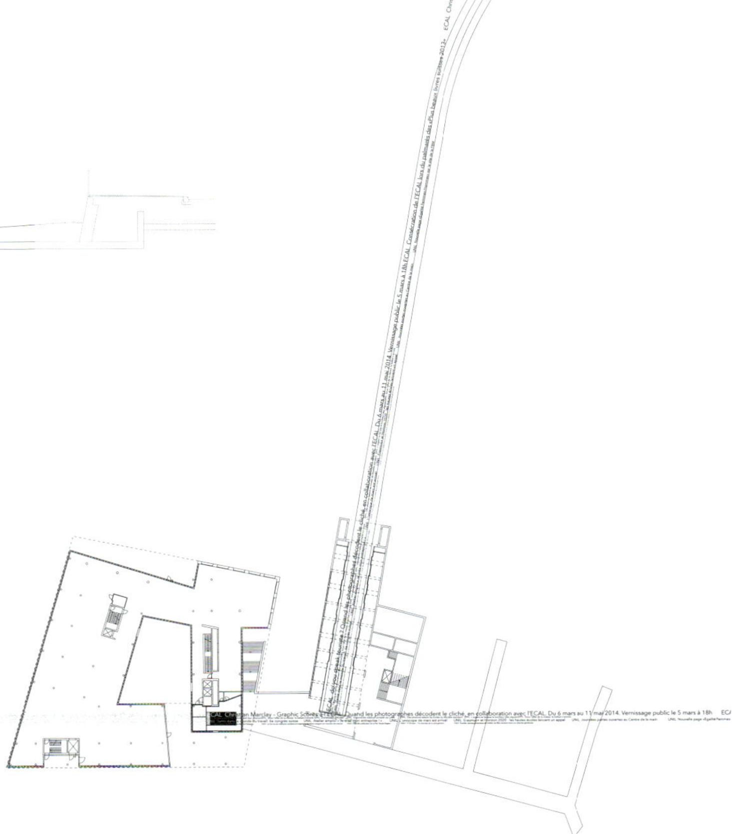

548 The large visual stimulus is achieved thanks to the contrast between the light and the 25 square metres of flat screen distributed throughout the entire space. The speed of the information creates a sense of gravity that transports visitors to a floating space.

549 The installation plays with perception and can evoke a sensation of blurred vision. The intention is that the content can be read and understood, accompanied by a landscape of scales and rhythms.

550 The strong interactive character of the project is made possible by the floor being sensitive to touch, which creates a relationship between reading, the visitor and a sensation of immersion in the space that has been created.

X-hibition

LIKEARCHITECTS

PORTO, PORTUGAL, 2012
SURFACE
250 m^2
CLIENT
UPTEC – PORTO UNIVERSITY
PHOTO
© DINIS SOTTOMAYOR PHOTOGRAPHY

551 An area of 250 m^2 is created with a total of 4,000 crosses printed on 6mm thick cardboard. The aim is to temporarily decorate the interior of the venue where the *BIN@ Porto International Event* is to be held.

552 Reusable and biodegradable cardboard is used to create a flexible and light structure with different graphical qualities to those offered by other materials. The blue colour of one side and the stripes of the other change the appearance of the room in just a few hours.

553 It is exhibited in a space of 250 m^2, in which two programs are carried out on different days: an exhibition room with newly created technological items and a conference room.

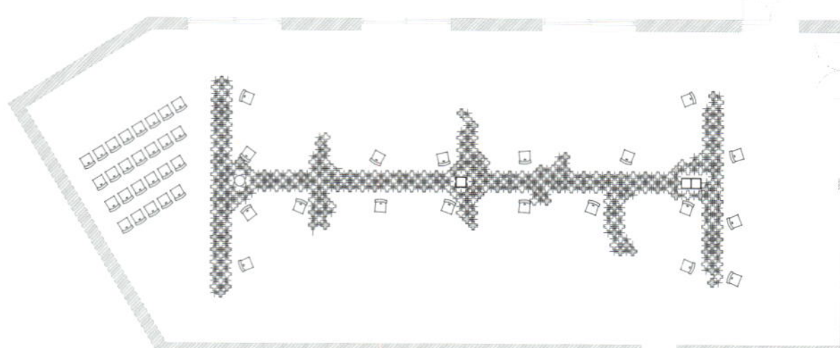

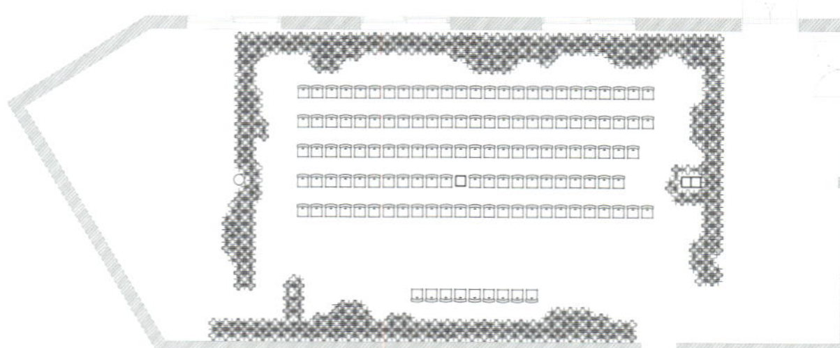

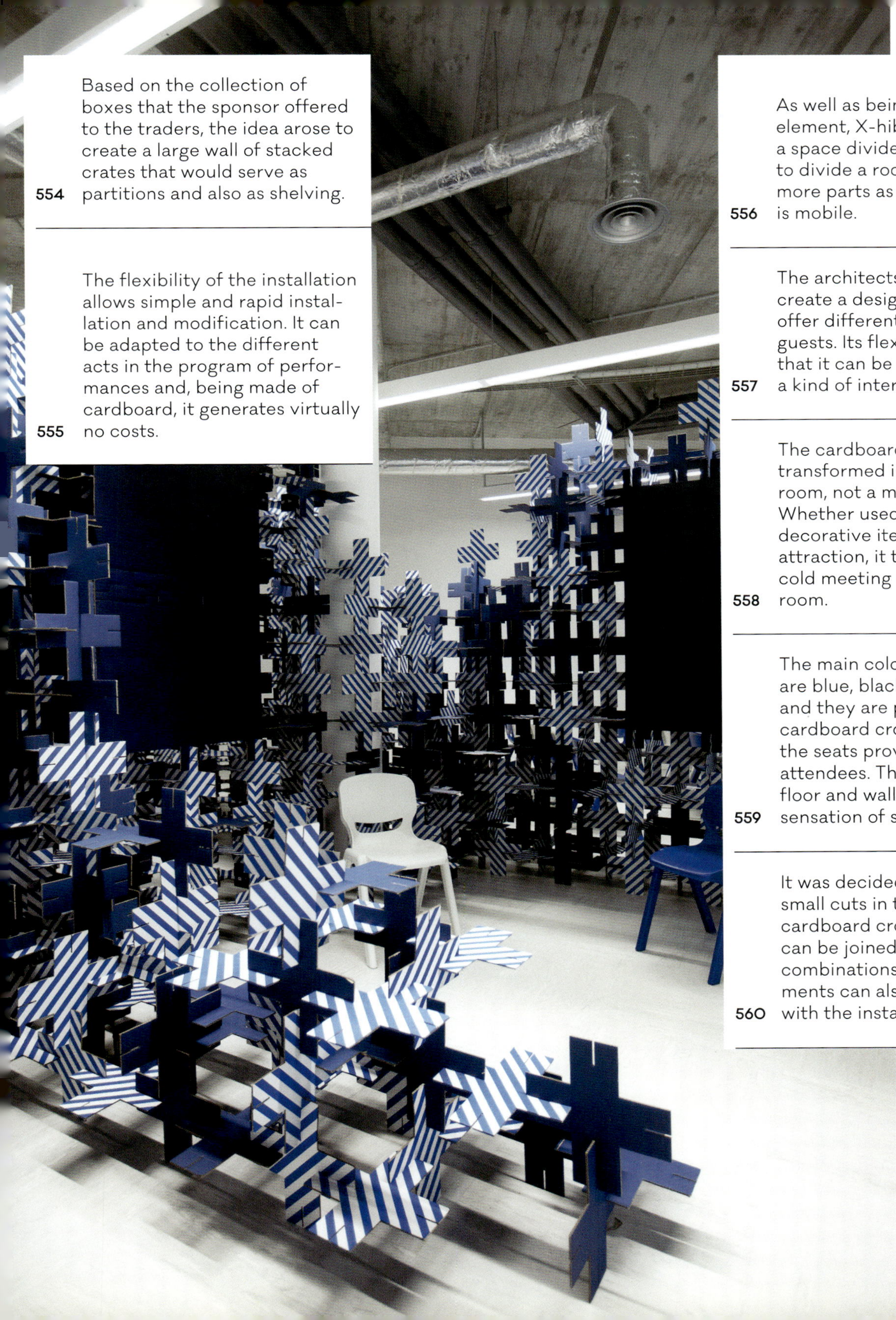

554 Based on the collection of boxes that the sponsor offered to the traders, the idea arose to create a large wall of stacked crates that would serve as partitions and also as shelving.

555 The flexibility of the installation allows simple and rapid installation and modification. It can be adapted to the different acts in the program of performances and, being made of cardboard, it generates virtually no costs.

556 As well as being a decorative element, X-hibition can act as a space divider. It can be used to divide a room into two or more parts as the installation is mobile.

557 The architects decided to create a design that would offer different perspectives to guests. Its flexible nature means that it can be converted into a kind of interactive art.

558 The cardboard crosses are transformed into part of the room, not a mere decoration. Whether used as a partition, decorative item or visual attraction, it transforms the cold meeting and exhibition room.

559 The main colours of the room are blue, black and white and they are present in the cardboard crosses as well as the seats provided for the attendees. The pale-coloured floor and walls create a sensation of spaciousness.

560 It was decided to make small cuts in the sides of the cardboard crosses so that they can be joined together. More combinations and arrangements can also be created with the installation.

Cocoon

ANDREA GRAZIANO + CO-DE-IT, AMLETO PICERNO CERASO + MEDITERRANEAN FAB LAB

CAVA DEI TIRRENI, ITALY, 2013

AREA
717 x 513 x 310 cm

CLIENT
M.ART.E – MEDIATECA ARTE EVENTI

PHOTO
© CO-DE-IT, MEDITERRANEAN FAB LAB

561 The *Cocoon* is the result of a workshop run by Co-de-It, a digital creation laboratory, and organised by Mediterranean Fab Lab, a hub of ideas where they explore new types of computational design and production.

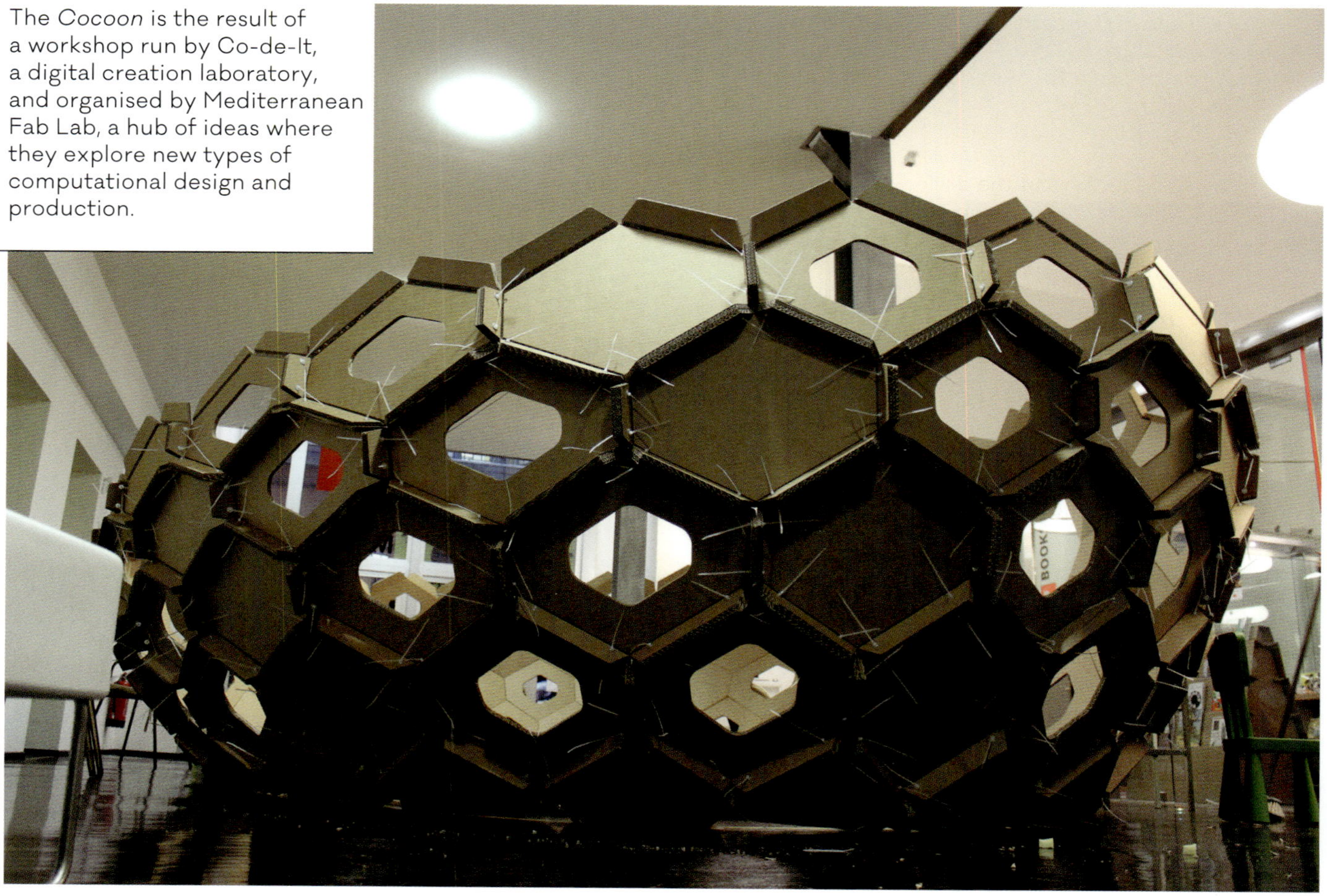

562 The project was conceived as an extension of a shop in an art gallery and as an exhibition room for temporary events, exhibitions, children's workshops, small-scale concerts, etc.

563 The structure was designed as a chrysalis, a space that is closed but at the same time visually permeable with the room that houses it, thanks to the alternation of opaque and perforated elements.

564 The choice of materials is not random; the workshop was the result of sponsorship from CRTS Cartotecnica, a local packaging company, who provided the 83 sheets of 1,190 x 1,590 mm triple corrugated cardboard used.

565 The pattern of the drilled tiles, as well as the position of the entrance opening, were carefully researched so that they did not compromise the stability of the structure.

566 After the shape of the interior was defined, the tiling of the structure following a viable pattern and its planning were carried out using the Rhino and Grasshopper design programs.

567 The shape and size of the 53 m^2 structure were previously defined in response to the plan of the available space. The circular shape and diverse planes of symmetry provide greater stability to the structure.

568 The pavilion consists of 231 pieces of cardboard, 115 open and 116 opaque, assembled with 1,500 plastic brackets and 1,500 metal rings.

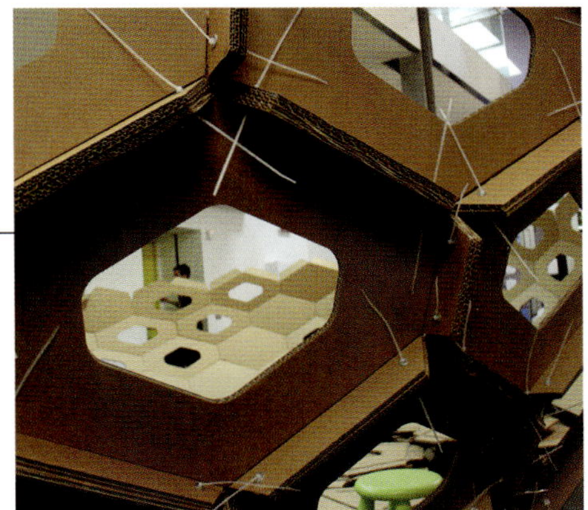

569 The flaps for each of the cells are folded and fitted by a 45° cut over the sheet of 14 mm thick cardboard, which ensures a 90° pleat and the correct assembly of the pieces without unwanted faults.

570 During the assembly phase of the panels, parts of the structure were anchored to secure items to support its weight. Once the construction had been completed and its stability tested *in situ*, these anchor points were removed.

Polyvagina

NEREA CALVILLO, MARINA FERNÁNDEZ, LAURA MIGUELÁÑEZ, FRANCISCO TRIVIÑO + C + ARQUITECTOS

MURCIA, SPAIN, 2014

AREA
650 m²

CLIENT
FAN RIOTS

PHOTO
© MIGUEL DE GUZMÁN

571 The Polyvagina pavilion was part of the Fan Riots artistic event for the SOS music festival. Videos, installations and performances were shown with the consequences of the punk phenomenon on the art world as leitmotiv.

572 The assembly took two days. Different areas and routes were created for the visitors, who saw themselves continuously reflected by the polyamide of the balloons.

Two of the main requirements
for the installation of this
ephemeral intervention were
artistic creation with a small
budget and a fast, two-day
construction. These conditions
were fundamental for designing
573 this spectacular intervention.

The installation was
constructed using undistin-
guished materials used in
conventional architecture.
For example, sandbags and
balloons inflated with helium
574 to create a curved structure.

The balloons containing helium
or airfunction as construction
units that are used to cover
large lights with double
575 curvature shapes.

576 The system used for joining the balloons was collectively invented with the help of architecture students from the Escuela de Alicante. When working with an unstable object, search and investigation form the research concepts: architecture and uncertainty.

577 Due to the lack of technical specifications, such as the behaviour of helium and air when used for elevation, the anchoring systems for balloons on a large scale; for the architects this design was an experiment because of its uncertainty.

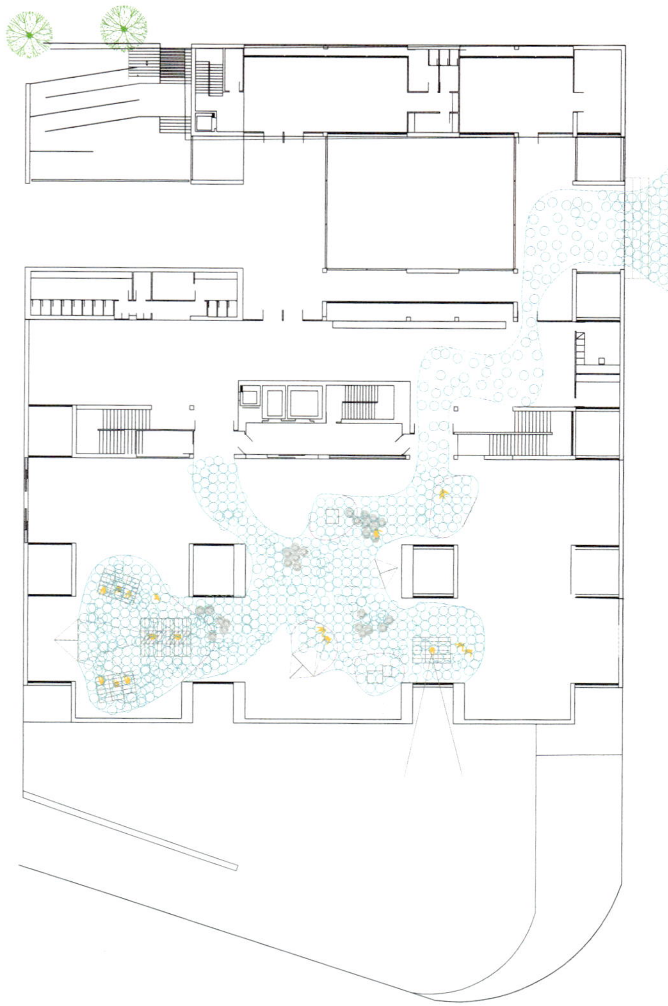

578 The aim of the installation is to include other elements that don't form part of the hegemonic repertoire of construction materials. For this reason, balloons used for celebrations and events were chosen.

579 **Polyvagina is a structure that has enabled exhaustive research and the establishment of a relationship between ephemeral architecture, action and performance.**

580 On the last day of the festival, participants were presented with the balloons. This gave relevance to the ephemeral quality of the installation and the success of the experimentation with unstable objects.

Positive-Negative

J. MAYER H. UND PARTNER ARCHITEKTEN

BERLIN, GERMANY, 2007

AREA
N/A

CLIENT
GALERIE KICKEN

PHOTO
© LUTTGER PAFFRATH

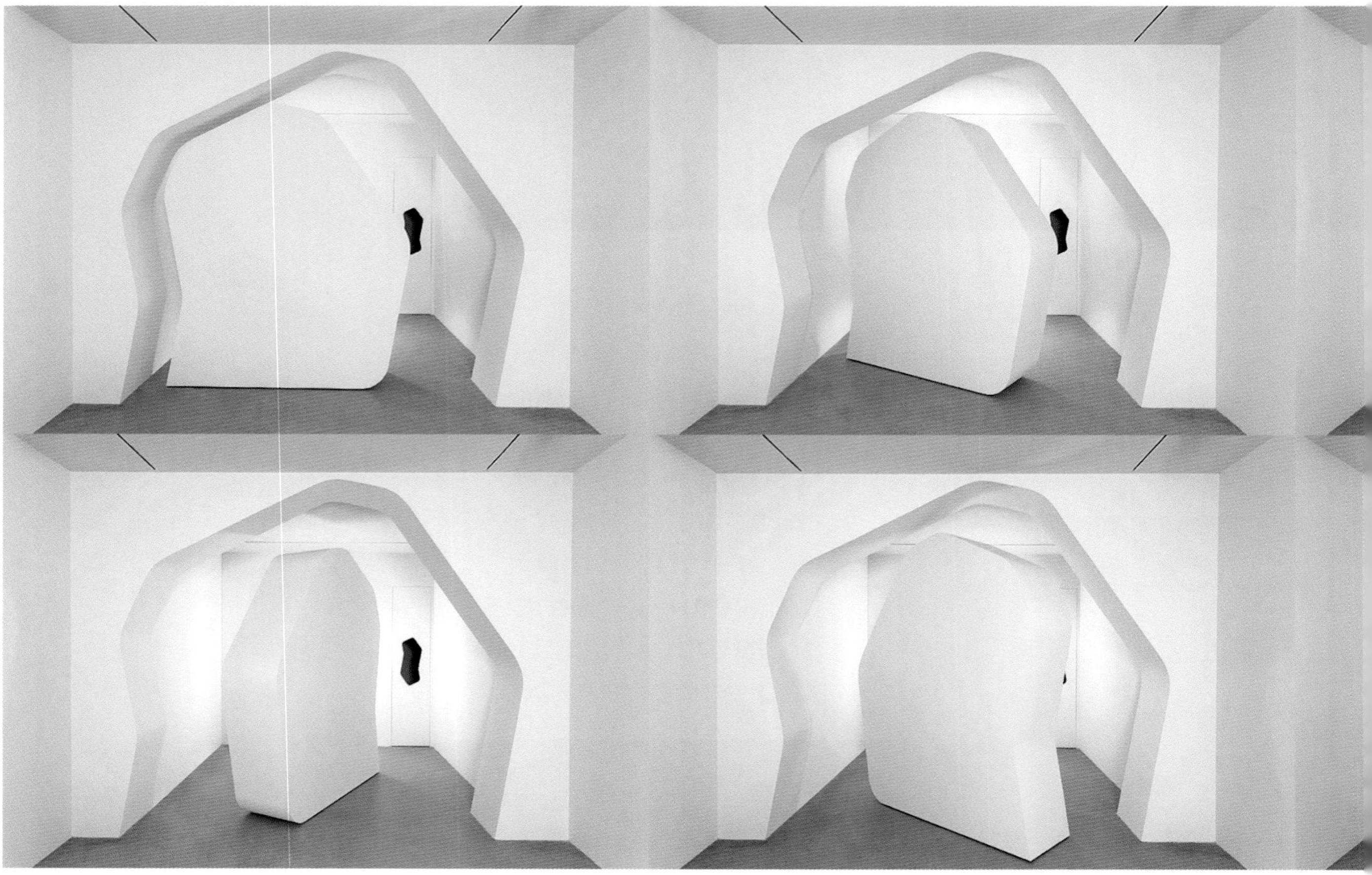

581 The project consists of installing a dynamic object in a gallery with the aim of generating a variety of spaces for exhibition.

582 The structure has a similar form to that of a white cube and serves as a decorative element, as a space divider and even as a static frame. One item with three uses that is easy to move.

583 *Positive-Negative* is presented as a changing and versatile structure. It consists of a frame and a filler that helps to change the space for potential exhibitions or performances.

The mutability of the gallery
means that unexpected pieces
such as *Positive-Negative*
can be displayed. A cube or
static framework that offers a
584 different way of enjoying space.

The design of the installation,
together with the white colour
and soft lighting create the
desired atmosphere. The visitor
can observe the installation
in its totality, without hurry
586 but without pause.

It provokes the changeability
of the space and reopens inter-
esting exhibition opportunities.
The typical artistic space
is thus transformed, fleeing
588 from convention.

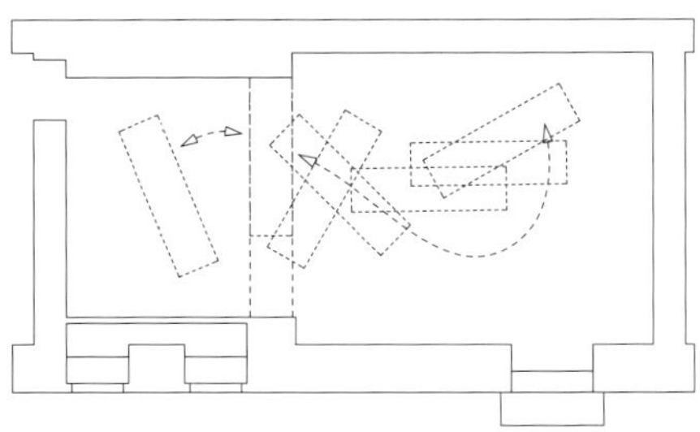

White was chosen to enhance
the different opportunities
to play with the light or obtain
a neutral ambience, devoid
589 of shadows.

The projects allows the space
to become more versatile
and innovative. It completely
changes the appearance of the
space and the way exhibitions
585 and activities are held.

The distorted arch has a double
function: to serve as an artistic
structure and act as a partition
587 for exhibiting different works.

The project proposes a new
form of art space. Various
performances can take place
on temporary stages with good
590 results.

591—594

Les Maîtres du Désordre

JAKOB + MACFARLANE

ORLEANS, FRANCE, 2010-2012

AREA
N/A

CLIENT
MUSÉE DU QUAI BRANLY

PHOTO
© JAKOB + MACFARLANE, NICOLAS BOREL

Jakob + McFarlane were commissioned to create an original and spectacular scenography for the exhibition *Les Maîtres du Désordre* planned at the Quai Branly Museum.

591

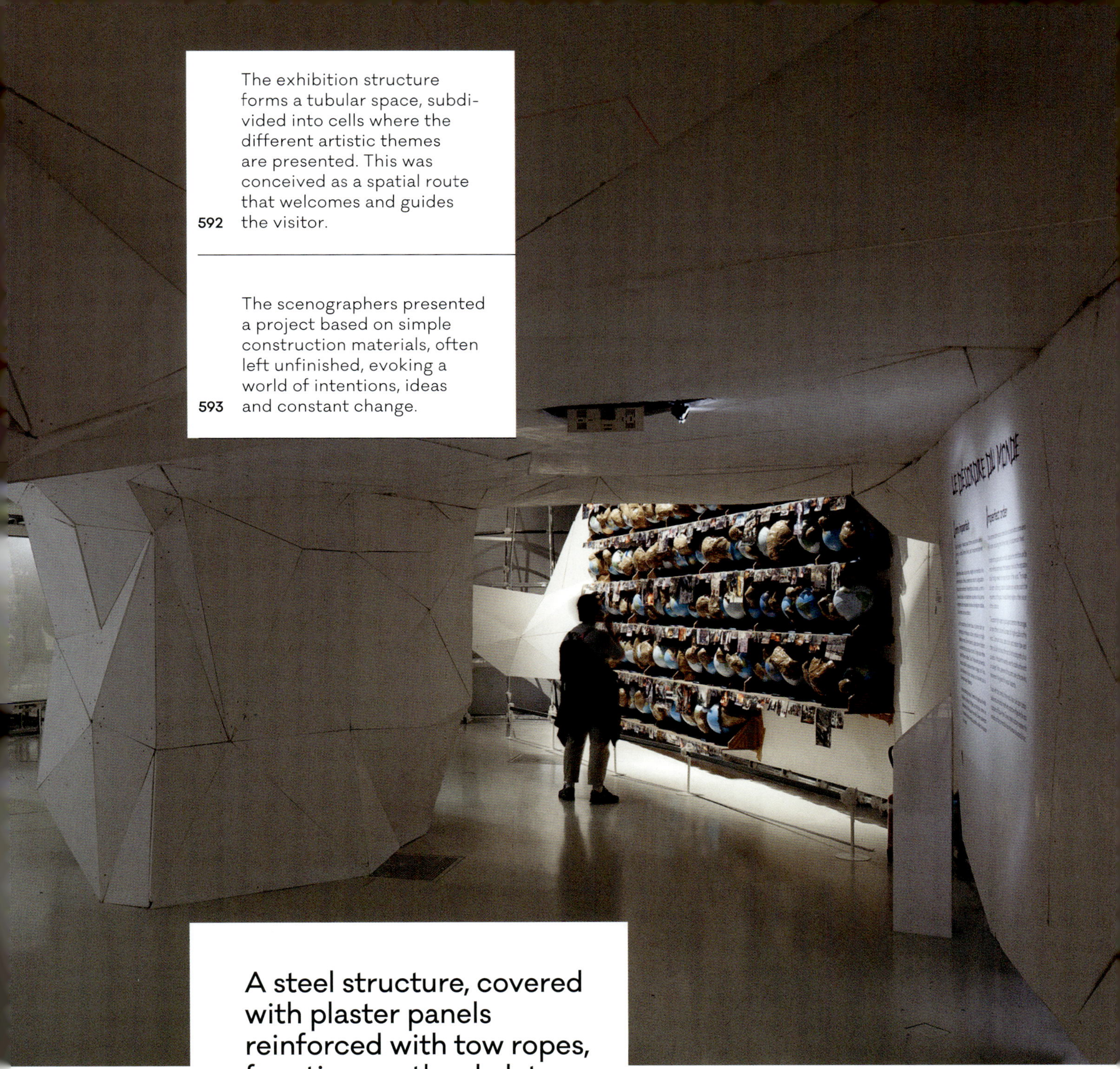

592 The exhibition structure forms a tubular space, subdivided into cells where the different artistic themes are presented. This was conceived as a spatial route that welcomes and guides the visitor.

593 The scenographers presented a project based on simple construction materials, often left unfinished, evoking a world of intentions, ideas and constant change.

594 A steel structure, covered with plaster panels reinforced with tow ropes, functions as the skeleton, ligaments and the skin of an organic body.

The assembly of the structure
oscillates between ancient
and modern, between manual
and industrial: it reinforces
the idea that a project could
595 appear as an evolution.

Illumination is used to
emphasise the primitive and
rough look with strong lighting
that highlights a journey
without freezing in time
596 or space.

Vortices have been installed
in the central unit with visible
power cables hanging from the
roof. These materialise the link
between earth and the beyond,
between the sacred and the
profane, between the percep-
597 tible and the intelligible.

598 The success of the scenography is due to the use of steel sheets covered with plaster and the fibrous tubular structure, which is used to display the shamans represented in the exhibition.

599 The scenography by Jakob + MacFarlane is impressive to the extent that the exhibition could almost work without the pieces displayed in the modules.

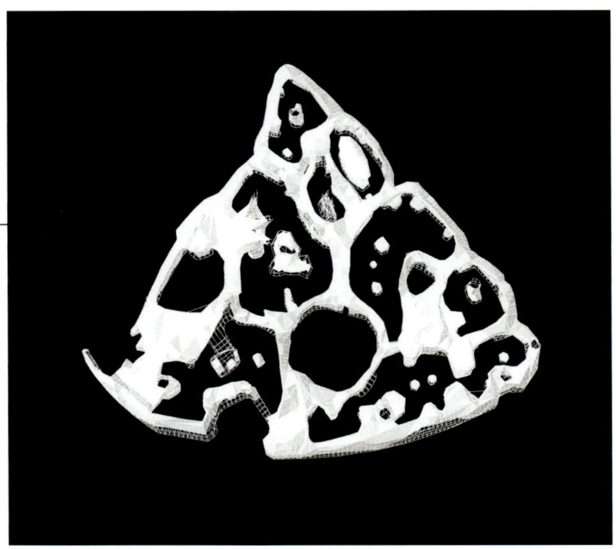

600 The purpose of scenographic design is to highlight the works of art and submerge the viewer in an experience of light and materiality through different atmospheres and emotions.

Garment Garden

J. MAYER H. UND PARTNER ARCHITEKTEN

FRANKFURT, GERMANY, 2009

AREA
39.5 m^2

CLIENT
NYA NORDISKA, DANNENBERG

PHOTO
© CONSTANTIN MEYRE PHOTOGRAPHIE, J. MAYER H. UND PARTNER ARCHITEKTEN

All cities need a space for
enjoying nature and leisure.
The structure aims to create
a relaxed area in an urban
context: Frankfurt's *Design*
601 *Annual*.

The vertical pillars are covered
with fabrics and curtains of
different colours and they
represent the medium-high
buildings and trees of the big
602 city.

The curtains that cover every
structure create rough surfaces,
imitating the bark of the trees.
The prints and colours of these
play a principal role in the
603 installation.

In 2008, the project was
honoured with the ADAM prize,
the most important award in
the field of innovative design
604 for fairs and events.

The cone-shaped sculptures
are more than three metres
high. They are covered with
curtain fabrics, which create
605 different patterns and textures.

606 Its different forms and features represent trees and futuristic skyscrapers. The combination of coloured fabrics and grand height completed the look.

607 Each tower was wrapped in metres of curtains with different colours and prints. The combination of these, together with the height and shape, make the installation even more pleasing.

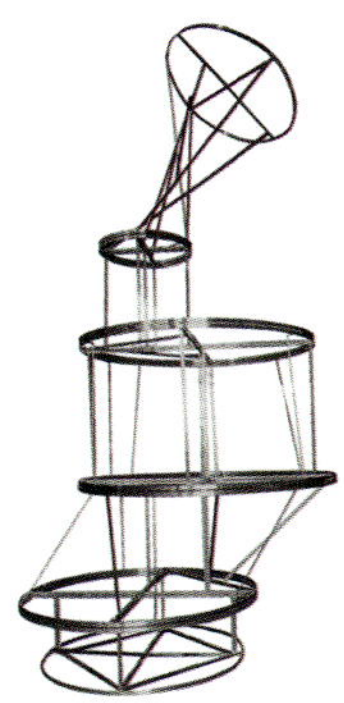

608 Separately, the structure and the curtains are not especially attractive by themselves. By putting them in the same space, they become an installation, a decorative project.

609 The collection of trees and buildings represented occupies a space of 39.5 m^2. In this small space, the large volume of the structures creates imposing shapes.

610 The structure of the towers was formed by joining different sized cylinders in an abstract manner. These were covered with the curtains, completely obscuring the main frame.

611—620

Cloud(e)scape

LIKEARCHITECTS

HAMBURG, GERMANY, 2014

AREA
25 m^2

CLIENT
SKYPRO

PHOTO
© MATTHIAS HEIDERICH PHOTOGRAPHY

611 The temporary exhibition was created for Skypro's shoe exhibition in the World Travel Catering Expo in Hamburg. The design and colour of the structure were key to its success.

612 The design's references were philosophy and the values of the shoe company. The aim was to visually represent the Skypro culture through the structure.

613 The blue colour and curvilinear form weren't randomly produced. The organisers wanted to transport visitors towards the sky while they contemplated the company's products.

614 The stand is composed of hundreds of foam pool noodles. Their alignment creates different levels so that all the articles can have the same importance.

615 Soft blue hues were selected in order to transmit peace and tranquility, some of the values the company wants to promote.

The ends of the noodles act as
perfect supports for the articles
to be exhibited. The stand is
accessible, low cost, easy to
assemble, disassemble and
616 move.

With this project, Skypro
proves that it is possible to
create a unique, innovative
stand with a minimum budget,
thanks to the use of low-coast
617 foam noodles.

The space was composed
of two separate volumes which
people could walk between.
They acted as shelving, storage
618 space, a table and a seat.

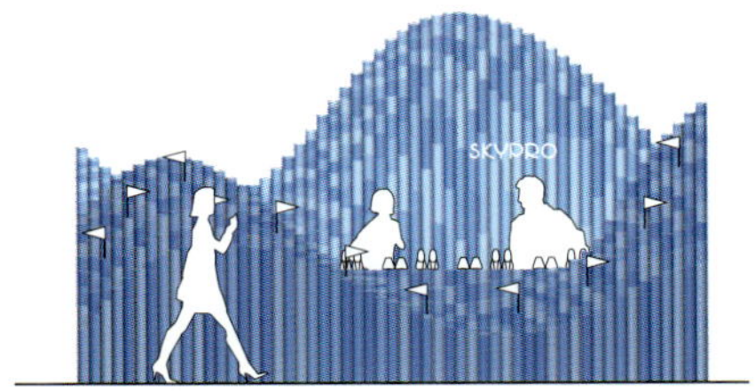

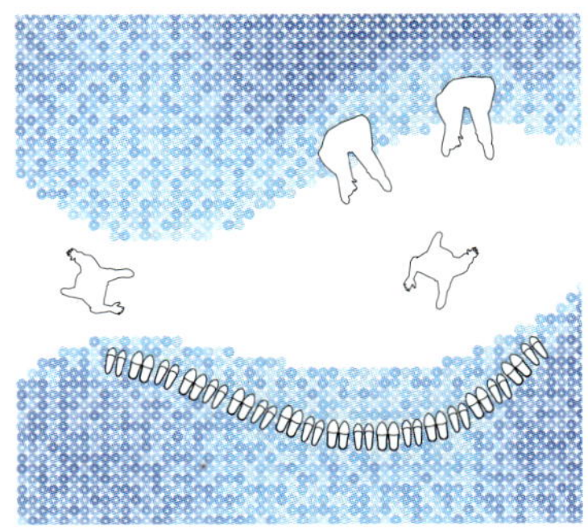

The foam noodles are different
shades of blue that create
a pleasant visual effect for the
visitor. The contrast with the
white wall makes them more
619 visible.

The material combines with
the tubular form and blue
colour to make a soft and
simple structure. The final
style achieves the company's
620 purpose.

621—630

Honda Stand

MARIA DE ROS, O2_BASSO ARQUITECTOS

BARCELONA, SPAIN, 2013

AREA
N/A

CLIENT
HONDA

PHOTO
© DANIEL LOEWE

621 The main objective is to create a design that is different to the other exhibitors, recreating a green outdoor space that contrasts with the inside of the venue, making it more visible and original.

622 The approach was to create an urban garden that serves as a stage for exhibiting the cars. It represents an exterior space with Mediterranean breezes that transport the visitor away from the fair.

623 What distinguishes the stand from the others around it is its simplicity and sobriety, which makes the car on show the main focus.

624 A series of pale-coloured wooden platforms decorated with delicate trees and little shrubs create an elegant stand that reflects the company's image.

625 The project is divided into clearly differentiated zones: the outside exhibition space with cars and wooden platforms and a more private area where the potential client can be provided with customer service.

626 This project reveals the potential impact of ephemeral architecture and the fact that great quality doesn't require large structures or exotic designs.

627 Knowing how to play with a wooden platform and a collection of plants and trees has earned the project leaders the achievement of a prestige that, unlike its stand, will not be ephemeral in nature.

628 With its simple assembly, dismantling and transport, the Honda stand is perfect for any fair. In a short time, an ambience can be created around the product to be exhibited.

629 The arrangement of the different wooden platforms is perfect: the visitor can pass comfortably between them without coming across obstacles.

630 The combination of simplicity and naturalness with which the stand has been created led to the creators winning the first National Award for Emporium Ephemeral Architecture in the best fair stand design category.

80 Sheets of Mountains

NENDO

STOCKHOLM, SWEDEN, 2013

AREA
N/A

CLIENT
STOCKHOLM FURNITURE
& LIGHT FAIR

PHOTO
© JOAKIM BLOCKSTROM

As the guest of honour at
the International Furniture
Fair 2013 in Stockholm, the
Japanese design studio Nendo
created this montage for the
main entrance hall at the
631 exhibition.

The prolific designer Oki Sato,
founder and lead designer at
Nendo, wanted to emphasise
that which defines the spirit
of the fair: treating materials
honestly and making design
632 transmit emotions.

The thematic thread followed
by the installation illustrated
how, starting with a small initial
idea (the sheet), the whole
design process is developed and
expanded, which according to
the creator defines the working
633 philosophy of the studio.

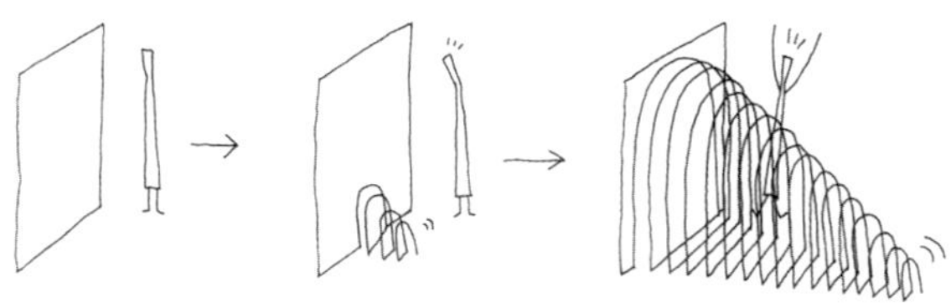

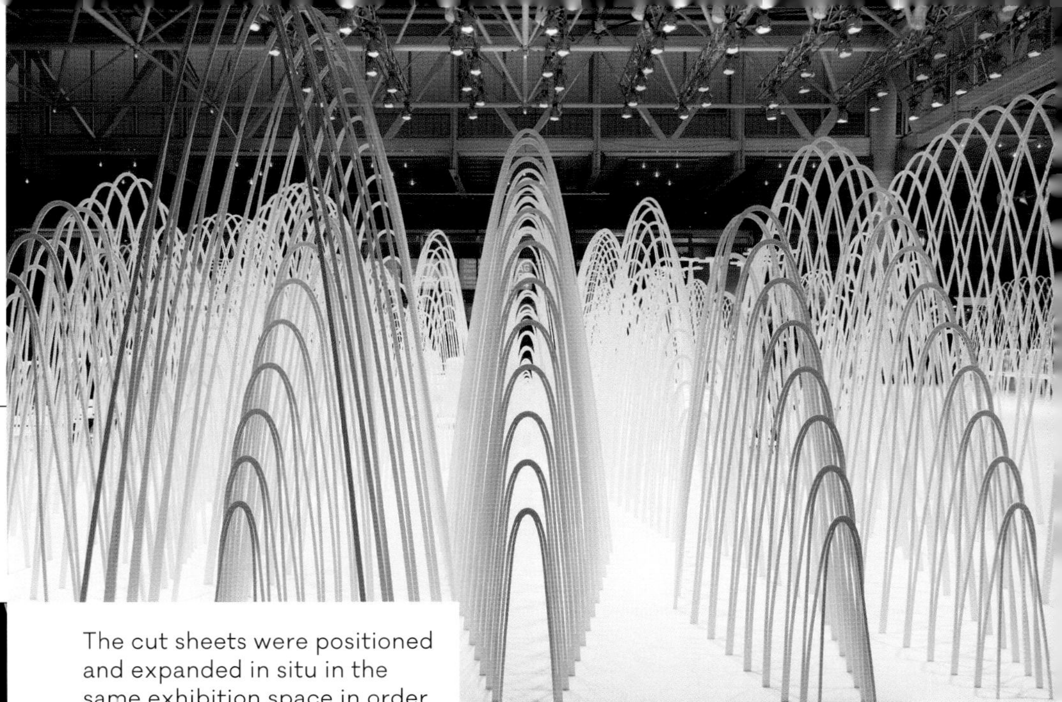

The installation represents a chain of snowy mountains, a profiled topography that gives the idea of an existing shape, but is not a visual wall, it is
634 lightly traced in the air.

Eighty flat sheets of 5 mm thick polystyrene were laser-cut, expanded and positioned in alignment so that visitors to the
635 fair could wander among them.

The installation also served as the framework for the launch of the Nendo w132 lamp and other items such as the Cape and Curve chairs, designed
636 by the same studio.

The project provides a blank space where time can be taken to take in an international fair full of great ideas and
637 innovative proposals.

The cut sheets were positioned and expanded in situ in the same exhibition space in order to reduce transport costs and to make it easier to fold and
638 take them away.

The *mountains* integrated chairs and armchairs that were also white and lightly interspersed, inviting rest
639 and conversation.

The invisible landscape made it more interesting to wander around and see it move, capturing the changing light
640 effects, shapes and shadows.

Alumafel Stand

ESTUDIO ATRIUM

MADRID, SPAIN, 2008
AREA
378 m^2
CLIENT
ALUMAFEL
PHOTO
© MARÍA LLORES MARTÍN

641 Exhibition pavilion dedicated to manufacturing aluminium structures. According to the client's premise, aluminium should have a remarkable role in the image of the installation.

642 The objects included in the exhibition have been carefully positioned on the floor of the stand: the more novel and sophisticated objects are positioned around so that they stand out.

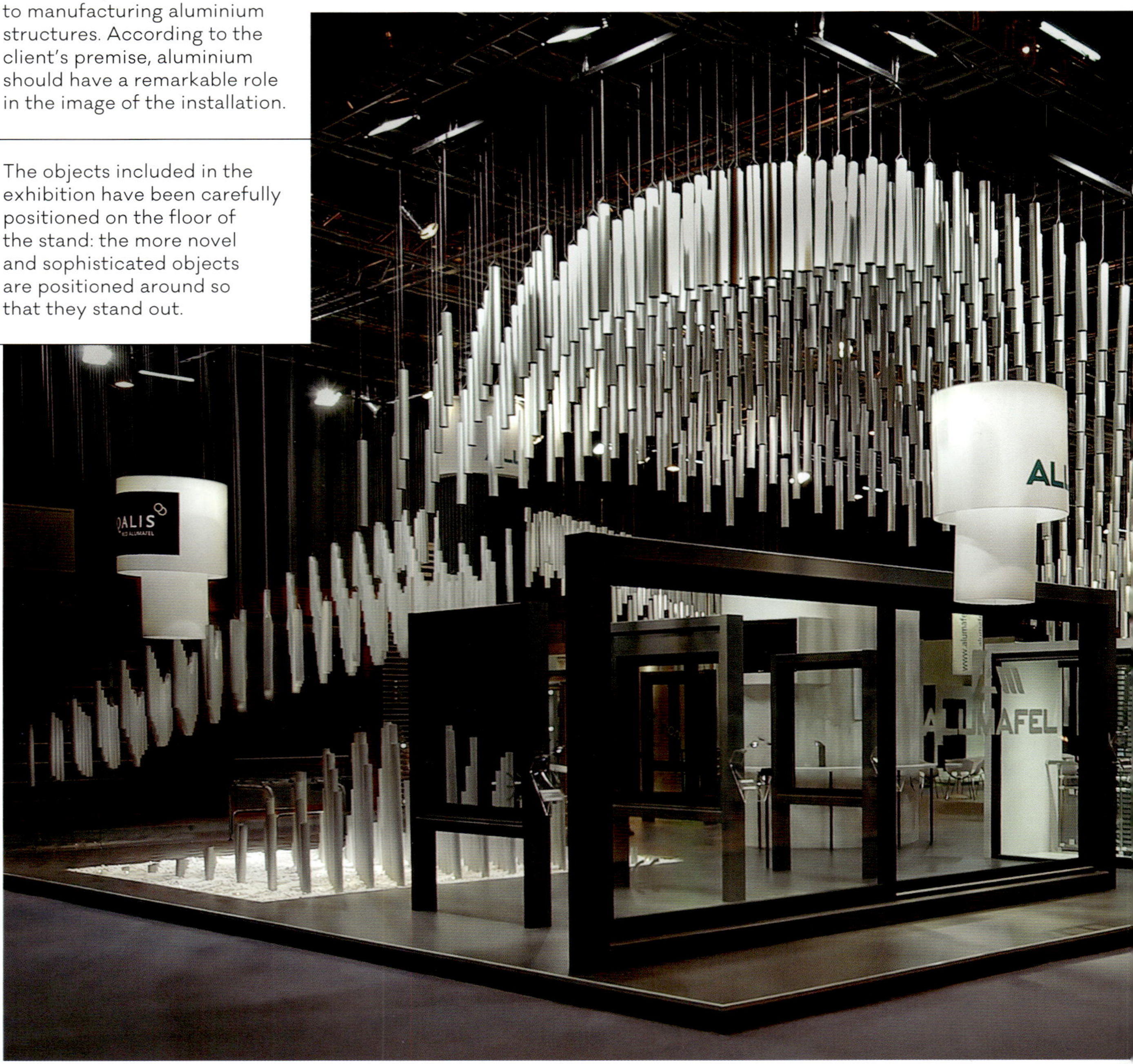

643 More than 1,933 aluminium cylinders, 4,523 metres of metallic thread, and over 1,720 kg of metal extrudate descend from the roof and emerge from the ground to make the space curved and transparent.

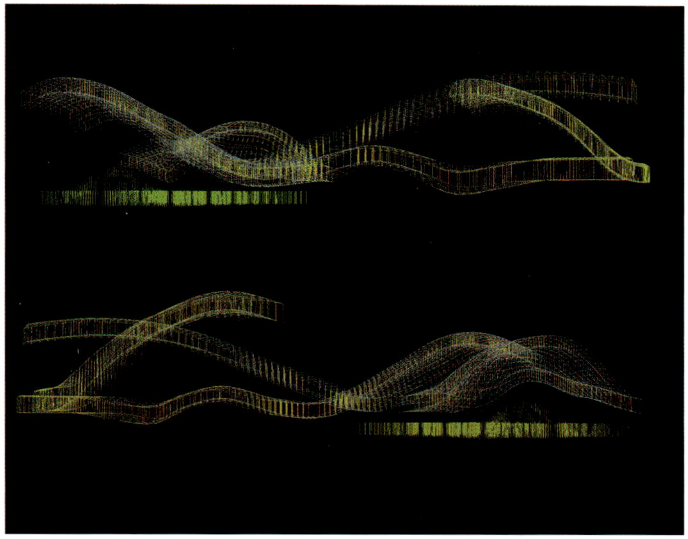

644 The architects began with an imaginary surface: a sort of cloak that gravitates over the samples displayed and distorts to make virtual bubbles visible.

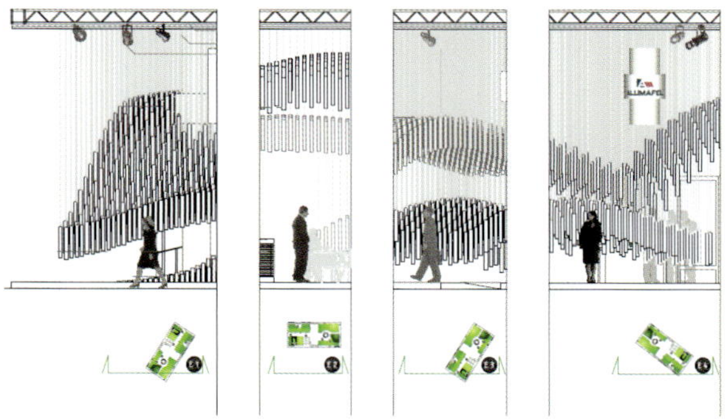

645 As the exhibition space was limited because it housed storage areas and a café, the arrangement of the objects needed to generate routes that would unite different environments.

646 These virtual bubbles rise and descend into the distance, generating a spectacular transparent landscape.

647 Tubular bells, anodised reflections and curved forms are used to create a light and meticulous atmosphere with great transparency.

648 **The main focus of the project, the imaginary membrane, was designed with digital software and constructed using cylindrical pieces that conformed with the quality requirements.**

---

649 The light atmosphere is obtained by using geometric rigour when positioning the silver-coloured cylinders in the air. However, the discontinuity disguised as transparency causes, with movement, the dematerialisation of an item we thought was opaque.

---

650 With extreme precision and in record time, the recycled cylinders were arranged to create an atmosphere of clarity and transparency that envelops the exhibited objects.

Neula

ENRIQUE SORIANO, PEP TORNABELL, GERARD BERTOMEU, MIRIAM CABANAS, XAVI SANTODOMINGO, RAMON SASTRE, ANNA RIZOU + CODA-OFFICE

BARCELONA, SPAIN, 2014
AREA
N/A
CLIENT
GERMANS GABARRÓ
PHOTO
© ANDRES FLAJSZER

651 During Timber Week, organised by the Barcelona guild of carpenters, Gabarró commissioned a canopy to shelter the events at the El Prat golf course.

652 The project connects with CODA's interest in lightweight structures. In this case, the aim was to create a compact flat frame, maximising portability.

653 The strategy for deploying the structure and curving it at the same time was to use a rigid grid that was lifted by a crane and fixed to four points of the frame marking its planned final position.

654 The Barcelona Fabrication Hubs network is an experiment in using a new production and consumption model derived from social fabric developments and changes in the economic and environmental circumstances of cities.

655 In this particular case, a configuration of flat planks was created that could be expanded into a strong double-curved shell of six times the original surface.

658 The team works with recyclable and economical materials, mainly wood or membranes, in order to minimise production costs, ecological impact and waste from the construction process.

659 The 15 mm thick wooden planks were rough on one face, for connections, and very smooth on the other to reduce friction during deployment.

656 The CODA team investigates the integration of forces, materials and processes, focusing on the generation of geometric systems to create efficient low impact structures through digital manufacturing.

657 The focus is on computational design, which enables complex and efficient systems to be created based on low profile technical systems. A commitment to high-tech design and low-tech fabrication.

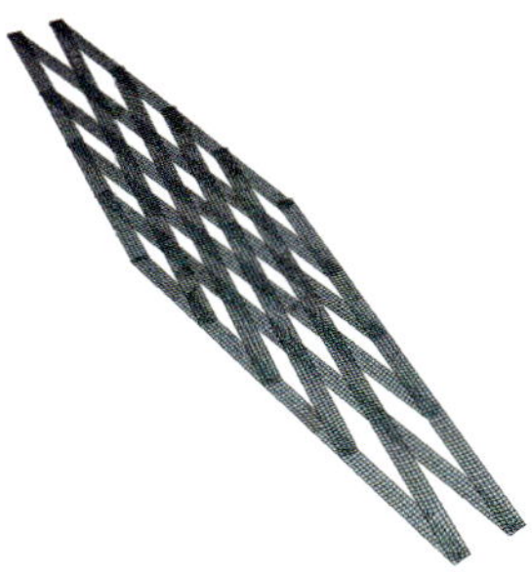

660 The Les Corts Hub of Fabrication, in Barcelona was commissioned to cut and mill the planks. Joining and assembly were done on the site where the pavilion was to be assembled.

Almond Pavilion

ENRIQUE SORIANO, PEP TORNABELL, GERARD BERTOMEU, MIRIAM CABANAS, XAVI SANTODOMINGO, RAMON SASTRE, ANNA RIZOU + CODA-OFFICE

BARCELONA, SPAIN, 2013

AREA
N/A

CLIENT
DEAV

PHOTO
© ANDRES FLAJSZER

661 The pavilion is the proposal for the redevelopment of an area of the Escola Tècnica Superior d'Arquitectura del Vallés (ETSAV) campus. The proposal is for a structure on an embankment near the bar terrace to serve as a shelter for the university community's various collective activities.

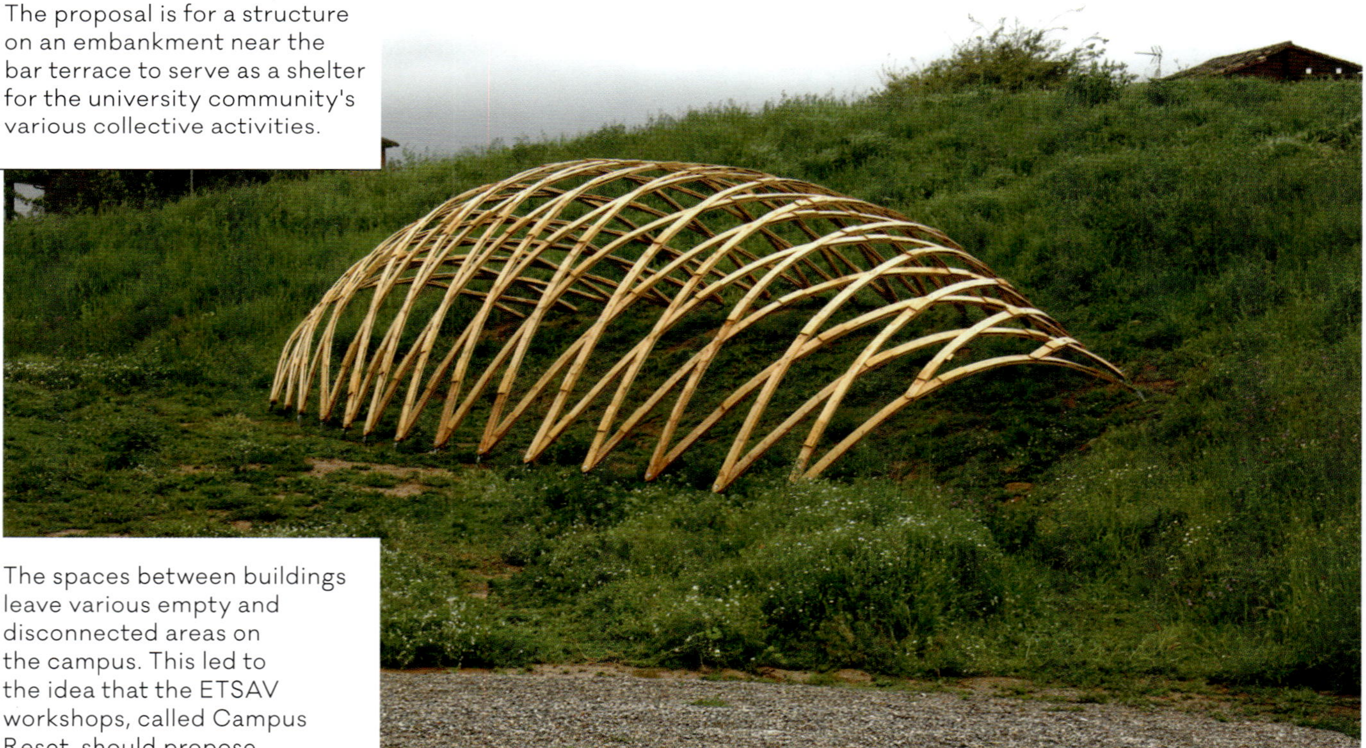

662 The spaces between buildings leave various empty and disconnected areas on the campus. This led to the idea that the ETSAV workshops, called Campus Reset, should propose different uses for these areas.

663 A shell-shaped roof with double curvature was designed to be constructed by crossing flat straight slats to form a frame with geodesic curves.

664 At the team's request, they were delivered having been recently cut from damp green wood in order to take advantage of its elastic properties and facilitate the assembly of a light shell.

665 The team asked for the planks to be as thin as possible, so that they could flex them using their elasticity without compromising their strength.

666 Planks of 2.4 m in length and 2 cm thick were joined in the same position to create the planks of up to 15 m needed to form the frame of the pavilion, which measures 15 m in length, 4 m in height and 8 m in width.

667 Resembling an almond shell, the cover of the structure is also formed using the same standardised planks used for the axes. These planks, like scales, form the bracing system.

668 The active bending of the woods streamlines thecon-struction process because the entire structure hardens and strengthens as it dries, being cured by the sun and increasing in rigidity and stability.

669 The proposal is framed by research carried out in the school to look for a way of minimising the environmental footprint of this type of construction.

670 A week to think of and create a design and a weekend to construct it. This is the time it took twenty ETSAV students to create the new pavilion.

Focaccia Bianca

ENRIQUE SORIANO, PEP TORNABELL, GERARD BERTOMEU, MIRIAM CABANAS, XAVI SANTODOMINGO, RAMON SASTRE, ANNA RIZOU + CODA-OFFICE

BARCELONA, SPAIN, 2014

AREA
N/A

CLIENT
N/A

PHOTO
© ANDRES FLAJSZER

The pavilion was designed
for the FAB10 Barcelona
conference, an international
meeting of more than 350
Fab Labs from 40 countries
who were researching new
designs for the society of the
future, applying open and
671 accessible technologies.

This is an evolution of
the *Juikbuin* pavilion, a
winning project at the Eme3
International Architecture
Festival that took place in
672 Barcelona in 2013.

A flat compact structure was
designed to build an open air
kiosk, a light shelter that is easy
to assemble and disassemble
with minimal use of materials
and hardly any waste from the
673 construction process.

Research into the mechanical
characteristics of wood,
such as its plastic and elastic
potential, is the cornerstone for
establishing this triaxial plait as
674 a reliable construction system.

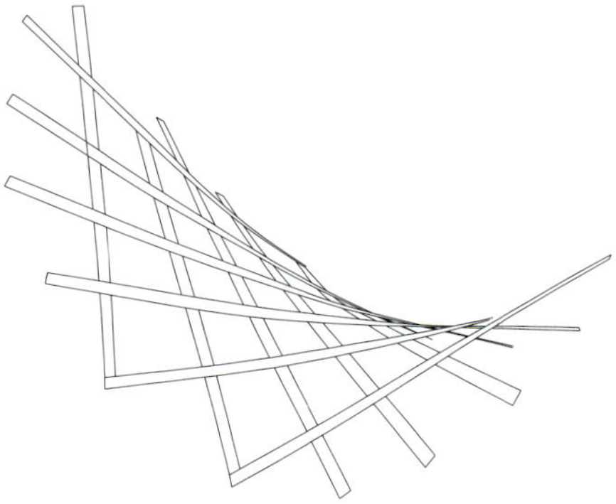

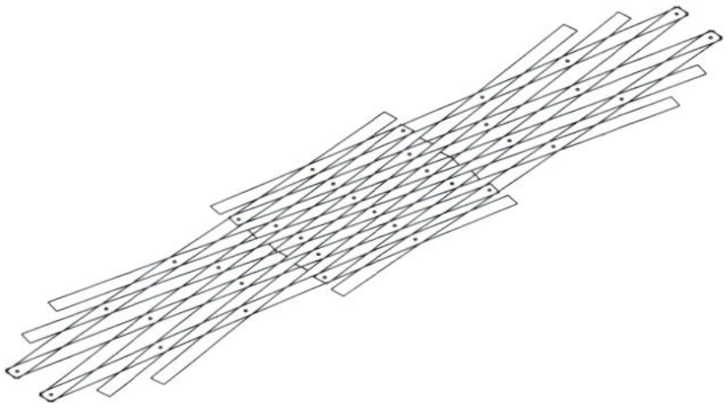

676 The structure has four times the surface area of the solid wooden boards. Each "petal" presents a variable opening, which ensures that the structure is adaptable for different topographies and needs.

677 Six boards of 1 cm thick birch plywood were used, each one cut into twelve slats to produce a "shell" or section of the pavilion.

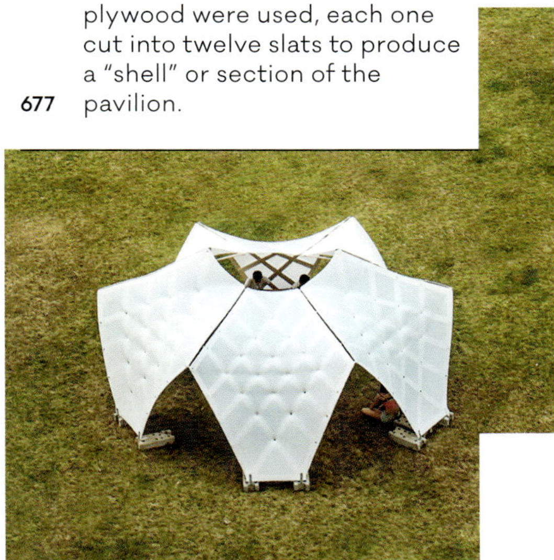

675 Fixing the membrane with simple bolts and washers and hemming the perimeter with staples added to the simplicity of assembling this pavilion.

678 The formula used to create an efficient structure with minimal energy requirements includes a high design value, high quality materials and minimal machining.

679 The elastic deformation of the materials determines the final form of the structure. In this case, the very nature of the plywood.

680 Research was carried out into construction techniques in places with a shortage of timber resources to look for new ways of using materials and new construction shapes as an efficient design mechanism.

BigO

ENRIQUE SORIANO, PEP TORNABELL + CODA-OFFICE

CSOROMPUSZTA, HUNGARY, 2013

AREA
N/A

CLIENT
HELLOWOOD

PHOTO
© DONAT KEKESI, SOMOSKOI GABOR

CODA researchers Enrique Soriano and Pep Tornabell were invited to participate in the *HelloWood* wood festival, which is held annually in Hungary and connects young
681 designers and architects.

Every summer, a multidisciplinary arts camp is held: an international workshop and festival in one. Participants are organized into teams of researchers and students to carry out projects that
682 respond to a proposed theme.

With the help of eight students, the CODA team spent one week creating the *BigO* project, a 75 m^2 wooden toroidal shell which took one day to design
683 and five to build.

684 The strategy was to create a simple framework of flat planks that would follow two geodesically curved beams over the torus, demonstrating the ease of constructing a very light curved structure with very simple elements.

685 One hundred identical 10.5 metre long planks were cut from four metre boards with a section of 1 x 10 cm. They were joined, marked, pierced and cut on-site.

687 Connecting the slats with simple metal pins, and joining them to the base using wooden blocks are all that is needed to stabilise the structure and give it stability and rigidity.

688 The parameters of the circular structure and the geodesic curves that the slats should follow were marked out on-site, based on the results of testing the wood's flexion and torsion.

686 Topology research determines the positioning of the structure's axes and defines its final form. The slats are positioned following a double beam of lines that cross on the same level to facilitate their connection.

689 The advantage of this type of flexible frame is that there is no need to shape and cure the wood, since the tension of the material during the assembly leverages its inherent elasticity.

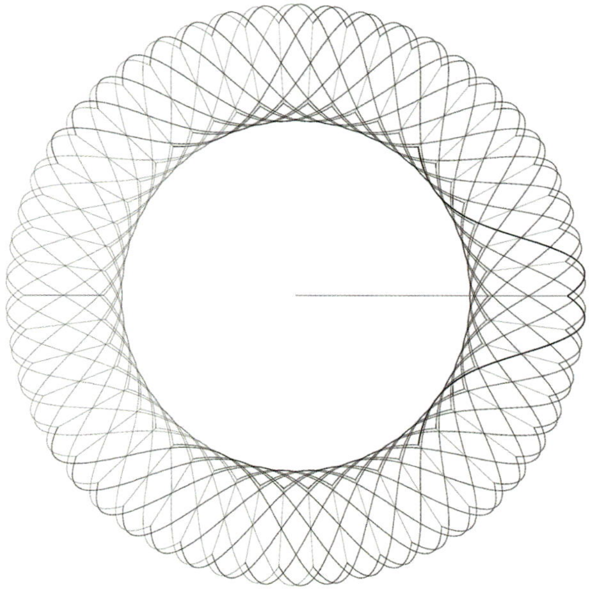

690 The architects' research focuses on the creation and optimisation of lightweight structures, seeking to reduce their environmental footprint through design and technological efficiency with solutions that can be generalised.

KA300

J. MAYER H. UND PARTNER ARCHITEKTEN

KARLSRUHE, GERMANY, 2015

AREA
N/A

CLIENT
STADTMARKETING KARLSRUHE GMBH

PHOTO
© FRANK DINGER

691 The temporary pavilion was constructed in the gardens of the Schlossgarten palace for the tricentenary of the city of Karlsruhe.

692 During the months when the installation is open, visitors can attend all kinds of events held in the palace gardens.

693 The structure comprises 170 wooden beams laminated in light grey. These are slightly tilted horizontally.

694 Artistic performances such as theatre performances, film projections and exhibitions can take place inside. It allows people to be in the fresh air and shelter from the sun when necessary.

695 A function room accommodates 250 seats or a total of 600 people standing. The café and the stage complete the different rooms inside the wooden structure.

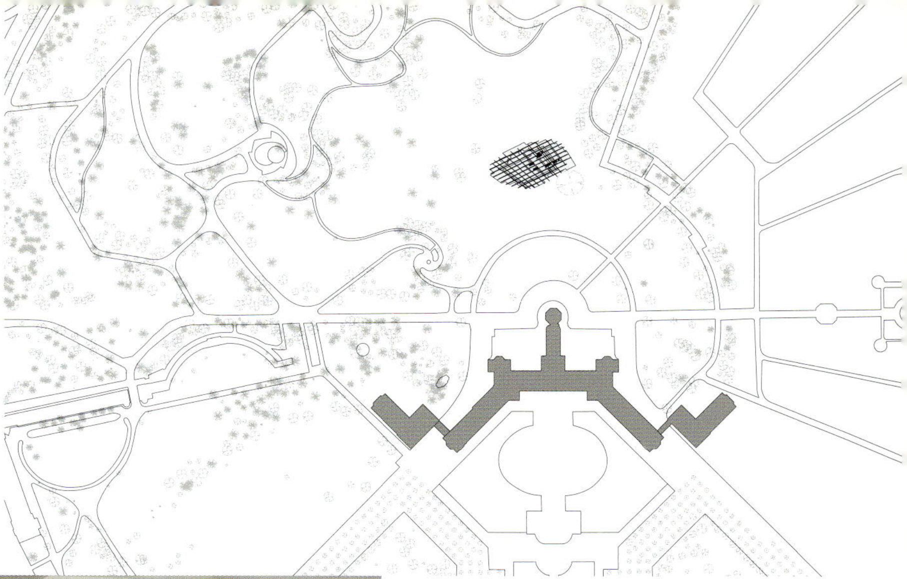

697 The ultramodern aspect of the wooden slats contrasts with the baroque style of the historic palace. This invites the visitor to contemplate it with more attention.

698 The structure is equipped with translucent membranes inserted between the beams, perfect for protection from the sun and bad weather.

696 The pavilion occupies a surface of about 1,000 m^2 and has a height of 16.5 m. It has a single floor where all kinds of activities and exhibitions will take place.

699 Once the structure has been disassembled, the wood and the steel used are recycled. This way they can be used in new projects.

700 The project is characterised by the reduction in the variety of materials used, permitting a very simple structure to be created.

Copper Droopscape

BALL-NOGUES STUDIO

INDIO, CA, USA, 2008

AREA
N/A

CLIENT
COACHELLA VALLEY
MUSIC AND ARTS FESTIVAL

PHOTO
© BENJAMIN BALL

701 Built for the Coachella Valley Music and Arts Festival in California, the structure had a double function: to create a visual impact and provide shelter from the strong desert sun for the visitors.

702 It only took ten days to construct the installation. The project was developed thanks to powerful made-to-measure software. The computer program made the form, controlled the degree of canopy opening and helped to speed up production.

703 When night falls and natural light disappears, the original structure is illuminated by strategically placed lamps, creating a magical atmosphere along with music, relaxation and decoration.

The canopy rests on strong
wooden slats and shows a
mosaic of interwoven elements
that provide protection from
the sun, while allowing the
704 breeze to flow through.

The tripods used were made
from local wood and, after
the structure was dismantled,
they could be reused for
various projects. This allowed
more ephemeral structures
sto be created, in keeping
with the architectural studio's
705 constructive philosophy.

Nylon fibres formed more
than 500 petals that were
carefully positioned to create
the large structure.
This material prevented the
wind becoming a problem;
instead, every time it blew, the
petals emitted a relaxing sound
706 and generated a gentle breeze.

Instead of drawing each
individual piece of Mylar fabric,
Ball-Nogues outlined the
qualities of the cup and then
the hundreds of components
that formed the canopy were
automatically generated
707 by software.

The movement of the trans-
lucent cover produces a
hypnotic effect as the light
passes through the canopy
and is reflected on the network.
This, together with the sound
of the breeze, creates a perfect
708 relaxing environment.

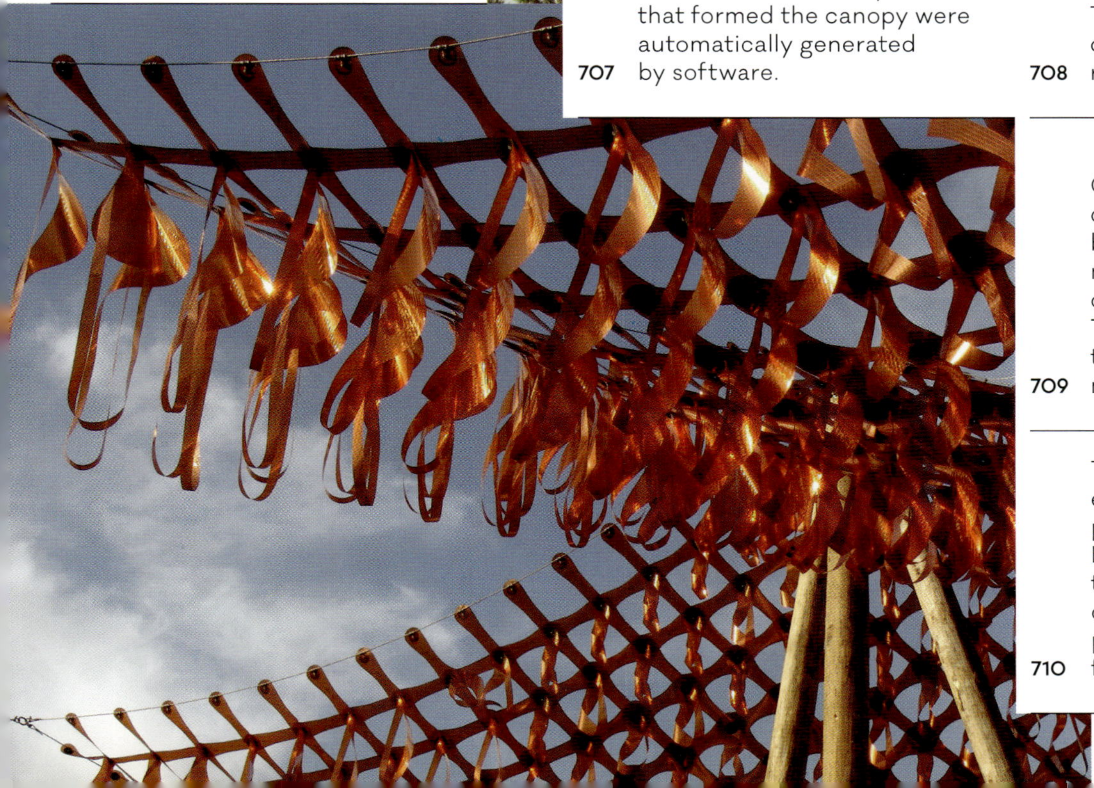

Once more, ephemerality has
demon strated the potential for
building structures which are
not bound by the restrictions
of conventional architecture.
This is an example that shows
the new lines of research for
709 manufacture.

The project also uses the
environment to create unique
patterns of light and shadow.
Ball-Nogues have shown that
their devotion to innovative
design that is not incom-
patible with magnificence nor
710 functionality.

Yucca Crater

BALL-NOGUES STUDIO

PALMS, CA, USA, 2011

AREA
N/A

CLIENT
HIGH DESERT TEST SITES

PHOTO
© SCOTT MAYORAL

Situated near the Joshua Tree National Park, 25 km from the nearest human settlement, *Yucca Crater* is a work of ephemeral art which functioned as creative equipment during the
711 *High Desert Test Site* event.

712 The project is inspired in of *Land Art* and abandoned suburban pools and is inspired by the ramshackle houses scattered across the Mojave desert.

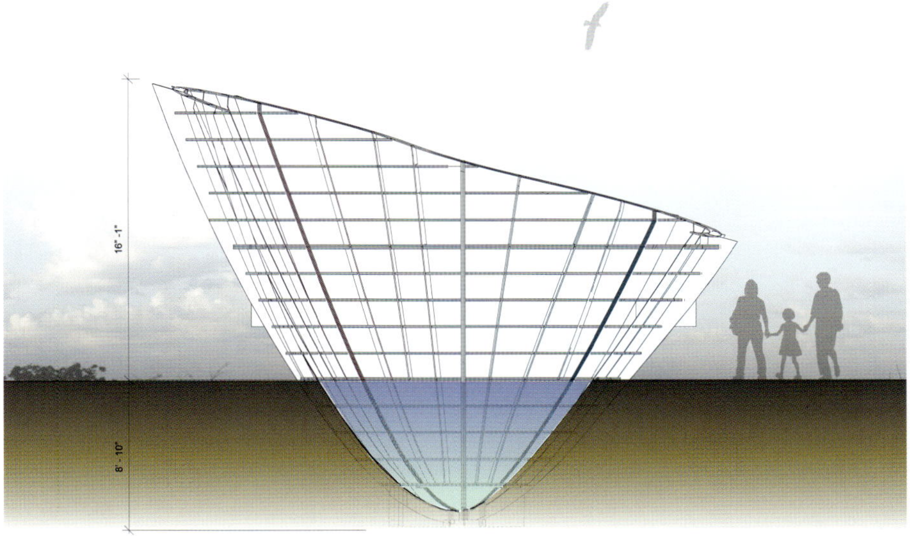

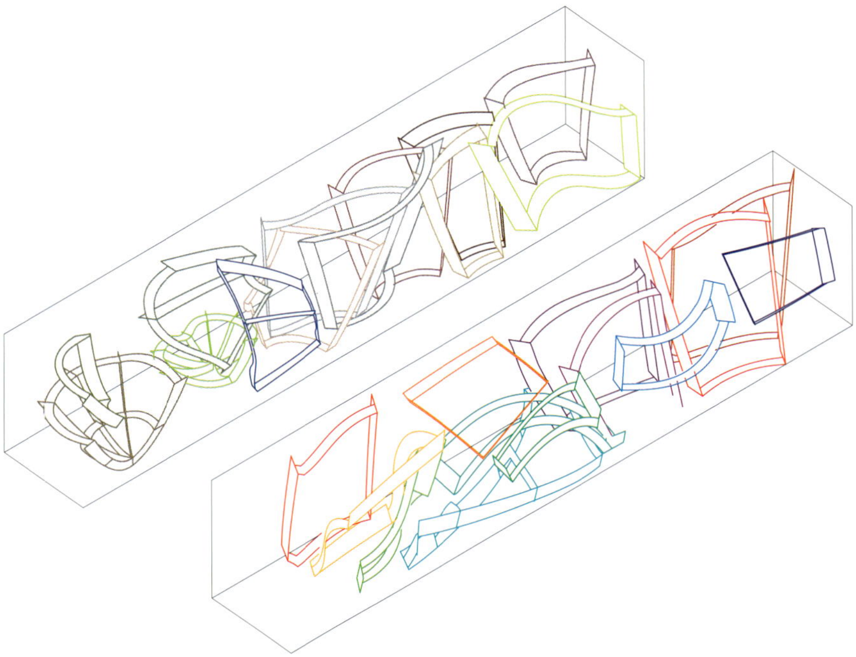

713 The installation is nine metres tall and is sunk three metres into the ground. An interior and exterior staircase allows visitors to descend into a deep salt water pool.

714 The High Desert test site initiative generates physical and conceptual spaces for contemporary art. In this sense, a very special pool was created for visitors to use.

715 Ball-Nogues have reinvented this type of intervention in the landscape, transforming manufacturing tools into objects for the exhibition.

716 Architects are reusing an increasing amount of recycled materials. For example, this plywood structure was the formwork used in the construction of another installation called *Talus Dome*.

717 The initial project plans had solar heated hot water pumped using a wind turbine.

718 The architects emphasize that *Yucca Crater* is a project designed to be abandoned. Like the majority of ephemeral art, it obliges its designers to relinquish ownership and materials.

719 **This project integrates aesthetics, social relationships and production. It invites the reconsideration of our relationship with the art of by-products, whose recovery is an alternative within the economical and geographical domain.**

720 The festival calls for the physical creation of spaces for art that explores the intersections between life and art itself. After the event, *Yucca Crater* was abandoned to the harsh weather conditions.

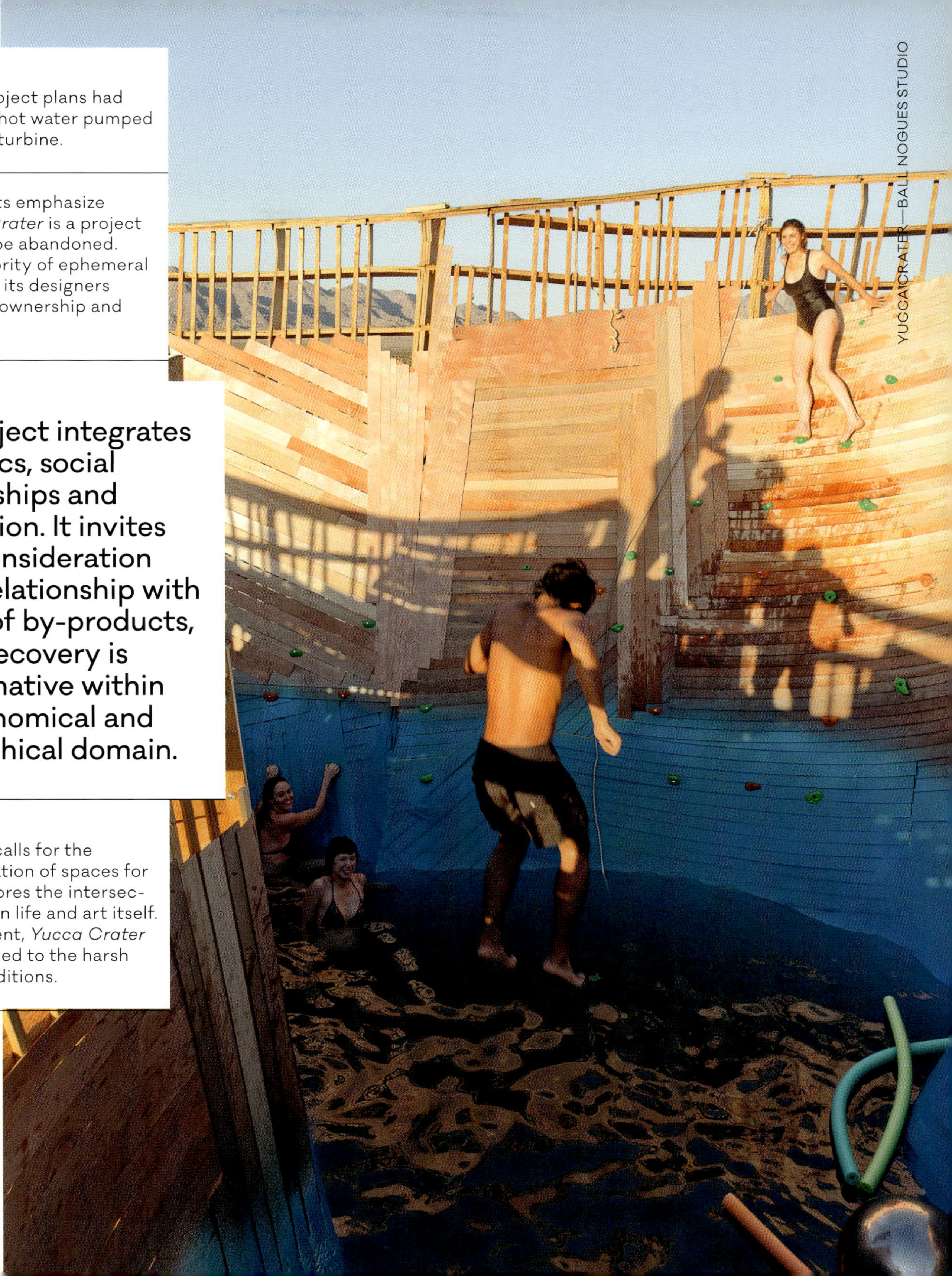

YUCCA CRATER—BALL NOGUES STUDIO

Luna St. Prex

DIETER DIETZ, SIBYLLE KÖSSLER, SARA FORMERY, RUDI NIEVEEN + ALICE STUDIO EPFL

SAINT-PREX, SWITZERLAND, 2013

AREA
719 m^2

CLIENT
FONDATION ST PREX CLASSICS

PHOTO
© ALAN HASOO, ALAIN HERZOG, JOEL TETTAMANTI + ALICE STUDIO EPFL

721 The ephemeral structure was designed to be installed in the Place de l'Horloge, in the medieval city of Saint-Prex. Luna was especially created to celebrate the sixth anniversary of the *St. Prex Classics* festival in 2012.

722 The pavilion was situated in the heart of Saint-Prex, next to the collection of historical constructions that acted as a background curtain during the shows. The installation was accessed from the clock tower, the most emblematic building of the old town.

723 The temporary construction is fully removable and easy to transport. The design had a very defined goal: to host music and dance performances with a capacity of between 500 and 700 people.

724 The idea was to create a floating hemisphere of around 25 metres in diameter with a polyamide skin. A spectacular visual impact was created with this material used to create a dome floating over the stage.

725 The dome was created with a polyamide membrane inflated with helium as if it were a balloon, so it could float above the stage and create a visual impact that completely changed the profile of the place.

726 The dome was illuminated from within the structure and was also used to project images during the various performances that took place inside.

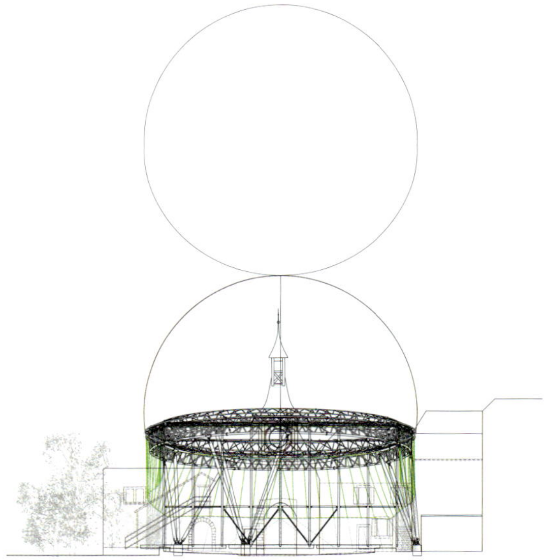

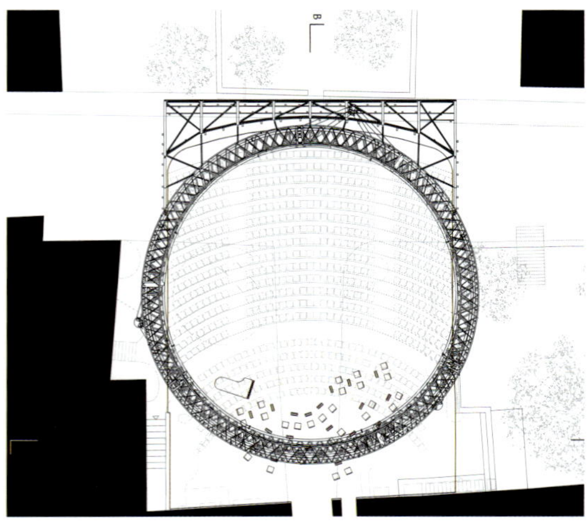

The design of the large helium dome, the materials used and the location were the key elements used to highlight the medieval character of Saint-Prex and, at the same time, create a magical atmosphere for each show
729 that took place.

Unlike the dome and the perimeter structure, the installation was created with wood. Its fully modular nature meant that it could house a variable number of spectators, according to the needs of each
730 show.

During rainy days, the balloon was attached to the perimeter structure composed of an aluminium lattice and supports. A waterproof curtain surrounds and protects activities from
727 changes in weather.

Inspired by the Epidaurus theatre of Ancient Greece, Luna sought to become a cultural landmark in Saint-Prex for the duration of its installation. With its large volume, the structure could be seen
728 from a distance.

Chrysalis

ADAM MARCUS + VARIABLE PROJECTS

STRAFFORD, NH, USA, 2015

AREA
N/A

CLIENT
N/A

PHOTO
© VARIABLE PROJECTS

731 *Chrysalis* is a complex structure composed of very simple pieces of wood. It is a design project proposal for a summer camp in New Hampshire.

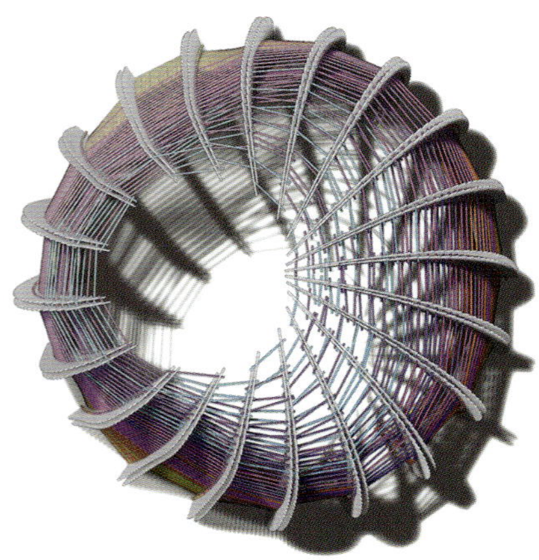

732 Its asymmetrical and curvilinear form is constructed from standardised 2 x 2 wooden slats. The different shades of the slats produce constant changes on a visual level.

733 The pavilion is conceived as a place to rest through which you can contemplate your surroundings. The forests of New Hampshire and the summer sky are the main scenery.

A screen-like structure creates
an ambience that is intimate
at the same time as being open
to the environment. The top
part is uncovered and creates a
734 direct relationship with the sky.

The interior of the pavilion
allow you to escape without
losing sight of the place you are
in and to create small bonfires
by the light of the moon or
735 contemplate the starry sky.

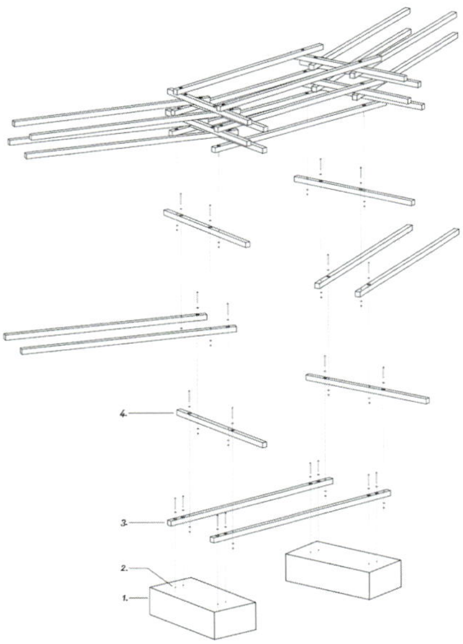

The installation acts as a space
for coordination and planning
for the campers. Inside it they
can carry out physical activ-
ities or engage in in discussions
736 and debates.

It is a temporary structure
created to be used for the
duration of the camp. Its aim is
to provide rest and distraction,
737 not perfection.

It was built in two weeks for the
100 campers who would enjoy
it later. A simple assembly
of wooden slats was all the
738 work needed toerect it.

It could be a small shelter.
Inside, you can be away from
your colleagues without
escaping one hundred percent
739 nor forgetting where you are.

The uncovered top part and
the screen-like framework
allow the breeze and natural
light to enter. This leaves the
installation exposed to the rain
740 and the sun's rays.

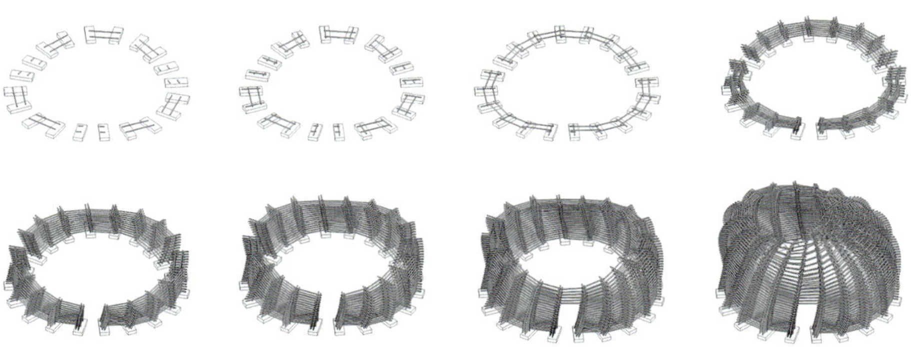

Trace Track

XEVI BAYONA

STANWICK LAKES, UNITED KINGDOM, 2014

AREA
N/A

CLIENT
CHANGING TRACKS NORTHAMPTON COUNTY C.

PHOTO
© XEVI BAYONA

741 The passage of time has barely left traces of the railway tracks by the water of Stanwick Lakes. The water has erased the forceful straight line which crossed its path.

742 The vertically located tracks defy gravity and give the place a new perspective.

743 The reflection cast on the water by the vertical installation reinforces the image of the structure floating in the water.

744 The project consists of a line of tracks that crosses the water and rises vertically next to the track coming from the opposite direction. The lines sinuously blend into the natural landscape.

745 The intervention aims to create an impact on the landscape. The act of installing the vertical structure in a green environment creates a predominant and even iconographic landmark.

746 The location's present and cultural heritage are fused by the installation.

749 The vertical structure of wooden slats intervenes resoundingly in the harmony of the landscape. It stands between bushes and trees as if it were a natural element.

750 The project was installed quickly with a minimal budget. Using wood and the design of the structure meant that it could be completed quickly and with hardly any cost.

747 The wooden slats that cross the river like a foot bridge aim to preserve the memory of the place. The former railway line is honoured with this subtle and practical installation.

748 According to the artist, the installation is erected to create a giant exclamation mark on the landscape. The result achieves his objective: to create a great visual impact.

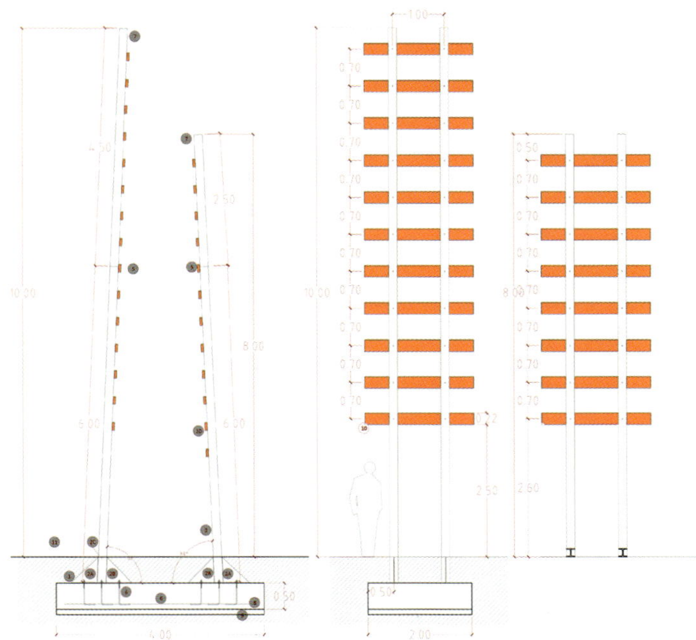

751—755

Roof and Mushrooms

NENDO, RYUE NISHIZAWA ARCHITECTS

KYOTO, JAPAN, 2013

AREA
N/A

CLIENT
KYOTO UNIVERSITY OF ART AND DESIGN

PHOTO
© DAICI ANO

751 An original structure covers the hill in a university area in east Kyoto. In the adjacent area, there is a woodland of Japanese plum trees that flower in the spring.

752 The pavilion was designed with a roof that gently inclines to follow the lines of its surroundings so that visitors are immersed and finally discover that it is a wall.

753 The main idea of the structure is to invite the visitor to go down the mountain where the woodland flowers and the surrounding fields act as furniture and bright gardens.

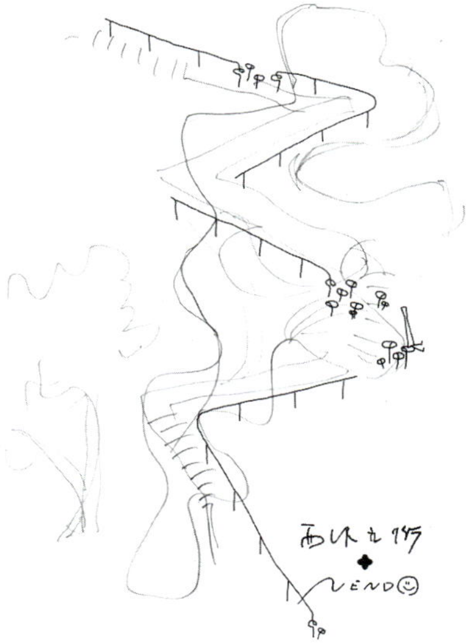

754 The large wooden structure contains a series of mushrooms that act as both a decorative feature and stools. These were hand-crafted and are different shapes and sizes.

755 The mushroom shaped stools were distributed throughout the entire installation in corners and cracks in the walls, and next to stairs or pillars. They act as furniture for decoration and rest.

756 The pavilion is at the University of Kyoto School of Art and Design. It aims to transform the walkway of a steep hill, that lacks charm where a simple modern structure merges with nature.

757 The undulating form of the wooden roof and the curves of the walkway create a spatial experience to remind visitors of a walk through the mountains, eliminating the boundary between the exterior and the interior.

758 Dozens of columns support the wooden structure, playing with the form of the hillside and alternating with the mushroom seats scattered throughout the entire structure.

759 The area left uncovered by the wooden roof allows visitors to contemplate the difference between the exterior and the interior. It also allows the entire structure to be discovered along the hill.

760 The simple installation, minimalist lines and small amount of materials encourage dialogue with the natural environment.

Warka Water

ARCHITECTURE AND VISION

NORTHEAST REGION OF ETHIOPIA, 2012

AREA
N/A

CLIENT
N/A

PHOTO
© ARCHITECTURE AND VISION

This is another example
of ephemeral architecture
seeking solutions to problems
presented by lack of resources.
The architects visited isolated
communities in the northeast
region of Ethiopia, where there
is a serious shortage of drinking
761 water.

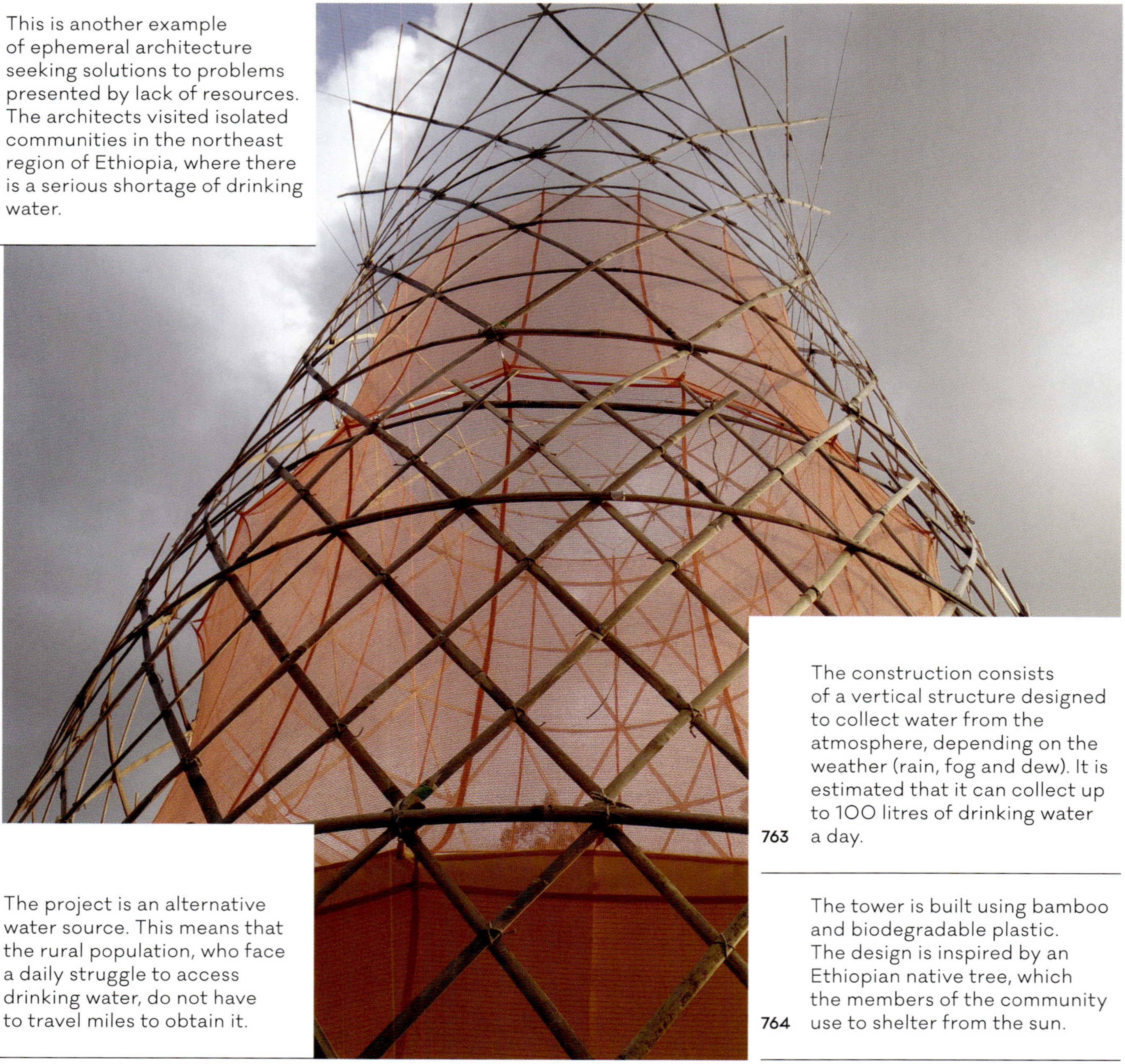

The project is an alternative
water source. This means that
the rural population, who face
a daily struggle to access
drinking water, do not have
762 to travel miles to obtain it.

The construction consists
of a vertical structure designed
to collect water from the
atmosphere, depending on the
weather (rain, fog and dew). It is
estimated that it can collect up
to 100 litres of drinking water
763 a day.

The tower is built using bamboo
and biodegradable plastic.
The design is inspired by an
Ethiopian native tree, which
the members of the community
764 use to shelter from the sun.

765 After moisture is captured, it is directed to a hygienic storage tank through a nozzle. No electricity is needed for maintenance, it is simple and can be carried out by members of the community.

766 The prototype measures 10 m in height and 4.2 m in width. The biodegradable plastic net helps to collect water from the mist. There is another system to collect water from dew.

768 Some of the prototypes have a structure with an awning under the canopy to create shade. They can be used as meeting places and schools.

767 Warka Water is a passive system that does not require electrical power. It is designed to be built by the local community with simple tools. Most of the materials are biodegradable.

769 The Warkino weather station was designed to analyse the qualities that each material offers for water collection and control of atmospheric conditions.

770 The architects and designers have constructed nine Warker Water prototypes. This was the prototype used as the first field test pilot in the rural Ethioian community.

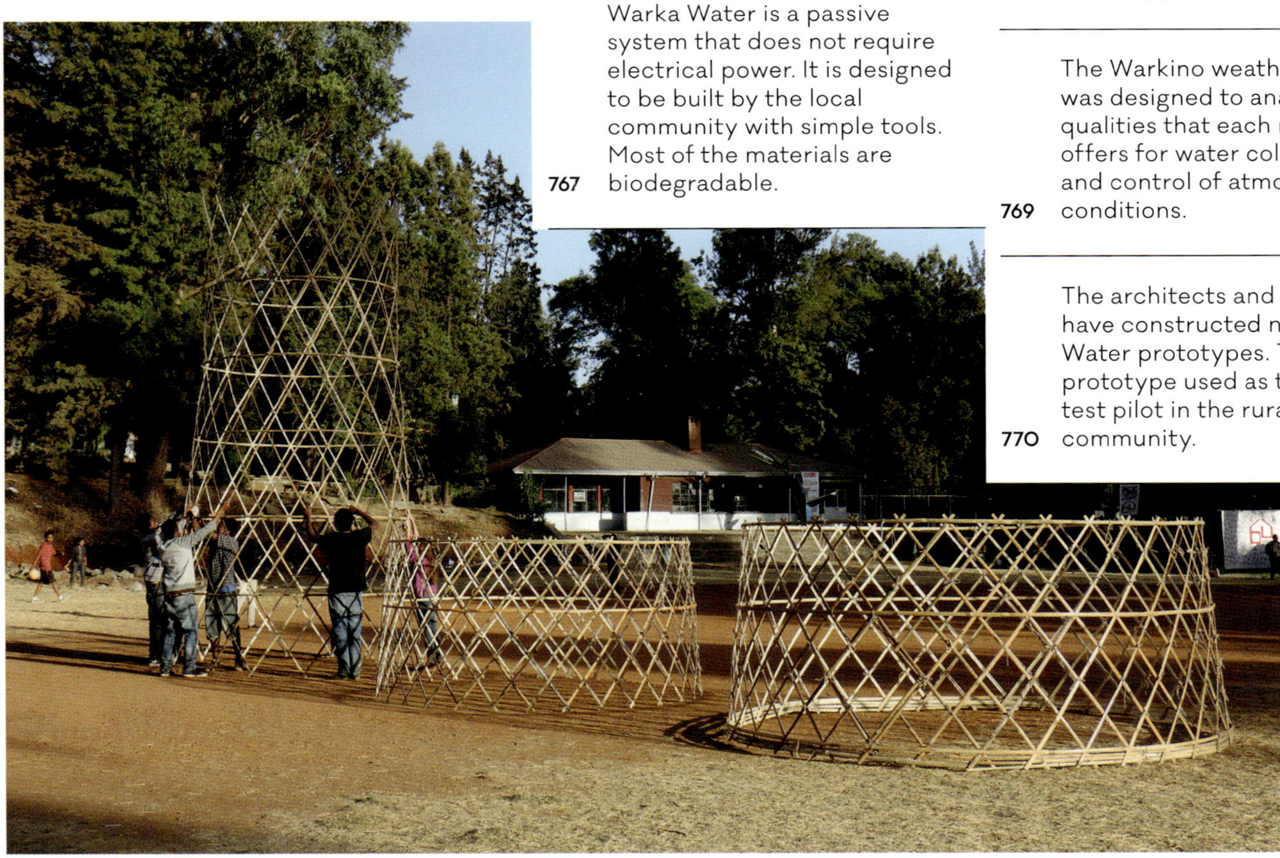

Water Paths

CAROLINA GUERRA GONZÁLEZ

PENCAHUE, CHILE, 2014
AREA
N/A
CLIENT
UNIVERSITY OF TALCA
PHOTO
© CAROLINA GUERRA GONZÁLEZ

The project, entitled is located
in the cemetery of the Chilean
city of Pencahue. The archi-
tect's idea is to create a new
architectural and scenic
771 landmark in the city.

The main construction material
is a steel structure clad in
recycled wood that reaches
a heigh of six metres, visible
from most of the city.
The aim is to signpost the
space as a place of rest and
772 contemplation.

Given the magnitude of the
project, the construction
material had to be economical,
so it was decided to use French
773 and American oak wood staves.

The staves are used in the
manufacture of wine casks
and were donated to this
project by Viña Concha
774 y Toro, a local winery.

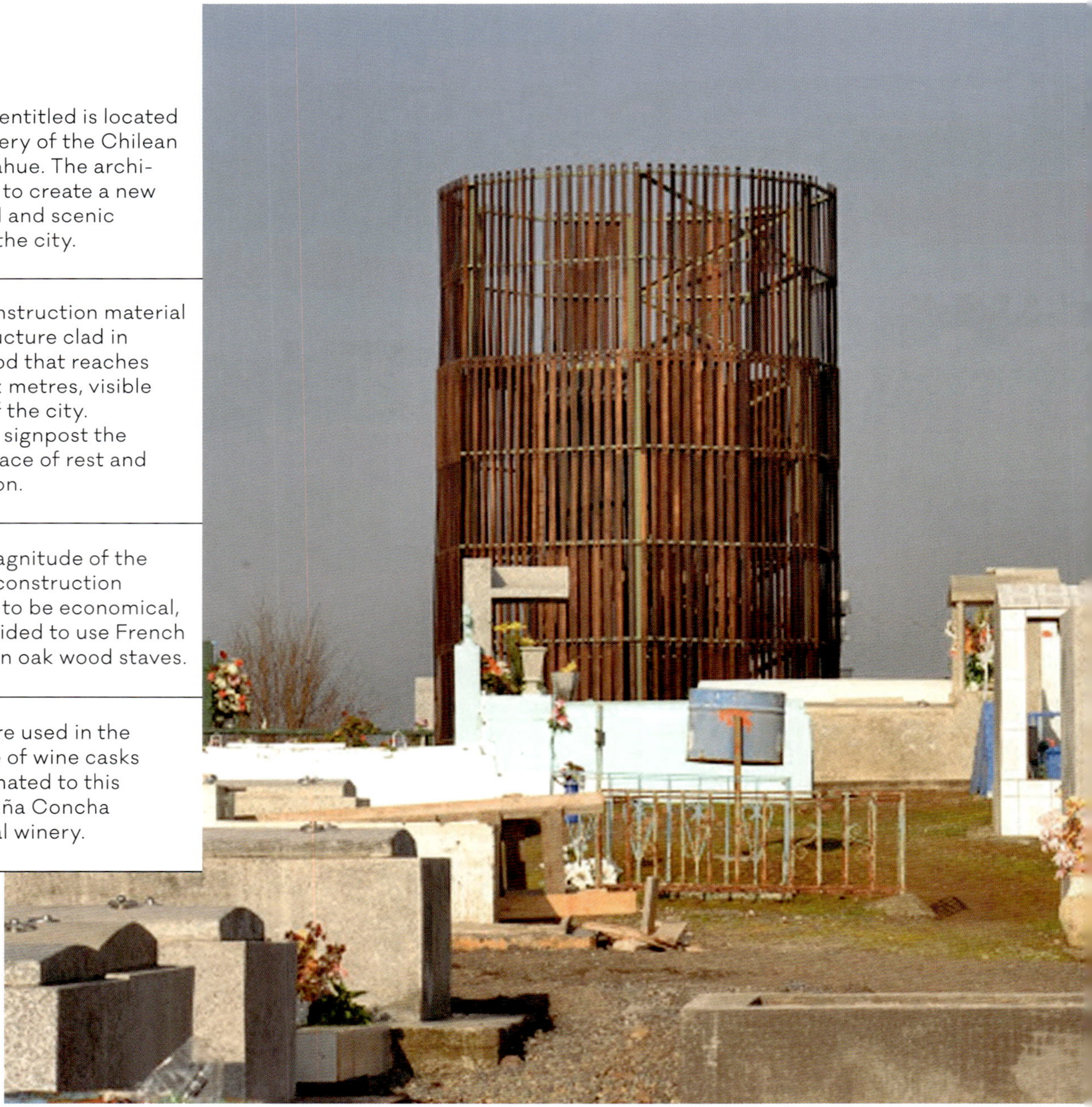

Nine new floors were made
at the existing water points
775 for the comfort of visitors.

The architect analysed the
cemetery and identified an
underground network that
carried water from the
"cup of water" to the various
distribution points. It is part
of a kind of hydraulic archi-
tecture with three water points
distributed throughout the
776 cemetery.

These three water collection
points are used by visitors
to collect water for the plants
and flowers that they are
bringing to their deceased
778 family members.

The main steel structure was
built in the shape of a dodeca-
hedron, with six pillars and six
spaces between horizontal
rings, with wood attached
to the interior and exterior
779 of the rings.

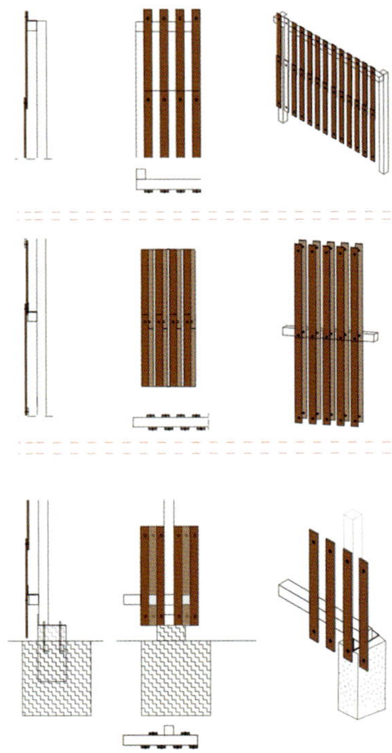

Six spaces are generated
between the horizontal rings
and these are divided into
three bands. In the first two
bands (from bottom to top),
the staves were attached
alternately on the exterior and
the interior. On the exterior, the
two central staves follow the
line of those that come from
below and the last two are
777 only attached to the exterior.

The redevelopment led to
better use of the area and
it created a space dedicated
780 to rest and contemplation.

Temporary Dormitories

A.GOR.A ARCHITECTS

MAE SOT, THAILAND, 2013

AREA
72 m²

CLIENT
MAE TAO CLINIC

PHOTO
© FRANC PALLARÈS LÓPEZ

781 A few kilometres from the Burmese border, many schools and orphanages offer accommodation and education for immigrants and refugees from the armed conflict in Myanmar. The Children's Development Center (CDC) School and Mae Tao Clinic accomodate more than 500 students.

782 In this context of a lack of space and the immediate need to accommodate new students, a new model of provisional residences has been created which is economical and easy to assemble.

783 The Luxembourg Embassy in Bangkok financed the construction of these four dormitories. The first one was quickly built in April 2012 in just four weeks. This home accommodates 25 students.

784 The main requirement for the creation of these temporary schools is that local recycled wood and renewable bamboo should be used for construction. These materials were used because they are easy to maintain and are very economical.

785 The interior layout provides an extensive open space that is semi-private and includes a storage area for the students' use. The materials are local and well known by the users, which makes maintenance easy.

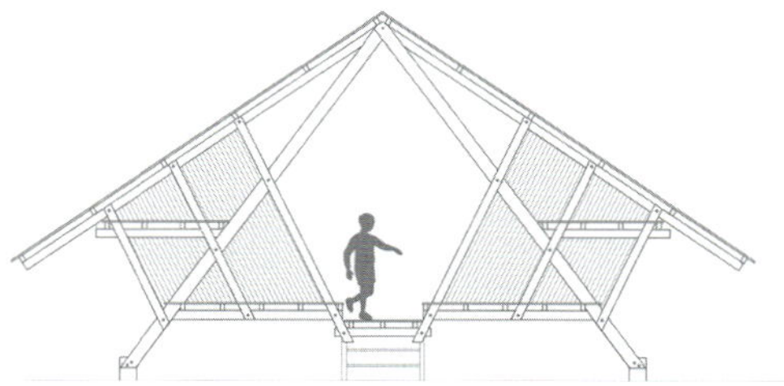

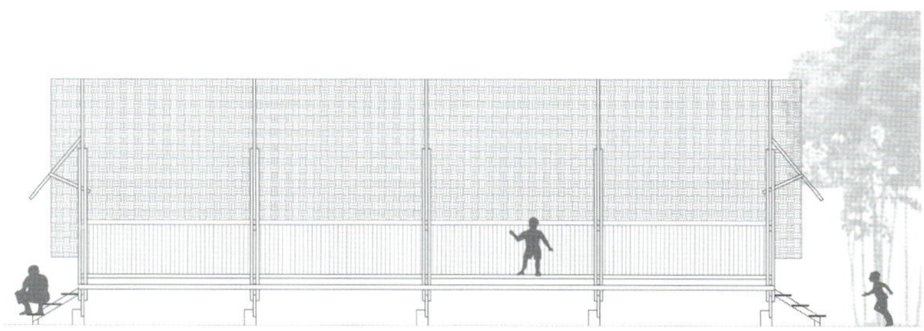

786 The main cost of the building is the structure of recycled wood, which represents 70% of the total construction cost. Bamboo and straw are also used for the walls, floors and ceilings.

787 Although the materials are not likely to last more than two years without any prior treatment, they are readily available in any season and the cost is affordable and stable for the local population.

788 The wood used for the dormitories comes from old buildings in the city; it was been carefully removed then sawn and polished to the necessary size. Each wooden structure is easy to disassemble then assemble in a new location.

789 The use of wood as the main construction material has helped to preserve indigenous traditional construction techniques. Recycled wood is a construction product that raises awareness about deforestation in the local communities.

Each of the five 72 m² bedrooms built costs approximately 1,700 euros. The construction of a clinic has been planned using the same system: environmentally friendly practices and helping local communities.

Temporary Schools

A.GOR.A ARCHITECTS

MAE SOT, THAILAND, 2014

AREA
130 m^2

CLIENT
MAE TAO CLINIC

PHOTO
© FRANC PALLARÈS LÓPEZ

791 The construction of this school wouldn't have been possible if it hadn't been part of a shared project between a.gor.a architects, Science and Technology Training Centre (STTC), and Ironwood, a local organisation.

792 The project is the first prototype of an ephemeral temporary school for immigrants from the Thai city of Mae Sot. Construction costs are minimal since local materials are used.

793 This entire architectural complex forms part of the new Mae Tao Clinic Training Centre. The idea is that in the near future, more classrooms, hostels and a clinic will be built.

794 This prototype school is closely linked to the first project designed by the same architects: the temporary hostels that accommodate refugees arriving from neighbouring Myanmar.

795 A minimal structure that forms the iron frame supports the pitched roof. Once more, straw, local wood and the indigenous construction system has been used for the creation of this prototype school.

796 The construction materials are readily available and endemic to the area so maintenance is easy and economical. Bamboo was used for the support, hay for the roofs and iron for the main structure.

799 The price of teak wood that comes from the border between Thailand and Myanmar has greatly increased, due to being considered as one of the best in the world. This has led to recycled wood becoming popular among the local population.

800 The main feature of this school is its iron structure that can be assembled and disassembled easily to move it to a new location. The frames can be stored and used again.

797 The interior has been divided into two similar spaces that have room for two classes in each. The centre is used as a corridor towards the exterior and as communication space between the two classrooms.

798 The architects opted for the design of a single horizontal floor and double pitched roof. This design shelters the building from the weather and gives the interior good visibility for carrying out school tasks.

Bird-apartment

NENDO

KOMORO, JAPAN, 2012
AREA
N/A
CLIENT
ANDO FOUNDATION
PHOTO
© DAICI ANO, MASAYA YOSHIMURA

Nendo, the Japanese studio,
designed this installation for
the Momofuku Ando Centre
in Komoro, a centre dedicated
to the promotion of nature
801 and outdoor activities.

The centre is located in
the Nagano prefecture, a
mountainous region known
as the Japanese Alps in the
centre of the island of Honshu.
The area has great ecological
value and very beautiful
802 landscapes.

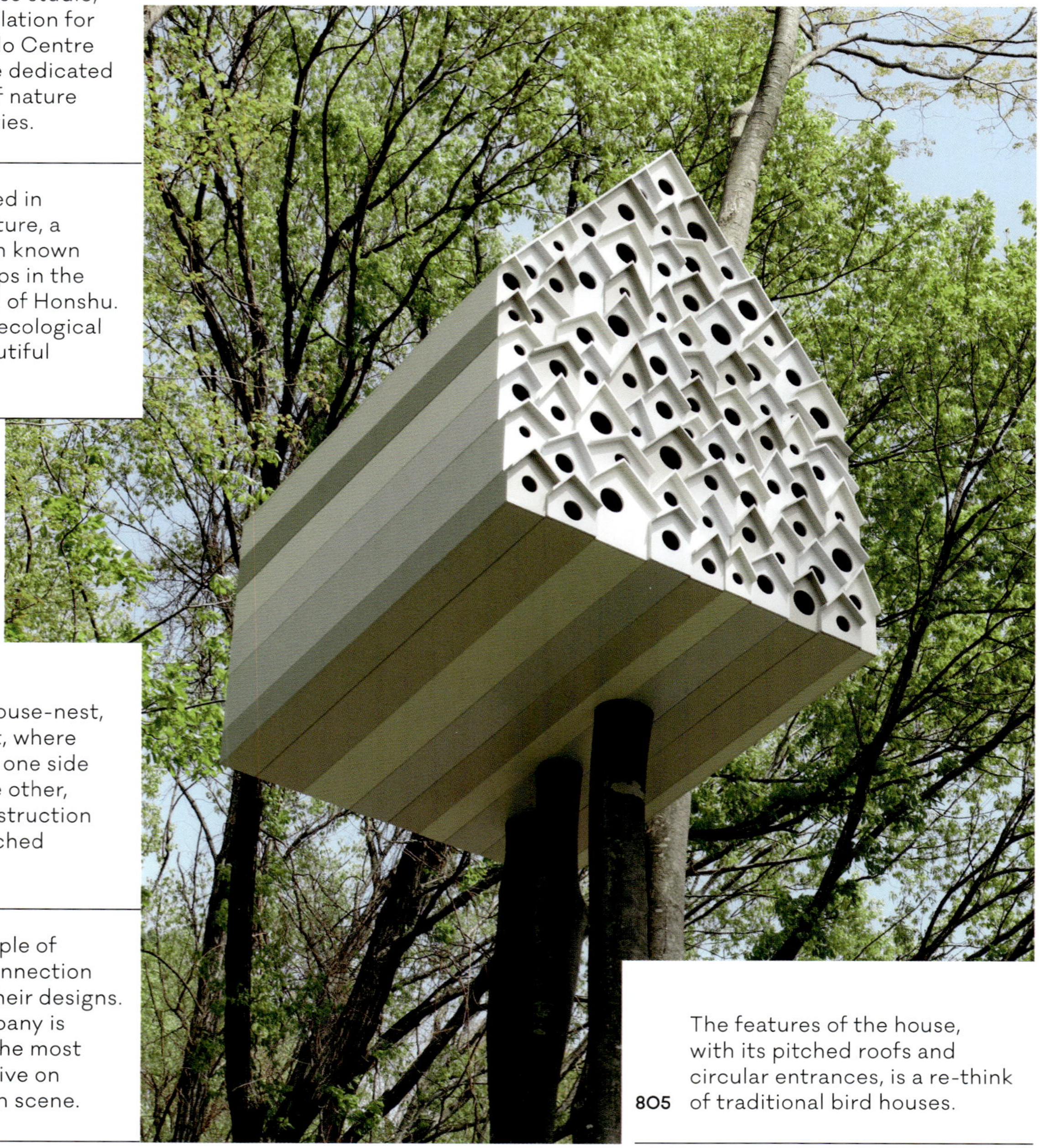

Nendo planned a house-nest,
a shared apartment, where
78 birds can live on one side
and a human on the other,
and placed the construction
between trees, perched
803 on three trunks.

This is a good example of
how Nendo seek connection
and emotion with their designs.
The Japanese company is
considered one of the most
prolific and innovative on
804 the industrial design scene.

The features of the house,
with its pitched roofs and
circular entrances, is a re-think
805 of traditional bird houses.

806 The repetition of the characteristic motifs reflected on both sides of the installation balances the specific weight of the two homes, reinforcing the concept of respect and peaceful coexistence between species.

807 The house-nest was constructed as a birdwatching hide but goes beyond putting the spectator behind a window: it seeks empathy and identification with the birds.

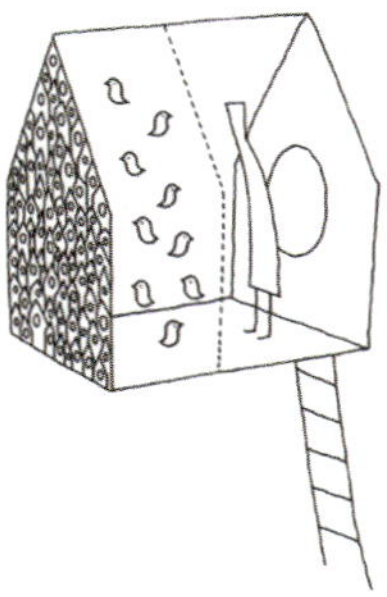

808 The interiors of birds' nests can be viewed from the observer's side of the house through the many peep-holes in the middle wall.

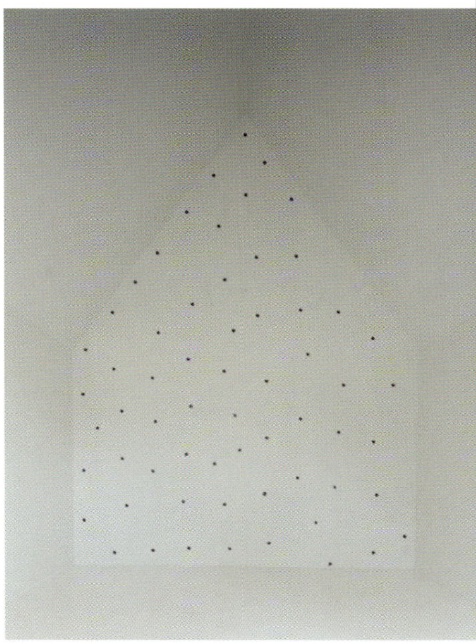

809 The delicate job of stabilising and balancing the house is especially noticeable in its interior, where the parts of the tree that support the structure as well as the fixings are invisible.

810 The interior is bright white with no other furniture or features, so that the only thing noticeable from the house is the inside of the nests and the birds' eye view of the forest, as if we were just another tenant in the house.

811—818

Antoine

BUREAU A

SWISS ALPS, SWITZERLAND, 2014

AREA
N/A

CLIENT
N/A

PHOTO

811 The project, named Antoine, was commissioned to accommodate artist residences within the program run by the Verbier 3d Foundation and was presented in the *Mutations* exhibition held on July 5th, 2014.

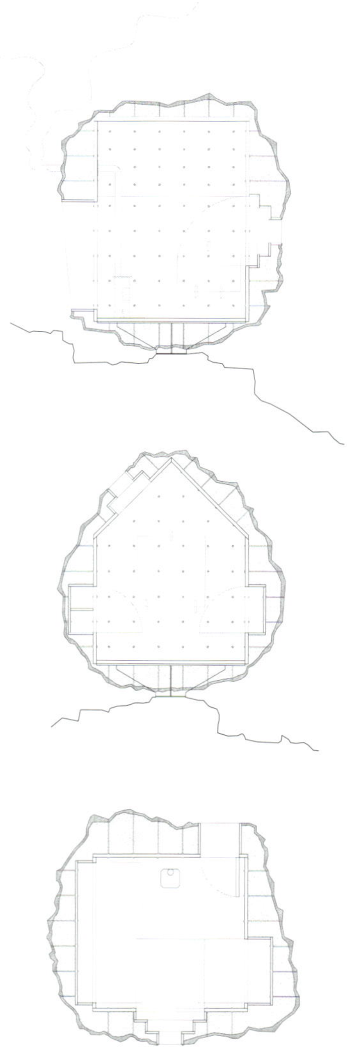

812 The originality of this project is the creation of a wooden cabin inside an artificial rock, transported to a remote site in the Swiss Alps.

813 The architects who designed this ephemeral shelter named it Antoine as a tribute to the main character of *Derborence*, the famous 1934 novel by Swiss author Charles Ferdinand Ramuz.

816 A crane and truck are used to literally position and leave the shelter in a field where there are rock falls. This was intentional: the architects had planned the design as a camouflaged bunker.

814 The project is based around a simple wooden hut, enclosed within a large boulder-shaped concrete shell. The exterior design was intended to have dialogue with the surrounding mountains.

815 The project contains the characteristic architectural features that are the basics in any house: a bed, table, seat, window, door and fireplace. It is a place where one can enter and hide without being seen.

817 For the interior, the architects decided to use wood as the material most in line with the basic concept: respect for the environment. The treated wood is used for the walls as well as the floor and ceilings.

818 The only openings in the interior are two small windows in the top and side of the structure and a small door on one of the sides.

819 The design was inspired by the landscape in the novel. Antoine, a Swiss shepherd is trapped between the rocks after a landslide and survives for seven weeks before finding his way back.

The architects based the design on their observations of the physical geography of the mountainous terrain. The location's rocky structure inspired a narrow rough exterior.

Landscape Fence

HERI&SALLI

VIENNA, AUSTRIA, 2011
AREA
N/A
CLIENT
N/A
PHOTO
© PAUL OTT

821 Approaching the task of redefining a property with an existing garden and making provisions for views and separation from surrounding properties, the idea of a classic rustic fence was rejected.

822 A geometric relationship is established with the original construction. Steps, seats, surrounding areas and a table with back rest are integrated into the structure. The project presents a number of possibilities contained in the same space.

823 The structure should not close off the space. The architects experimented with adapting the opening process of a cocoon. When it opens, different spatial qualities are created.

824 The source of inspiration for the creation of this steel structure was a cocoon. The owner wanted an ephemeral cover installed over his outdoor pool. The architects were able to experiment with the creation of a usable surface.

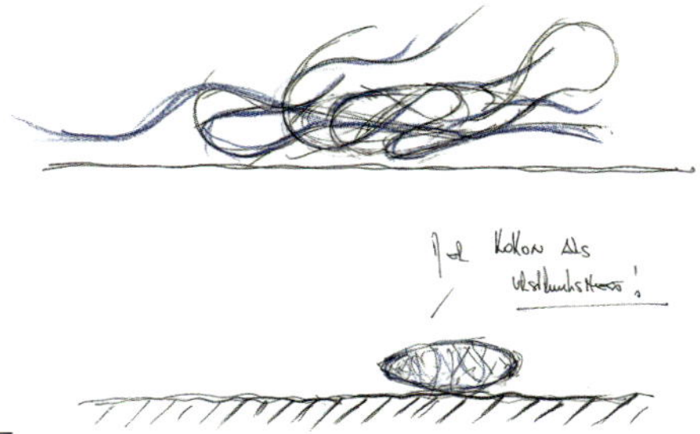

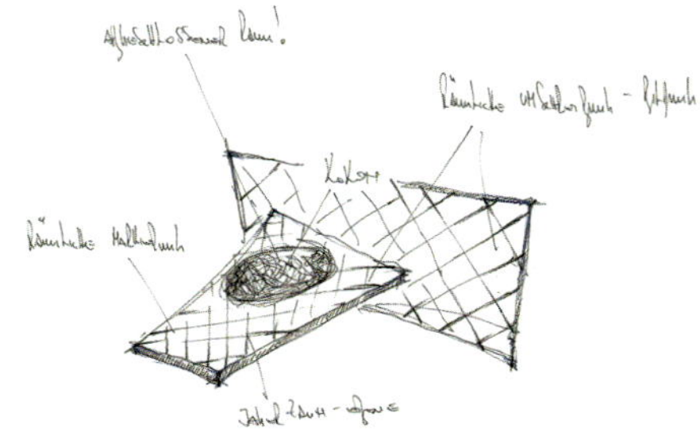

825 The diagonal pattern is the main focus of this architectural installation. This pattern continuously envelops the structure from the plane of the roof to the floor, as if it were a liquid.

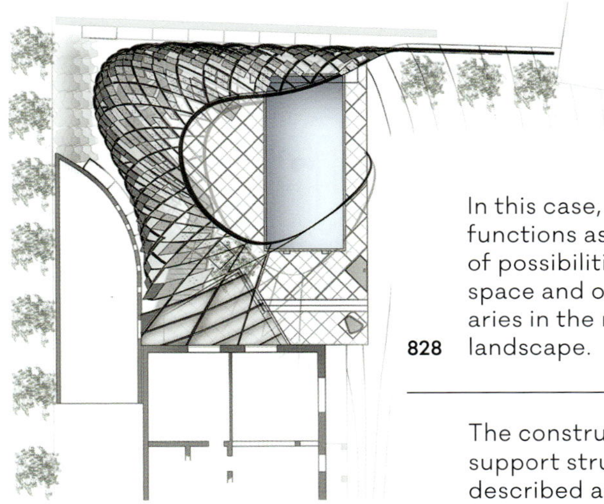

828 In this case, architecture functions as an accumulation of possibilities described in a space and only creates boundaries in the middle of a vast landscape.

829 The construction of the support structure can be described as a overhanging free concave form. The frames consist of welded solid steel flat profiles.

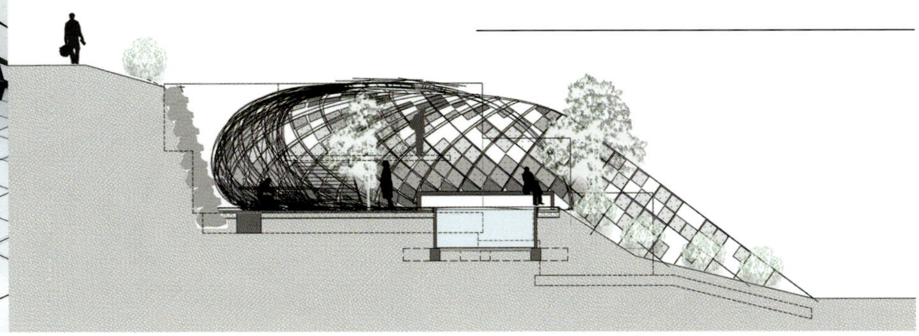

826 The shell of the structure is not completely closed. It is made using plates in the shape of a diamond, which are fixed using tabs in the diagonals. Many of them can be turned around on their axis.

827 The construction is partially covered, withdrawn and protected at first. It then opens out and finally gives way to the water of the pool. The curves of the structure make the space seem bigger than it actually is.

830 One of the main achievements of the architects has been transforming the concept of the typical metal fence into an aesthetic element that envelops the residence to provide privacy from the neighbours.

Monte Verita

BUREAU A

ASCONA, SWITZERLAND, 2015

AREA
N/A

CLIENT
N/A

PHOTO
© DOROTHÉE THÉBERT, BUREAU A

831 The architects decided to create a temporary theatre so that it could be moved to different towns and villages. It is easy to transport to different places thanks to the construction materials and its quick to assemble format.

832 The project's scenery comprises basic items, such as benches, chairs, simple partitions, stairs, canopies and standard lamps. Items that are ordinary, economical and easy to handle and transport.

835 Free public education, sexual diversity, family break-ups and the various types of family, concern for the environment and commitment to an ideology are the main issues examined in the theatre.

833 The aim of the project was to create a quick and easy to assemble structure and versatile scenery. This was achieved using basic materials such as pine wood and natural wool.

834 Bureau A envisioned a temporary theatre that could travel with the artists for performances. This is another reason for the decision to create this mobile, economical and sustainable structure.

836 The project resembles a large-scale cabin with removable scenery. A structure that is not too heavy and can be easily handled and transported is created using light and easy to assemble materials.

837 The project includes a communal sauna and shower, which invite both actors and guests to get naked and experience Utopia freely, without prejudice and without the need to worry about looks and appearances.

838 The basic idea for this project is "minimal architecture", which involves materials that are easy to use and acquire, such as pine, wool and a drum as a water tank for the shower.

839 **A sauna, or "sweat lodge" was also created using basic architecture. It aims to be functional and utopian, not modern, and the design is not overwhelming, since this implies costs and difficulty with assembly and disassembly.**

840 The project seeks to be Utopian from architectural, ideological and cultural points of view. It aims to show that with wood, wool and liberation we can pursue ideals and create a very different society.

Jellyfish Barge

LINV, PNAT, STUDIOMOBILE

NAVICELLI CHANNEL,
(BETWEEN PISA AND LIVORNO),
ITALY, 2014

AREA
9.7 x 9.7 m / 3.5 m HIGH

CLIENT
ENTE CASSA DI RISPARMIO
DI FIRENZE AND REGIONE TOSCANA

PHOTO
© MATTEO MAYDA

A multidisciplinary team of architects and botanists offers a revolutionary proposal to combat the scarcity of resources that the world is enduring: the Jellyfish Barge. It is an agricultural, ephemeral and floating structure that produces food.

841

842 Simple recycled materials are used for this construction. The project consists of an approximately 70 m^2 wooden base, floating on 96 recycled plastic drums.

843 This structure produces a greenhouse effect without consuming land, freshwater or energy. It was designed and envisioned for vulnerable communities prone to water and food shortages. It is built with simple low-cost technologies.

844 Seven solar stills arranged along the perimeter provide the freshwater needed for agriculture. They produce up to 150 litres of clean, desalinated water and salt water per day.

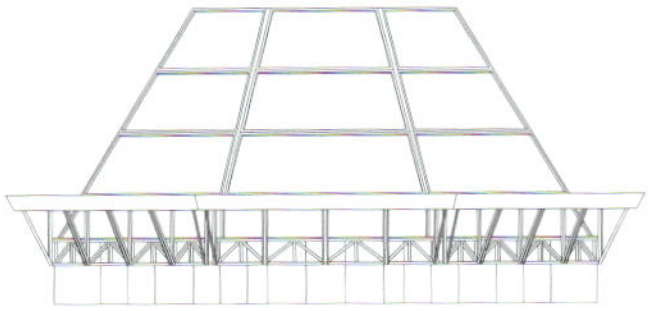

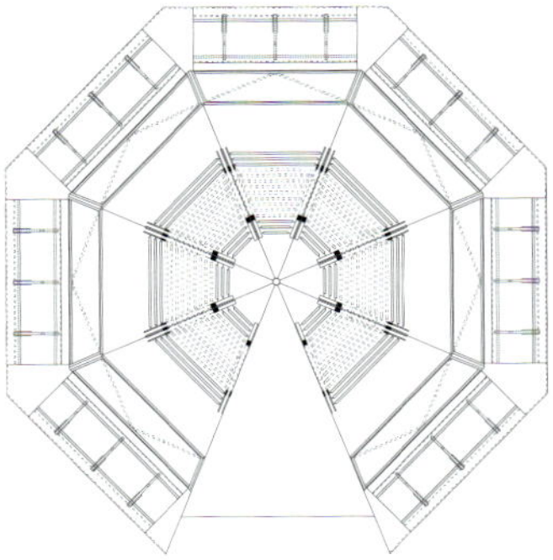

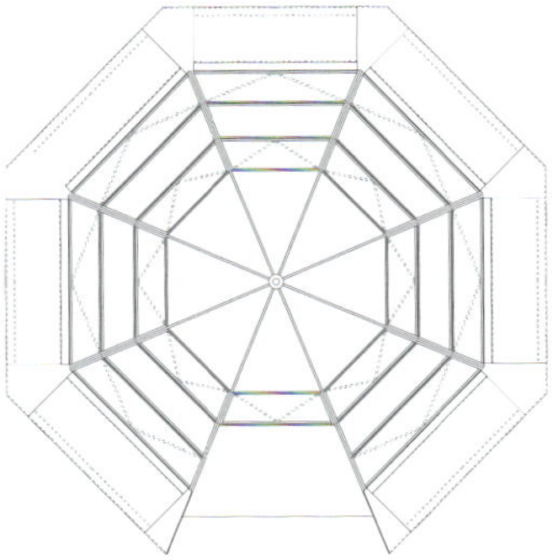

845 The solar desalination system replicates the natural phenomenon that occurs in oceans: the water evaporates and falls as rain. In this case, on a small scale, humid air is sucked in and condenses on drums cooled by contact with the cold surface of the sea.

846 Two of the project's successful aspects are the small size and low cost. A single module is completely autonomous and several can ensure food security for an entire community.

847 Renewable energy systems integrated into the structure provide the low energy requirement for the pumps.

848 An innovative hydroponic system creates a greenhouse effect. Hydroponics is a crop production technique which uses 70% less water compared to traditional cultivation, thanks to the continuous re-use of water.

849 The Jellyfish Barge uses about 15% sea water mixed with distilled water to ensure even better water efficiency. The whole complex has an innovative automated monitoring system with remote control.

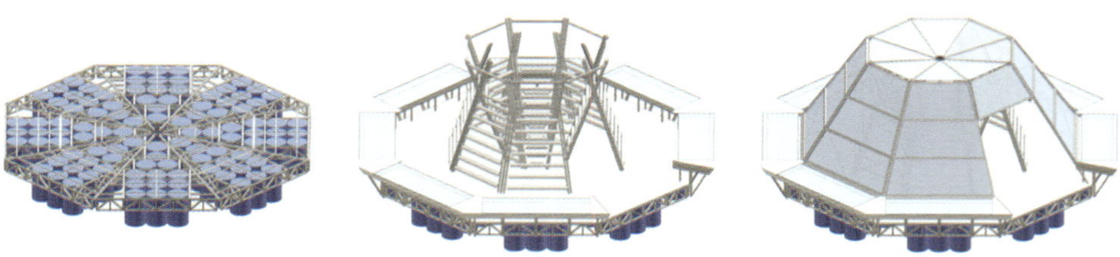

The octagonal shape of the platform allows different modules to be combined by connecting them with square floating bases. This way the assembly can be converted into small markets or small community spaces.

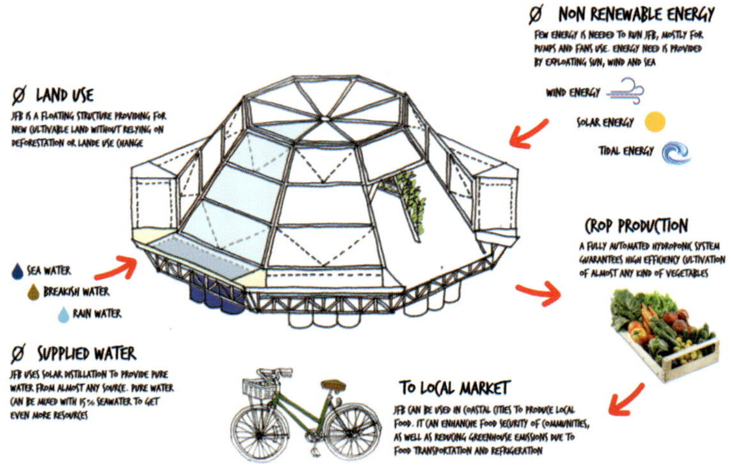

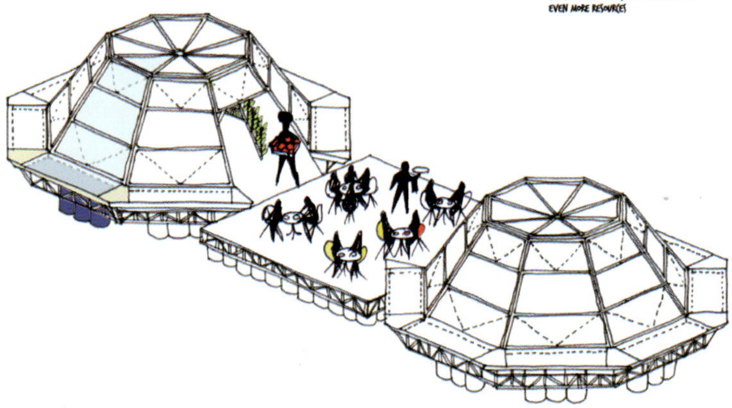

Smoke Train

XEVI BAYONA

NEWPORT, IRELAND, 2014

AREA
N/A

CLIENT
CHANGING TRACKS,
XARXA TRANSVERSAL

PHOTOS
© XEVI BAYONA

851 The aim of the intervention is to represent the memory of the train that used to cross the old bridge. Now, the speed of the railway has given way to the calm rhythm of people and bicycles.

852 The large spiral aims to represent smoke and steam coming from the train. Tubes, steel cables, water sprinklers, a water tank and a small pump were used to achieve this.

853 When night falls, a series of bulbs lights up the spiral as well as the lower part of the bridge. This creates a play of lights, colours and materials reflected in the river.

854 Twenty two tubes of six metres in length and six centimetres in diameter are joined with steel cables to create a substructure of more than 1,200 metres of plastic tubing.

855 A 1,000 litre water tank and a pump supply 120 sprinklers. These spray water with the idea of creating a cloud that resembles the steam from a train.

856 The project involved recreating the silhouette of the smoke and steam of an old train with the objective of enhancing the image of the bridge with a somewhat nostalgic touch.

857 It took 27 days and a lot of effort to create the final structure. The appearance of the bridge was changed radically since the tube construction could be viewed from a distance.

858 The spiral structure contrasts with the traditional shape of the bridge. On the other hand, red emphasises the natural colour of the stone that forms part of the traditional Irish landscape.

859 The steel of the base structure, together with the tubes and the brick of the bridge create an interesting visual impact. This combination, together with the countryside that surrounds the place, shows that things that are different can fit in.

860 During the day, the bridge and the structure are visible and attractive. When night falls, it is illuminated creating an attractive silhouette that is reflected on the water of the river.

Shadows of Memory

XEVI BAYONA

TORTOSA, SPAIN, 2014

AREA
N/A

CLIENT
CHANGING TRACKS,
XARXA TRANSVERSAL

PHOTOS
© XEVI BAYONA

861 The site of the intervention is the railway bridge in Tortosa. Specifically, on the shoreline where the two banks of the river Ebro are joined.

862 The site chosen is the 230 metre long metal framework that connects both sides of the river.

863 The coloured image blurs the geometric forcefulness of the of the bridge's horizontal structure. A traditional hand rail becomes a point of visual attraction.

864 Playing with colours and their arrangement creates a measured rhythm of tectonic elements that form a changing chromaticity. The fading shades generate a unique atmosphere.

865 Part of the European cultural project *Changing Tracks*, the project intends to open contemporary art to new audiences by exhibiting works in large spaces.

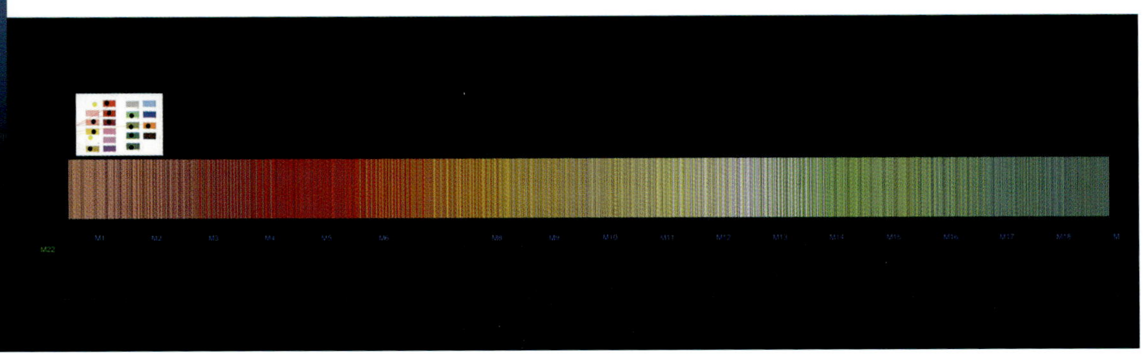

866 A total of eleven kilometres of tape was used. During the day, it helped to capture the sunlight and at night, it was illuminated by a collection of bulbs.

867 The light effects emphasise and intensify the sunlight during daytime hours. While the light of a bulb shows silhouettes of unhurried people and bicycles, peacefully passing by.

868 The silhouettes of pedestrians and bikes crossing the bridge can be seen through a back-lit membrane.

869 The intention is to carry out Goethe's colour theory. If the collection of these is offered as an object, they cause the eye to feel pleasure and see them an actual object.

870 A set of coloured tapes is all that is required to change the appearance of the bridge. A more colourful and visually appealing bridge is created for the duration of the installation.

Rainbow Station

DAAN ROSEGAARDE + STUDIO ROOSEGAARDE

AMSTERDAM, NETHERLANDS, 2014

AREA
45 x 25 m

CLIENT
AMSTERDAM FUND FOR THE ARTS, NS STATIONS, PRORAIL, STICHTING DOEN, STERRENWACHT LEIDEN UNIVERSITY

PHOTO
© DAAN ROSEGAARDE

871 The large-scale light intervention created in Amsterdam Central Station. It commemorates the 125th anniversary of the station's construction by architect Pierre Cuypers and engineer Dolf van Gendt.

872 This artistic and ephemeral intervention was visible on the east side of the station after sunset every day for about a year.

873 This intervention is a unique collaboration between the Daan Roosegaarde studio, astronomers at the University of Leiden and Optical researchers at the University of North Carolina.

A rainbow is portrayed using
lighting on glass, offering
874 travellers a moment of magic.

To achieve the desired light
effect, a lens was developed
that is capable of creating a
refractive dispersion, which
adapts to the dimensions
of the building's curve. It is a
collaboration with astronomers
875 at the University of Leiden.

The duration of the chromatic
landscape projection is just
a few minutes and it is visible
from inside as well as outside
876 of the building.

The artistic lighting piece
also commemorates the
International Year of Light,
announced by UNESCO.
The project has been made
possible thanks to the collabo-
ration of the Amsterdam
Fund for the Arts, NS, ProRail
877 y Stichting Doen.

Using this lens, white light
is fragmented, projecting
a rainbow onto the glass to
create a chromatic landscape
that is integrated into the
878 architecture.

According to scientist
Frans Snik from the Leiden
Observatory: "Thanks to new
liquid crystal technology
developed for exoplanet
research, the Rainbow
Station takes on the exact
879 shape of the 45 m station roof".

The liquid crystal spectral filter
distributes most of the light
inside the arch of the station.
It also limits its escape and
achieves a wide dispersion
of colours, obtaining the
880 desired shades.

Fabra i Coats

XEVI BAYONA

BARCELONA, SPAIN, 2012

AREA
N/A

CLIENT
BARCELONA CITY COUNCIL

PHOTOS
© XEVI BAYONA

881 The project arose from the Three Wise Men's need to store all the presents ready for the night of 5th January, *Noche de Reyes*, when Spanish children receive presents that arrive while they sleep. A historic factory was used as a warehouse for toys and excitement.

882 Inside the factory, the Pages were receiving and organising the Three wise Men's presents. After night had fallen, these were distributed to all the houses in the city.

883 The image of a charming toy factory was shown on the front of the former factory. The large windows on all three floors were lit with all kinds of colours.

884 You could glimpse the activity going on inside the warehouse against a backlight. Silhouettes and projections could be seen, powered by a simple motor that emitted a range of coloured LED lights.

The exterior windows were covered with translucent paper, playing with the perspective created in the interior. A mixture of imagination, bulbs and silhouettes created
885 a magical atmosphere.

The rear façade served as a showcase for the warehouse. It displayed thousands of gifts that were shown in different colours by the changing light
886 that illuminated them.

The building's 33 large windows allowed you to see some of the gifts, symbolised by a total of six thousand boxes in gift
887 wrapping.

Outside the factory, a Royal Page collected letters and explained to the children what was happening inside. Everything was ready to make
888 the gift distribution a success.

A hidden narration was the protagonist of the project's second edition. This was synchronised with a moving changing light, creating an magical atmosphere full
889 of excitement.

The combination of heaped boxes, the role of the large windows and light effects was all that was needed to create a project full of magic. A different way of seeing a
890 factory that is rich in history.

Constell.ation I & II

LIKEARCHITECTS

LISBON, PORTUGAL, 2013 / AMSTERDAM, NETHERLANDS, 2014

AREA
1,200 m² / 110 m²

CLIENT

CLIENTE
MUSEUM OF THE PRESIDENCY OF THE PORTUGUESE REPUBLIC / AMSTERDAM LIGHT FESTIVAL

PHOTO

Constell.ation I and Constell.ation
II are two ephemeral lighting
installations that are designed
to invigorate spaces that are
normally closed to the public.
This allows visitors to stroll
891 through unusual locations.

The first project was installed
in the gardens of the presi-
dential residence in Portugal
during the Christmas period.
The second project was
presented at the *Light Festival*
892 held in Amsterdam.

893 The *Constell.ation I* project is a reinterpretation of Christmas lights. A large space was covered with multiple arches of light for this installation.

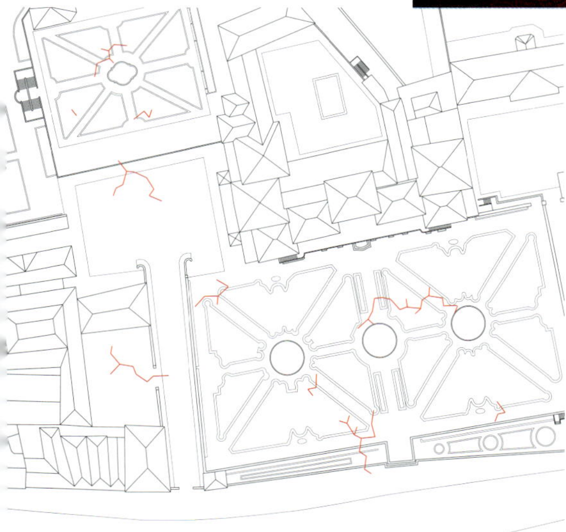

894 Light is used as a vehicle to evoke a poetic visual language in the form of calligraphy and drawings in the landscape. Arranged in small constellations, the arches created various illuminated frames.

895 The LEDs installed in the corrugated tube provide a strong red light, evoking Christmas and contrasting with the green of the gardens.

896 This network of nine adjoining arches was constructed using red corrugated tubes illuminated by a LED lighting system. The project connects with spaces and produces unexpected routes.

897 Here, the arch – a fundamental architectural element – has the inherent power to create a space and, at the same time, build a physical relationship between two places, giving rise to the idea of connection and unification.

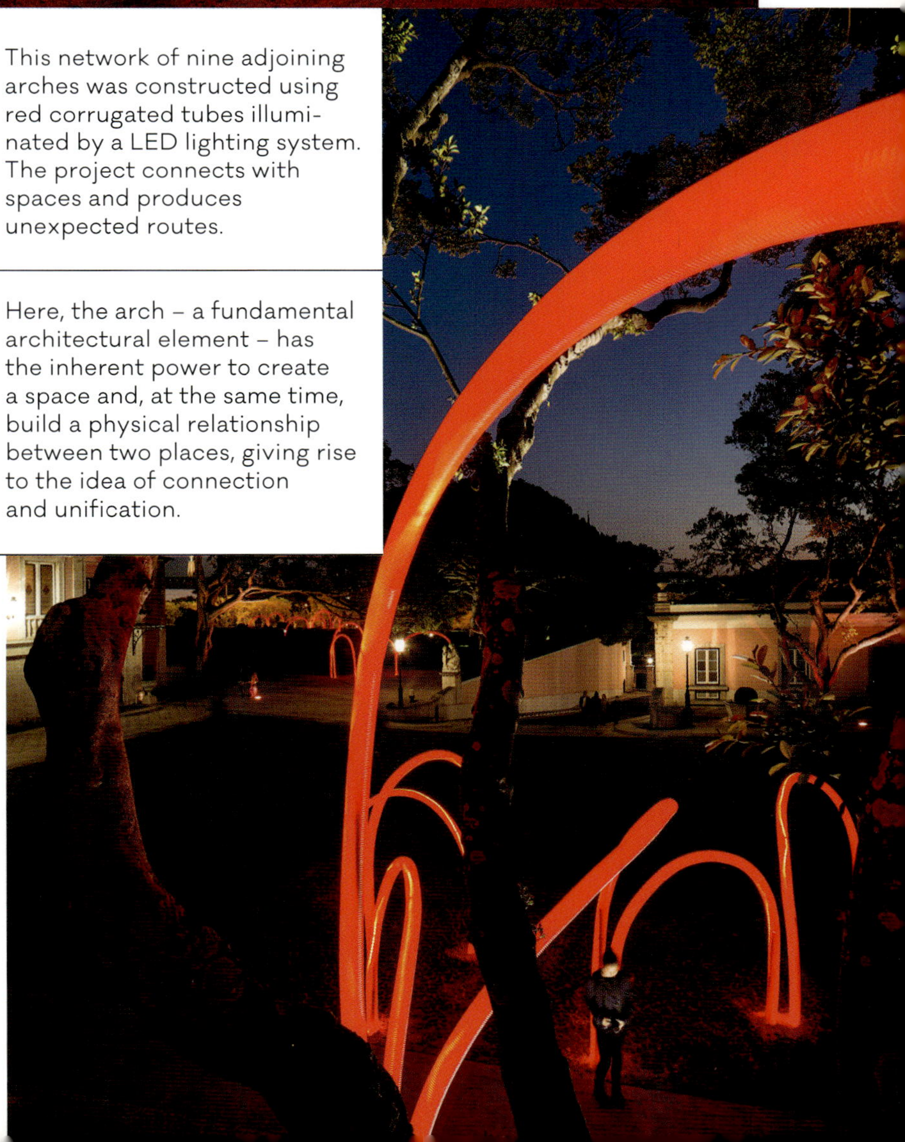

898 In the case of the Amsterdam installation, the red colour was also a tribute to the Dutch capital's famous Red Light District.

The *Amsterdam Light*
Festival is one of Europe's most
prestigious light festivals, where
the best light installations are
on display. The project provides
the viewer with an unexpected
899 and inspiring experience.

Regardless of its location,
Constell.ation II gives visitors
the impression that as they
pass through the arches,
they are entering into a physical
space: everything seems
different and time seems
900 to have stopped.

Light(wave)Flow

LOLA SOLANILLA, FABIENNE CUNY + COM UN LLUM, CARLA JARDIN, MARGA VICENS + APDI

AMSTERDAM, NETHERLANDS, 2015

AREA
N/A

CLIENT
AMSTERDAM LIGHT FESTIVAL

PHOTO
© TESSA VELDHORST

The intervention took place
within the framework of the
Amsterdam Light Festival.
The project sought to generate
a nocturnal dialogue with its
surroundings without changing
901 them.

The city's historic centre is
the stage where this forty day
festival is hosted. Light and
water are used to show the
902 city's charm.

The city is covered with
contemporary light sculptures,
projections and installations
by national and international
artists. A total of 33 projects
903 form the cloak of light.

904 The installations are divided into two routes: the boat route, or Water Colors, which can be seen along the canals; and the pedestrian route, or Iluminade, which runs through the city centre.

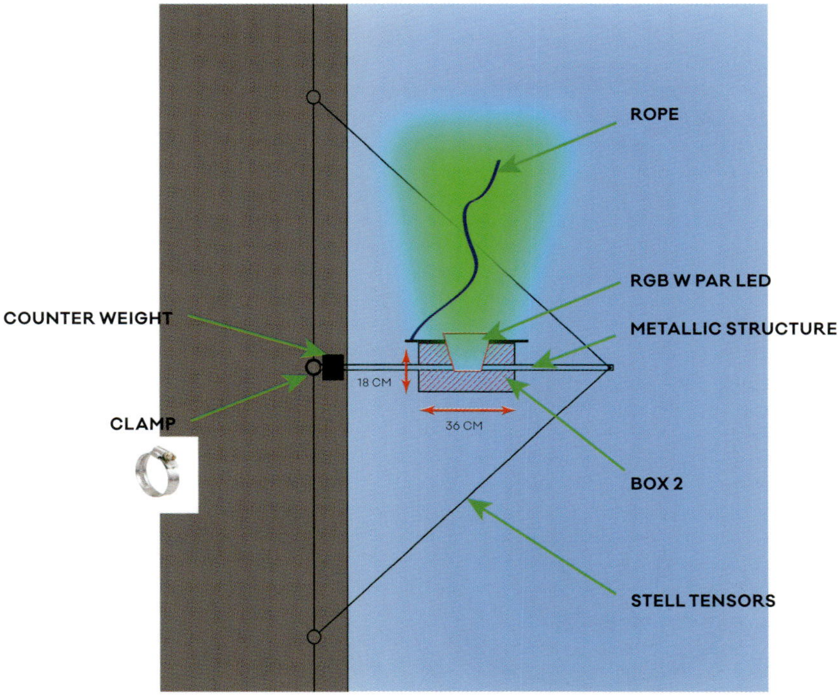

905 The main objective was to create a stunning visual effect. Light was combined with a wave oscillation, using kinetic art and movement as a reference.

906 The metal structure is submerged in water and secured with tensioning cables. At the top, there is a mechanism that is used to create the original light effects.

907 The coloured lights outline the modular trajectory of the waves and are reflected in the water, creating a unique dancing effect. This created a spectacular colourful look.

908 The project is designed as a homage to the city's canals, exploiting their visibility to the maximum with the installation of coloured lights over the water.

909 The wave of light is in continuous movement, suspended just a few centimetres over the water. It creates a kind of luminous serpent that radiates over the surface.

910 Assembly and installation of this project is not complicated but must be very precise. The structures must be arranged in absolutely the right places to achieve the desired effect.

Elastic Plastic Sponge

BALL-NOGUES STUDIO

INDIO, CA, USA, 2009

AREA
N/A

CLIENT
COACHELLA VALLEY MUSIC AND ARTS FESTIVAL

PHOTO
© BEN LLOYD GOLDSTEIN, CHRIS BALL

911 The project is made using one of the most simple and easy to use materials: plastic. It was planned and created by a group of students from the South California Institute of Architecture (SCI-ARC), directed by the Ball-Nogues studio.

912 Plastic can be folded, turned, curved and moulded. If this is applied to a large scale structure, the impact and ease of creation and installation demonstrate that simple things can be extravagant and impressive.

913 When the breeze blows, the combination of plastic and coloured fluorescent lights creates a sweeping effect that leaves nobody indifferent. This provides a view of the entire area and the structure emerges as the main axis.

914 The impressive effect created by the fluorescent lights when night falls attracts visitors and invites them to stay under the structure to gaze at it. A simple plastic construction can become the perfect installation for any festive event.

915 By day, the installation protects visitors from the sun then, when night falls, a combination of fluorescent tubes, attached using bungee cords, generate light and an ambience that invites you to lie there for hours.

The elastic is composed of 250 cells, which were produced using personalised templates designed by students. The nuclei of these cells are very transportable so the structure can be easily
916 moved.

Despite the large scale of the structure, the designers were able to outline and modify the style according to the conditions presented each day thanks to the versatility of plastic and how easy it is
917 to change its shape.

The strong presence of the construction, combined with the organic shapes of the plastic and changing lights, make the piece the festival's main icon. The project consists of a living room, a theatre and
918 a large sculpture.

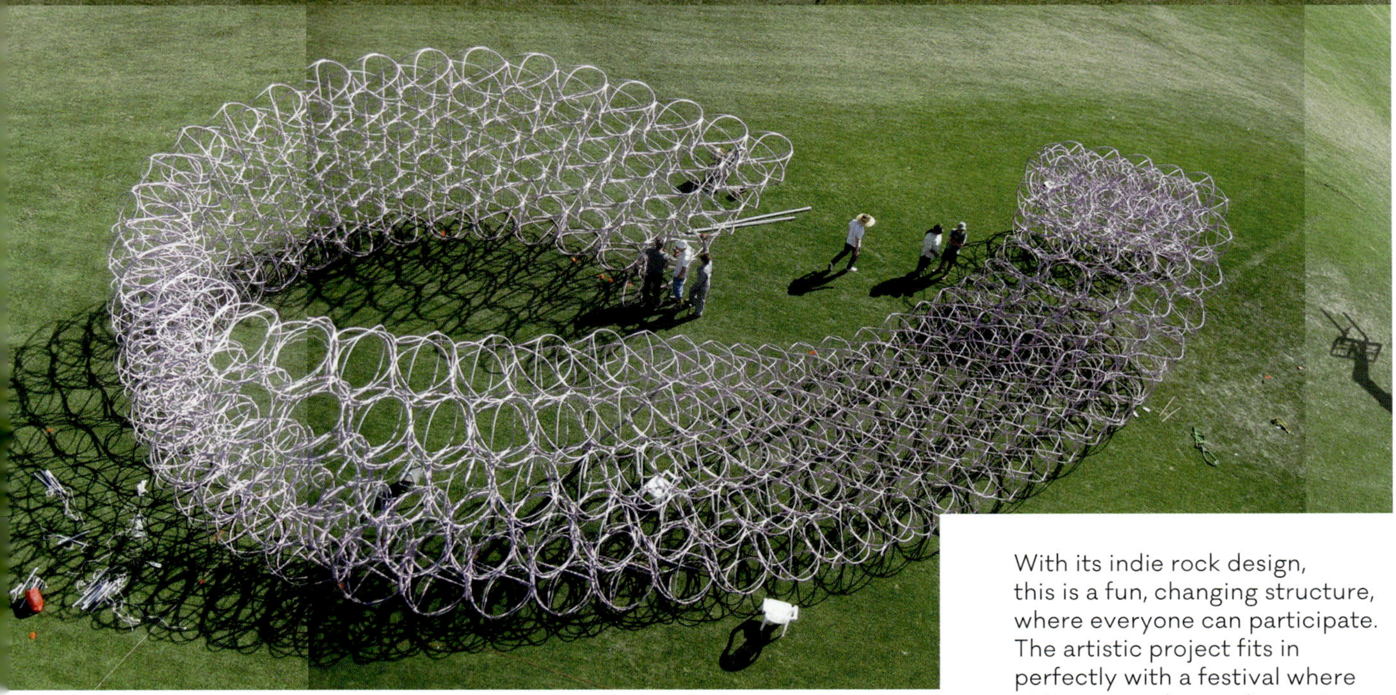

With its indie rock design,
this is a fun, changing structure,
where everyone can participate.
The artistic project fits in
perfectly with a festival where
visitors spend many hours: it
is decorative, it provides a sun
919 shield and is lit at night time.

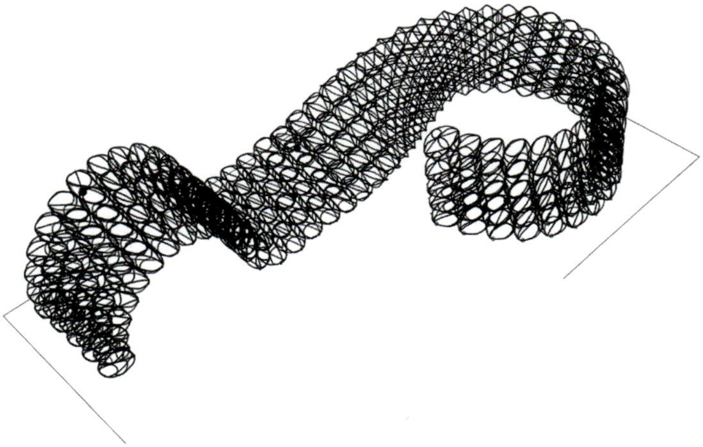

The mutability of plastic
allowed the students/designers
to play with shapes and sizes.
The fact that they could be
changed every day was inter-
preted as if it were a digital
920 model or a small scale piece.

921—930

Moon

BEN BUSCHE + BRUT DELUXE

MADRID, SPAIN, 2014-2015

AREA
1,300 m

CLIENT
MADRID CITY COUNCIL

PHOTO
© MIGUEL DE GUZMAN / IMAGENSUBLIMINAL

921 To celebrate Christmas, the Brut Deluxe architects designed the illuminations for one of the city's main arteries: the Gran Via.

922 The design consists of 31 luminous motifs which, all together, function as a human-scale flip book. Thirty one images vary gradually and produce an animation effect.

923 As you move along the avenue's 1,300 metres, the flip book effect appears as if you were flipping the pages of a book with your thumb.

924 The sequence of luminous motifs appears as if the moon is getting closer as you walk the ascent of the street. The reverse effect, of distancing, is produced in the descending stretch.

925 The architects planned a design which is repeated "n" times along the avenue to create an installation that changes at every point along its journey.

926 The sequence of images represents a hypothetical journey to the moon and also makes use of the Gran Via's specific topography.

928 The project is composed of grids of blue light with a white design in the centre, representing the moon's craters.

929 The Moon gets larger or smaller depending on the point of its trajectory.

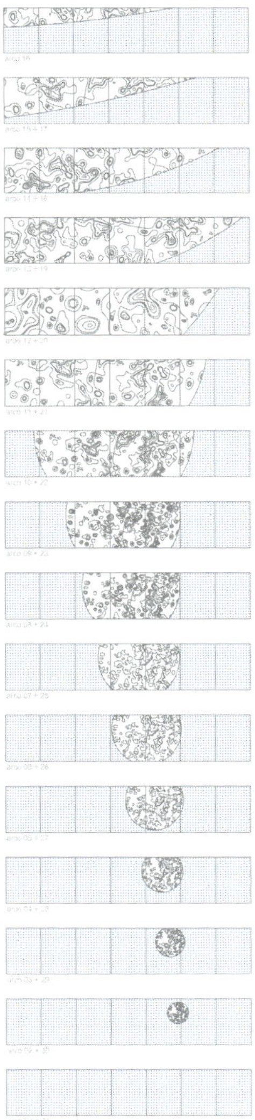

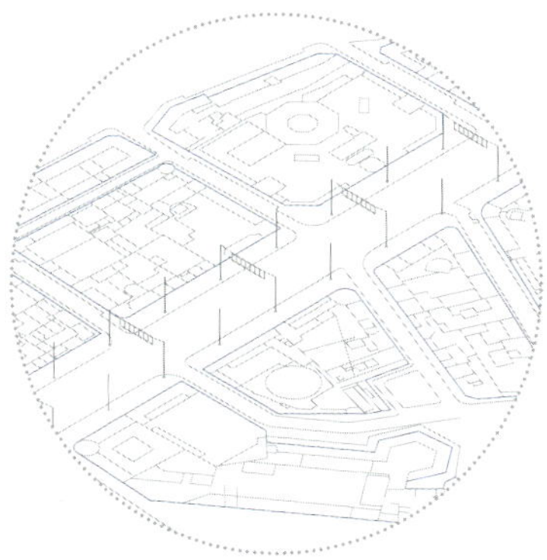

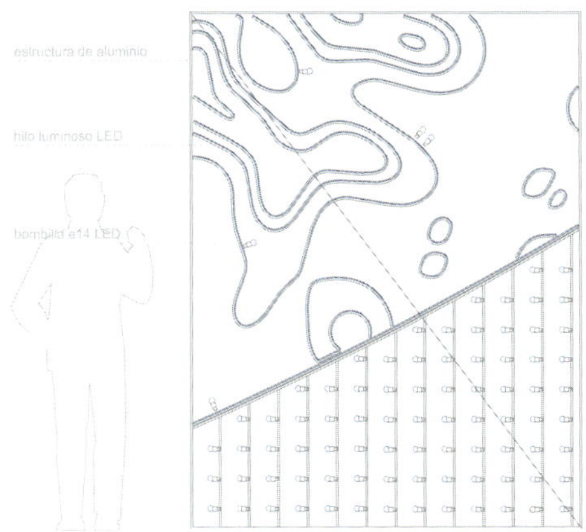

927 This successful project, created like an urban scale book, is the result of research and the creation of spaces, with a special focus on their atmospheric qualities.

930 The design was defined by the moon rising from one end of the street at the Plaza España and crossing with calle Alcalá to reach its highest point in the middle of its trajectory.

931—934

Berlin Lights

BEN BUSCHE + BRUT DELUXE

BERLIN, GERMANY, 2013-2014

AREA
N/A

CLIENT
WALL AG

PHOTO
© MIGUEL DE GUZMÁN / IMAGENSUBLIMINAL

931 This lighting project is part of the installations designed specifically as Christmas decorations. Three interventions take place in the famous Kurfürstendamm, in the centre of the German capital.

932 The first installation is on the Joachimstaler Platz junction, in front of the old traffic kiosk. It consists of an enormous dome of light with a diameter of 7.5 metres.

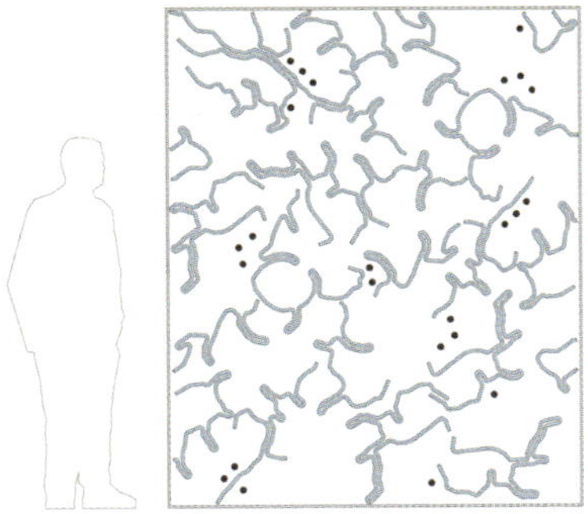

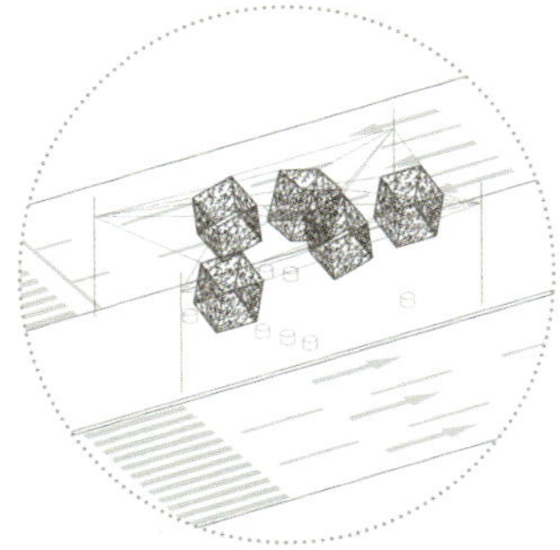

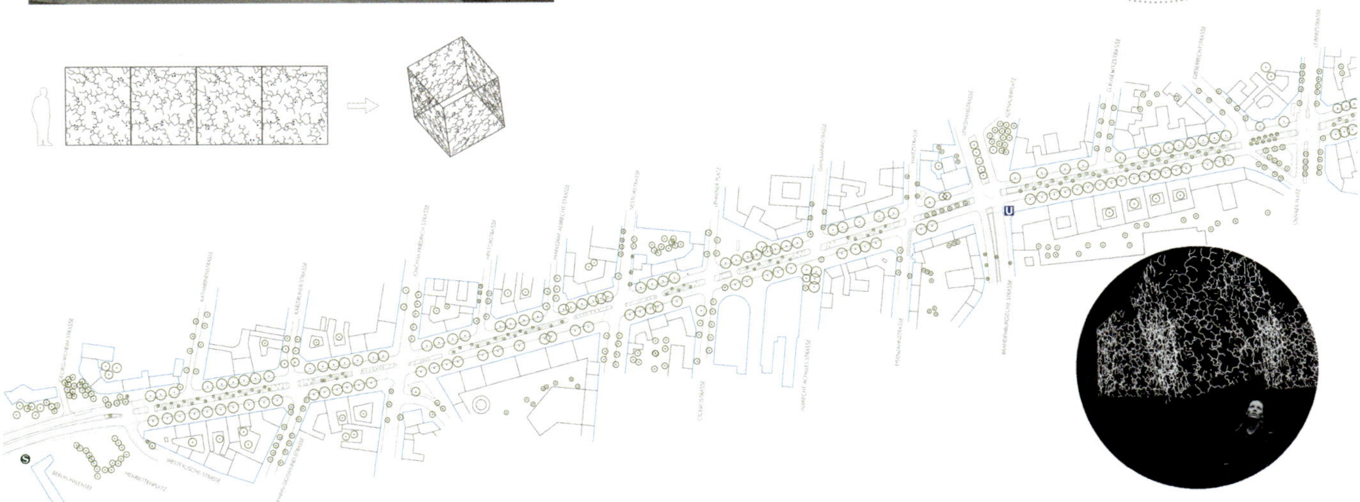

933 The second lighting intervention is on the Uhlandstrasse crossroads. The design consists of five large three dimensional cubes of light with decorative motifs.

934 Inspired by images and situations that we associate with Christmas, the architects abstractly converted them into landscapes of light.

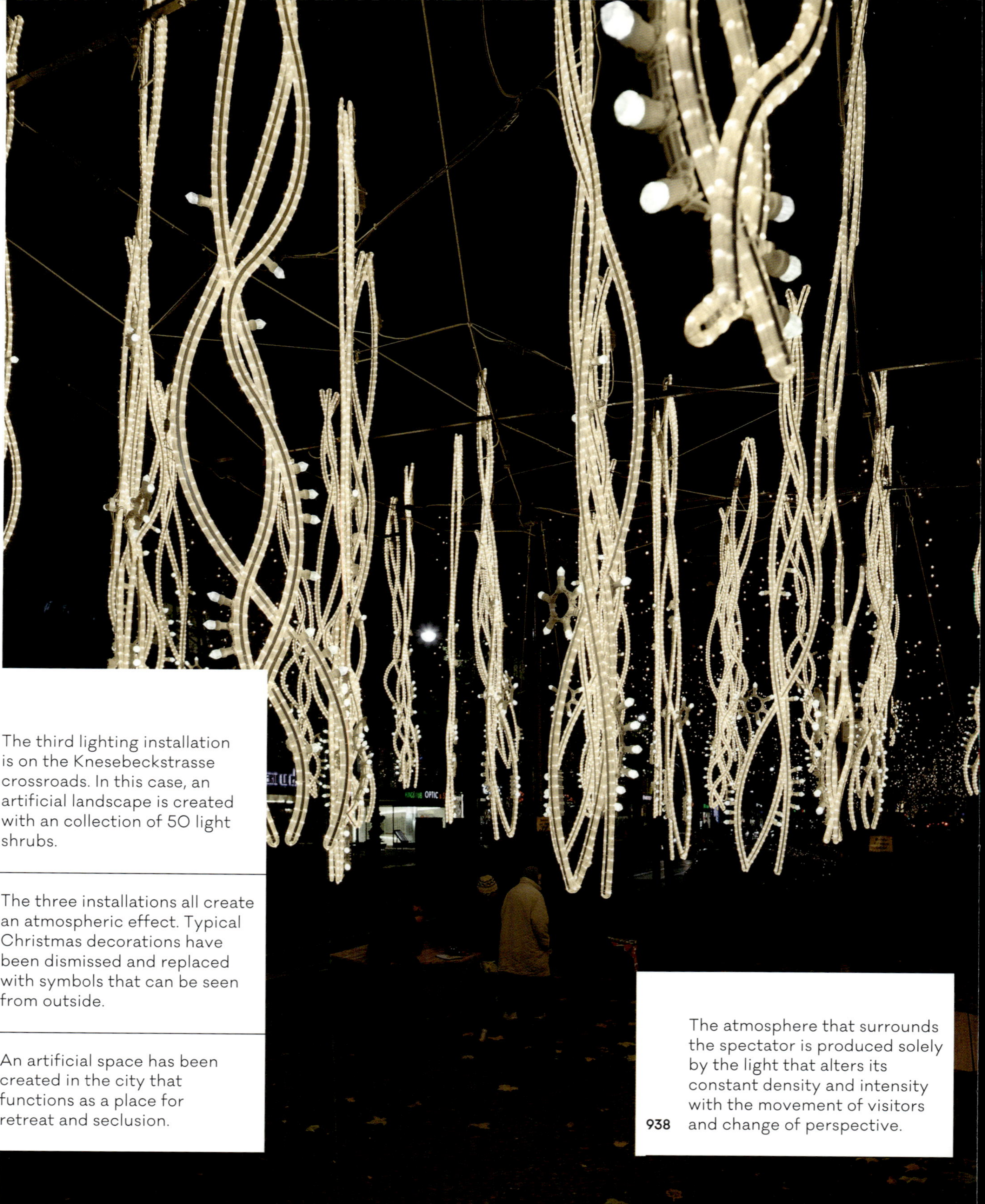

935 The third lighting installation is on the Knesebeckstrasse crossroads. In this case, an artificial landscape is created with an collection of 50 light shrubs.

936 The three installations all create an atmospheric effect. Typical Christmas decorations have been dismissed and replaced with symbols that can be seen from outside.

937 An artificial space has been created in the city that functions as a place for retreat and seclusion.

938 The atmosphere that surrounds the spectator is produced solely by the light that alters its constant density and intensity with the movement of visitors and change of perspective.

The installations propose a route that invites the passer–by to rest in the middle of the big city's urban landscape. This is achieved by using LEDs to project lights that change in intensity and movement according to perspective.

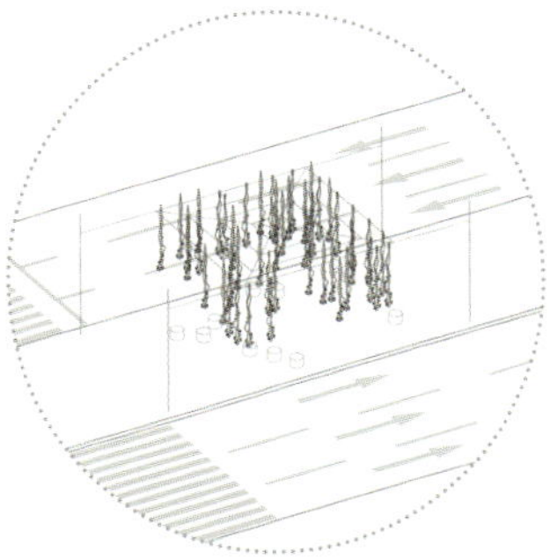

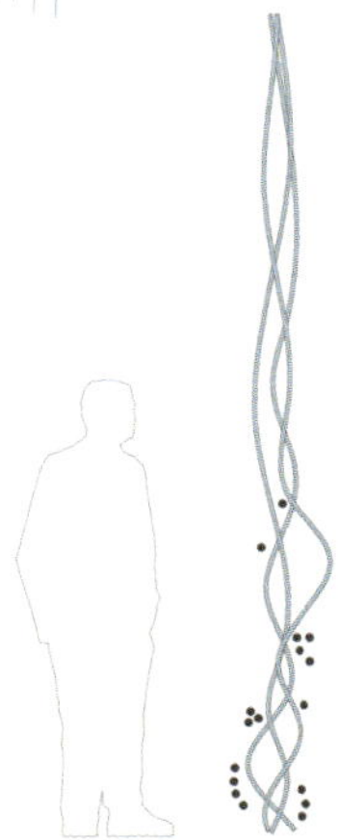

With this avant-garde design,
Brut Deluxe has created an
atmospheric effect where the
public can interact and exper-
iment with the space, shapes
940 and light.

MAZE Lights

BEN BUSCHE + BRUT DELUXE

HONG KONG, CHINA, 2014-2015

AREA
N/A

CLIENT
SUNG HUNG KAI PROPERTIES

PHOTO
© ROCÍO ROMERO / IMAGENSUBLIMINAL

941 The project was installed in an artificial park on the roof of an eight floor shopping centre in the New Town Plaza, Hong Kong.

942 The artificial park also functions as a connecting space between several homes of great height, hotels, office buildings and community installations. This entire architectural complex is at the top of the shopping centre.

943 Brut Deluxe was commissioned to design a series of light installations for a fun route that alternates labyrinthine concepts as the common thread throughout the different designs. These can be followed by the shopping centre's 350,000 visitors.

944 Instead of the typical light motifs, the designers created a series of installations inspired by the perceived atmosphere inside the shopping centre. The route begins with an artificial pink and white jungle of floral motifs.

945 The floral motifs on the first route are suspended in an apparently random order. The second ambience is achieved with a labyrinthine accumulation of transparent perspex panels with the same floral motif.

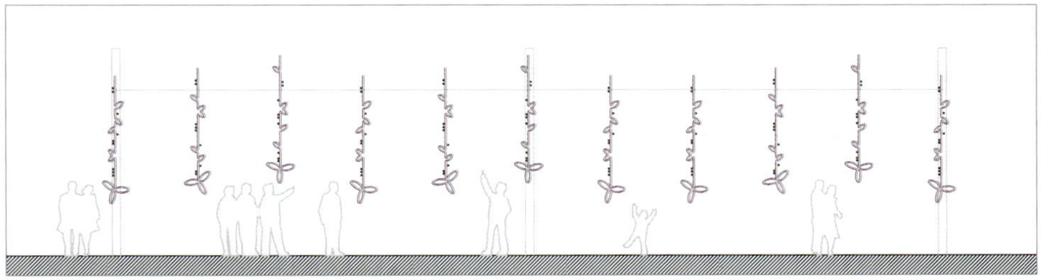

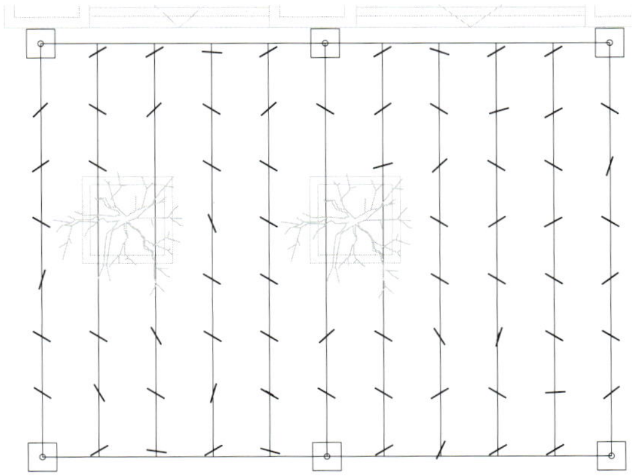

948 The materials used were: metal posts, steel cables, electrical fixings and connections, provided and installed by local companies. The existing natural trees formed part of the installation.

949 The schematic drawings consist of steel cables that can be laid in different directions, but they must function horizontally at approximately 3.5 - 4 metres in height.

950 The light installation consists of 72 light motifs grouped into three different types, randomly distributed in equal quantities.

946 The labyrinth was designed for NTP by the designer Adrian Fisher. The route ends in an ambience created by a blue geometric labyrinth that flashes and appears to float in the sky, creating a dome of single arches.

947 The light motifs are composed of tubes of pink LED light and tubes of 14 white LED bulbs, fixed onto an aluminium structure. The designers wished to interact with transparency and provide and infinite geometric spaces.

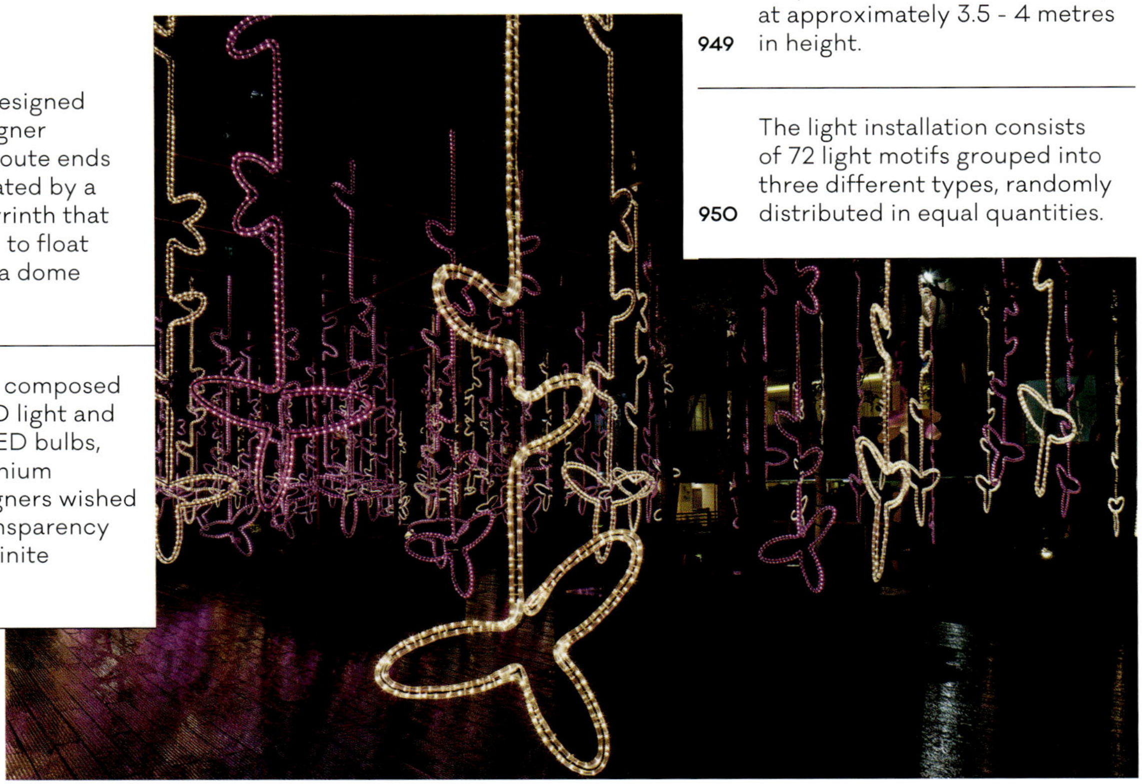

LEDscape

LIKEARCHITECTS

LISBON, PORTUGAL, 2013

AREA
112 m²

CLIENT
IKEA PORTUGAL

PHOTO
© FG+SG ARCHITECTURAL PHOTOGRAPHY

951 This installation uses light as a construction material for the space and landscape.

952 It is designed to show the visitor the importance of LED bulbs. It demystifies preconceived ideas about them and argues the need for responsible consumption.

953 LIKEarchitects decided to design the installation only using components from the large Swedish multinational. These were transformed to achieve an innovative effect.

954 An expressive light is created using a standard lamp. This is divided into three modular heights based on the company's style. Excess items were joined to make new units.

955 The installation is situated in the main courtyard of the Belem Cultural Centre in Lisbon, where a road lit by 1,200 points of light incite introspection.

956 *LEDscape* becomes an architectural labyrinth that challenges the visitor to an interactive experience.

957 The structure combines disposable resources and seeks to raise environmental awareness with the spectator. Economy played an important role and the installation was created at a very low cost.

959 A black base enhances the effect of the lights. The visitor can walk among them and enter the world of LEDs.

958 A total of 1,200 LED bulbs and 1,200 Hemma lamp bases were assembled at different heights. A combination of marketing, art and energy saving awareness.

960 The project is aimed at challenging the visitor to take part in an interactive experience, through a path of 1,200 points of light.

Filling the Void

XEVI BAYONA

GRANOLLERS, SPAIN, 2014

AREA
N/A

CLIENT
CHANGING TRACKS,
XARXA TRANSVERSAL

PHOTOS
© XEVI BAYONA

961 An experimental installation intended to stimulate discussions and discovery of new sensations and environments. It is an ephemeral intervention of space and light created in a former manufacturing complex now converted into a cultural centre.

Large moulds were placed in
the centre of the areas shaped
by pillars. The appearance
of the room was completely
962 changed by the installation.

Kilometres of elastic bands
were used to weave the residual
spaces, winding around the
shapes to generate a dense
pattern that would fill all
of the free space. The result
was an abstract and original
963 installation.

Empty interior spaces were
to be found between the woven
elastic bands. If you look at the
installation from the outside,
these spaces make the piece
964 seem larger.

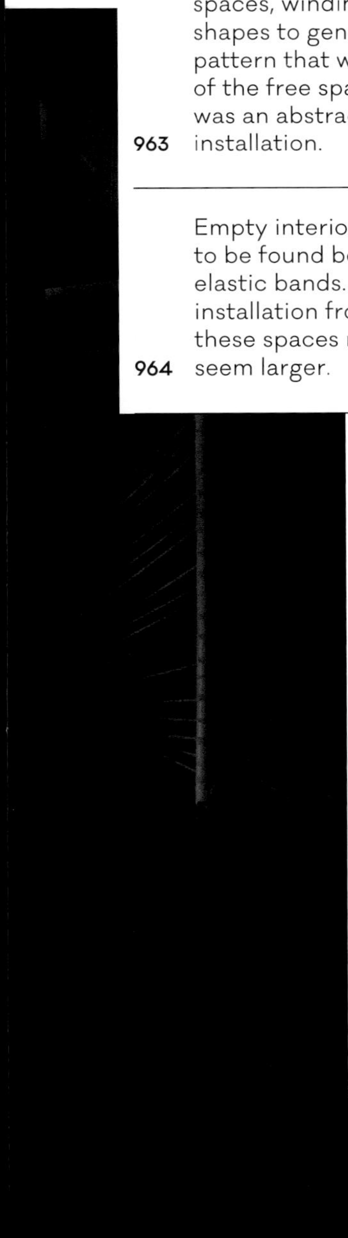

Lighting plays a very important
role. Although the installation
is stunning, the effect created
with the coloured bulbs makes
965 it more visually attractive.

Using elastic bands allows
the piece to be modified to
create different looks. If some
of the inner strips are removed,
966 visitors can view it from inside.

The main objective of was for
the participants in the artistic
event to create an ephemeral
installation inside the
967 warehouse.

Several local art schools and
art workshops collaborated
in the design and implemen-
968 tation of the installation.

Access to the exhibition was
free of charge but you had
to register beforehand if you
wanted to participate. The
installation in the workshop
was put together in about
969 three hours.

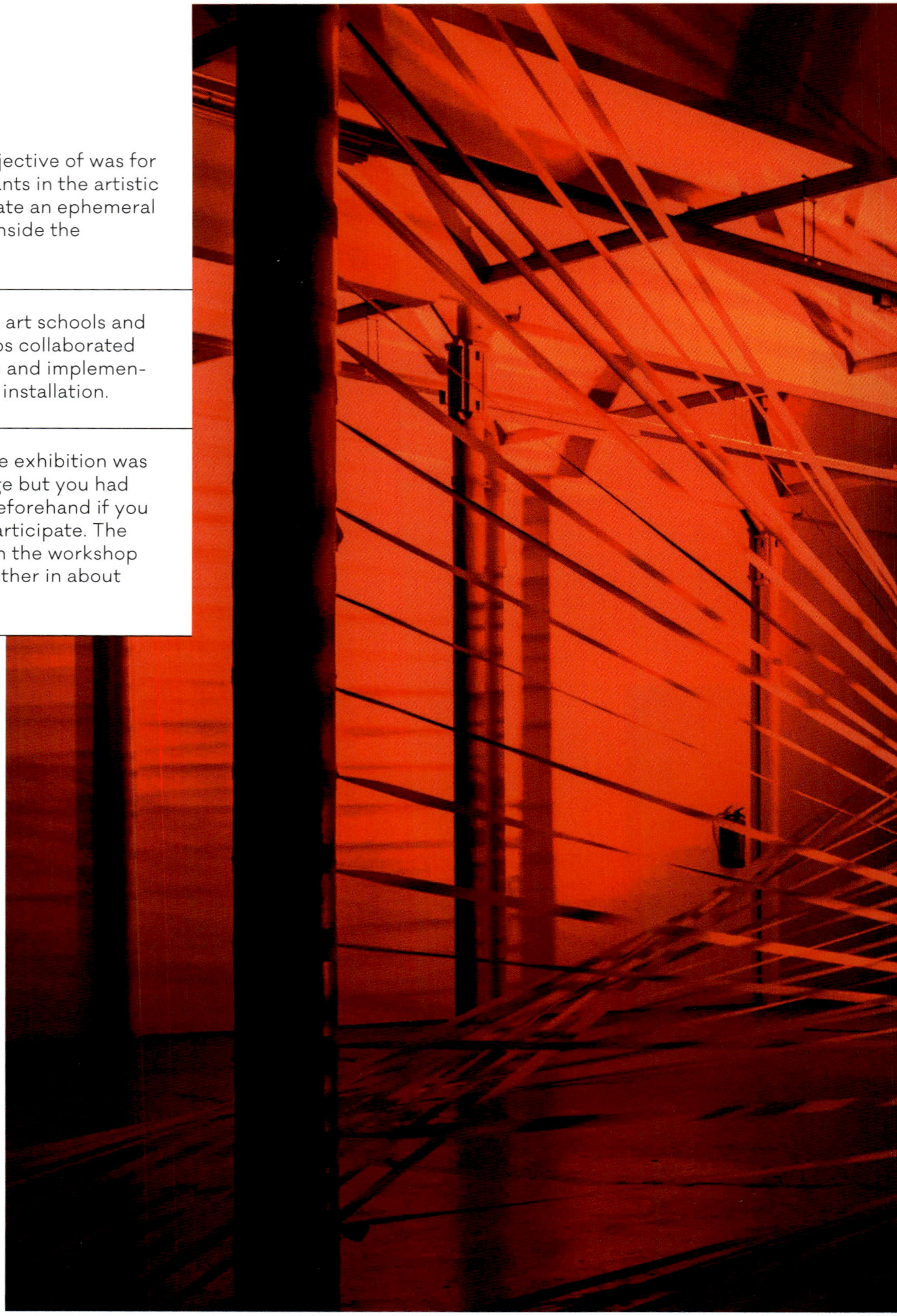

The *Changing Tracks* days are part of a European project that aims to engage new audiences in contemporary art through the placement of works of art in non-traditional exhibition spaces.

Orchard of Light

LOLA SOLANILLA + COM UN LLUM

OLOT, SPAIN, 2013
AREA
N/A
CLIENT
LLUÈRNIA FESTIVAL
PHOTO
© COM UN LLUM

971 The violet installation is in front of the Olot County Archive. The layout of the structures allows the visitor to pass between them and view them closely.

972 The project was created with a ton of shredded paper. An original layout and three 400W ultraviolet light bulbs created a unique exterior space.

973 The design seeks to transmit an experience through the reuse of shredded paper. Combined with ultraviolet light, it generates a magical atmosphere with a very compositional rhythm.

974 The space's perspectives and circular shape create a spectacular installation. The visual effect is different depending on whether it is viewed in daylight or darkness.

975 The design of the installation is inspired by Provençal lavender fields. Paper and ultraviolet light are used to represent the natural tapestries of the area.

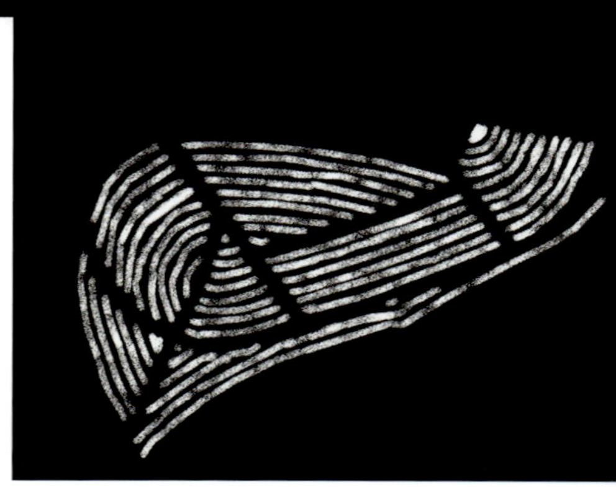

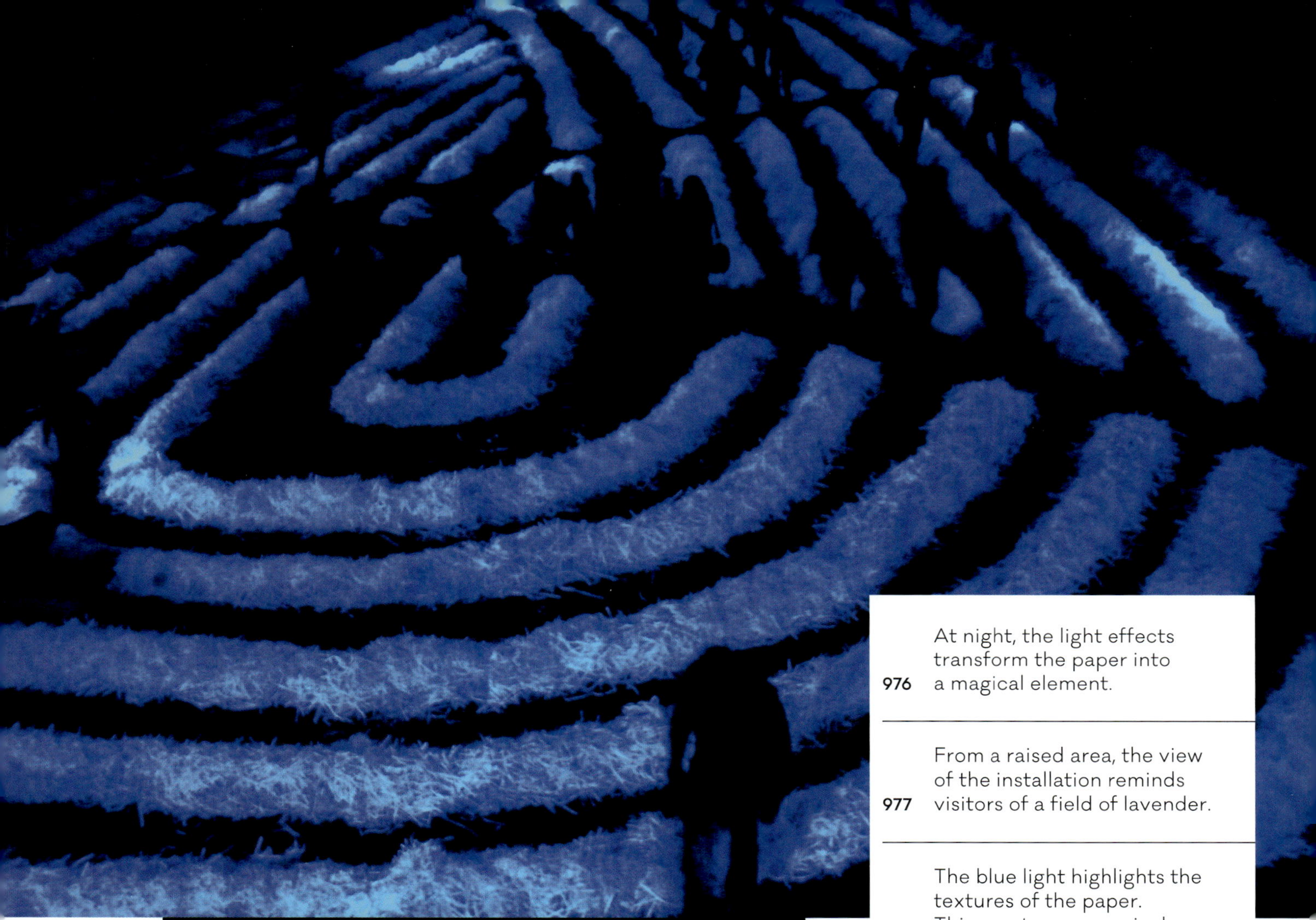

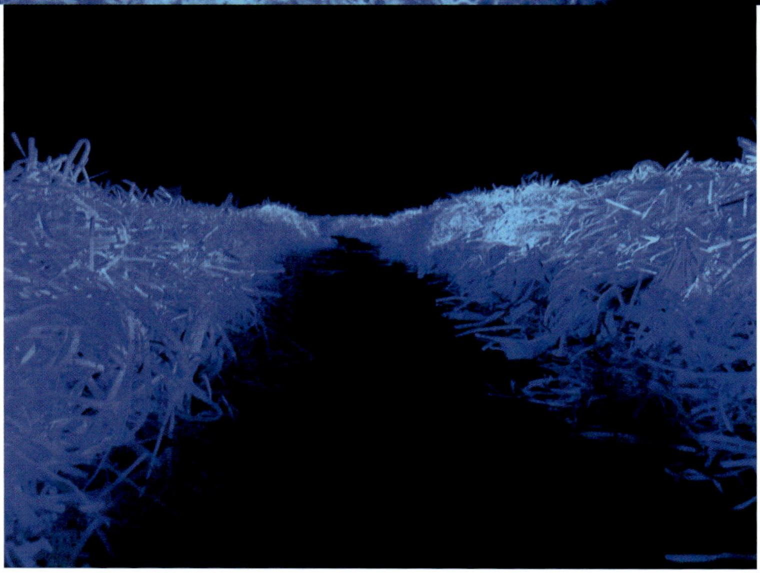

976 At night, the light effects transform the paper into a magical element.

977 From a raised area, the view of the installation reminds visitors of a field of lavender.

978 The blue light highlights the textures of the paper. This creates economical and reusable visual scenery.

979 The layout and order of the installation invites the visitor to walk through its interior. This proximity provides a close-up view of its assembly, simplicity and even its fragility.

980 Using shredded paper as the main material significantly reduced the cost of the project.

Star Immersion

CRISTINA MASFERRER, GUSTAVO TORRES, ÈLIA CLEMENTE, KARLA MEDINA

GIRONA, SPAIN, 2015

AREA
N/A

CLIENT
GIRONA CITY COUNCIL

PHOTOS
CRISTINA MASFERRER, GUSTAVO TORRES, ÈLIA CLEMENTE, KARLA MEDINA

981 The project transforms the initial appearance of the tank at the Museu d'Història de Girona during the flower show *Girona Temps de Flors 2015.* The result is a magical space.

982 The spectator enters an inhospitable place where the main features are flowers and stars. This erases all the space's original references.

983 The petals are suspended in the air by a network of black wires. Together with the ultraviolet light, they acquire prominence and independence.

884 **Large mirrored surfaces are incorporated into the base. These reflect and enhance reality to create a universe beyond the limits of the real world.**

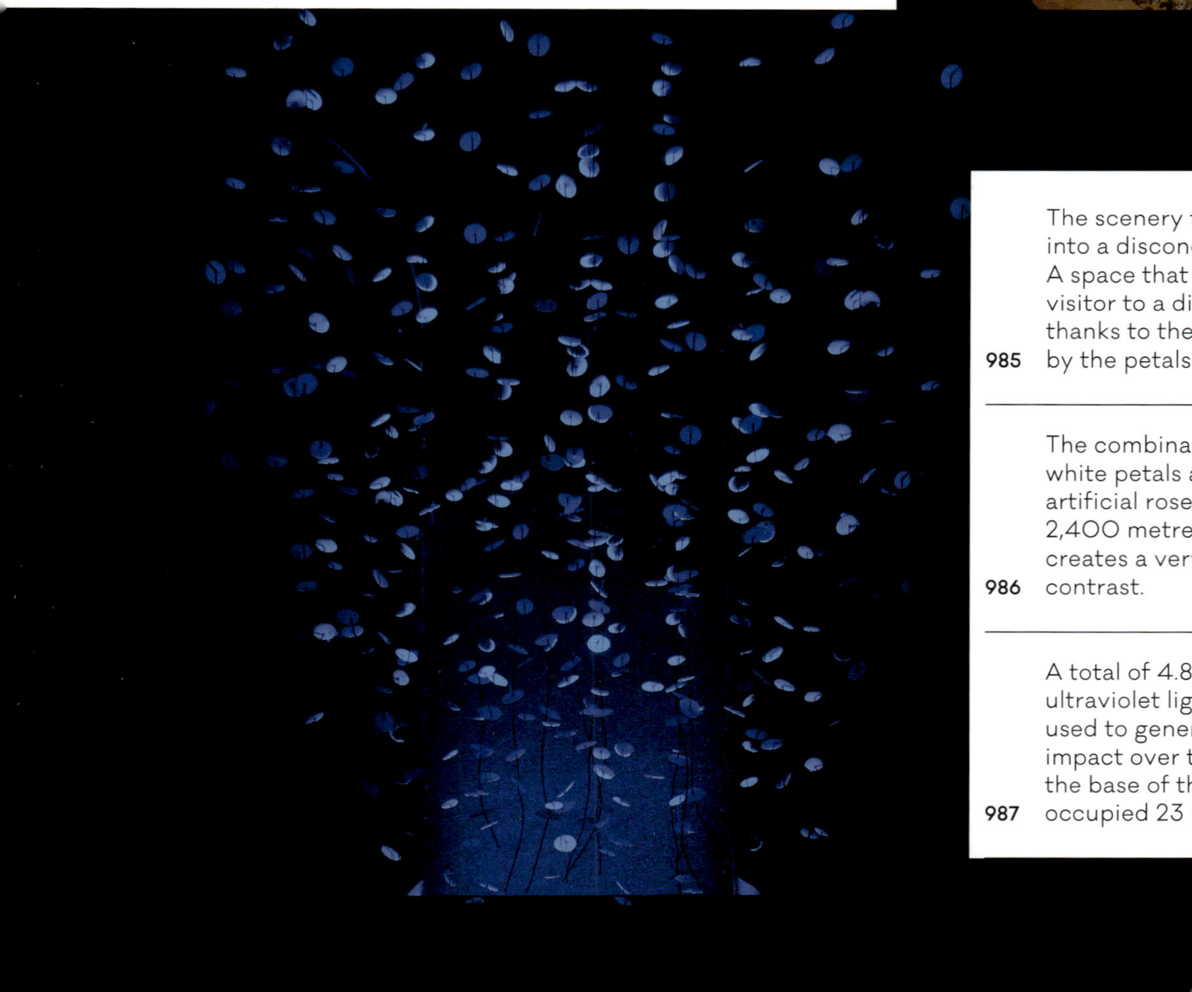

985 The scenery transforms a tank into a disconcerting place. A space that transports the visitor to a different universe thanks to the effect created by the petals and mirrors.

986 The combination of 4,000 white petals and 100 white artificial roses with a total of 2,400 metres of black thread creates a very appealing contrast.

987 A total of 4.80 metres of ultraviolet light tubes were used to generate the visual impact over the mirrors in the base of the tank, which occupied 23 m^2.

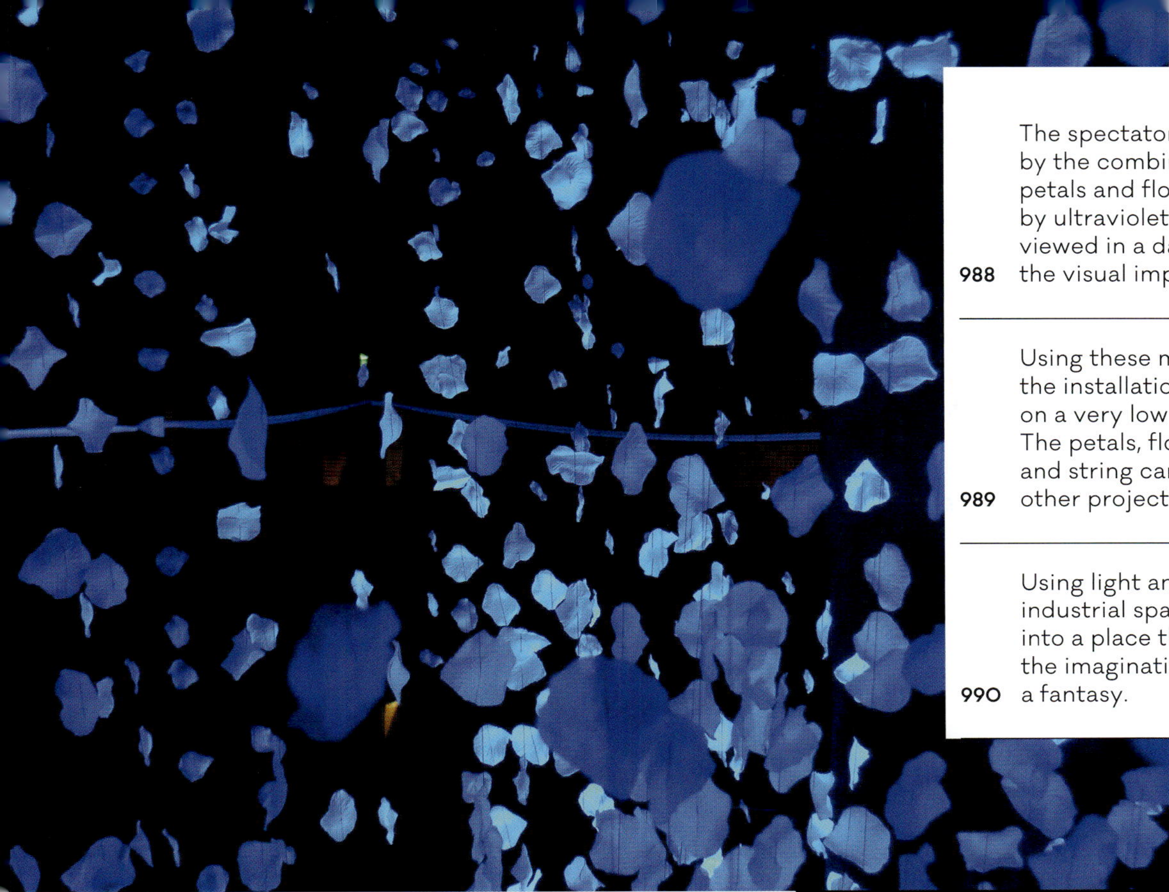

The spectator is enveloped
by the combination of white
petals and flowers, illuminated
by ultraviolet light. Being
viewed in a dark space makes
988 the visual impact even stronger.

Using these materials allowed
the installation to be created
on a very low budget.
The petals, flowers, mirrors
and string can be reused in
989 other projects.

Using light and colour, an
industrial space is transformed
into a place that stimulates
the imagination and creates
990 a fantasy.

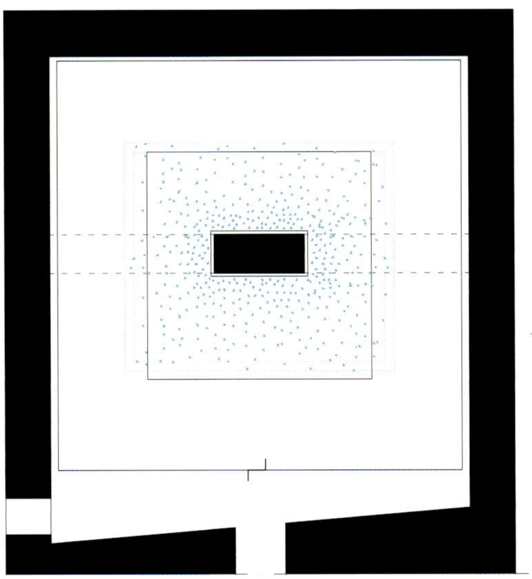

Waterlicht

DAAN ROSEGAARDE + STUDIO ROOSEGAARDE

AMSTERDAM, NETHERLANDS, 2015
AREA
N/A
CLIENT
MUSEUMPLEIN
PHOTO
© PIM HENDRIKSEN / STUDIO ROOSEGAARDE

Described by participants
as the *Dutch Northern Lights*,
this ephemeral intervention
took place between 26th
February and 1st March 2015.
It was created in the flood
channel of the Ijessel river
991 near Westervoort.

The Breach of St Anthony's
Dyke, portrayed by the Dutch
Baroque artist Jan Asselijn
in 1651, is the starting point
of the installation. The painter
immortalised the flooding of
Amsterdam which left several
992 thousand dead.

The designer, who specialises
in ephemeral artistic interven-
tions, connected with Jan
Asselijn's work through the
interaction they both establish
between man, nature and
993 technology.

Daan Roosegaarde raises the
following question: What would
happen to the Netherlands
if there were no dams to hold
back the waters of the ocean?
Of course, most of the land
994 would be underwater.

995 The installation consisted of wavy lines of light projected onto an area of more than 4 hectares. These lines were made using a system of LED lights to create a flood effect.

996 The wavy lines of light resemble the lights of the Aurora Borealis, a natural phenomenon created when charged particles enter the earth's atmosphere.

997 The LED lights are projected through lenses to focus their light. The energy sources are installed around the edges of the area, positioned so that the rays of light cross in the air and move up and down powered by motors.

998 The installation also reflects on the effects of global warming and the changes that will take place in vulnerable areas and affect daily life in coastal areas.

999 The designer wanted to demonstrate the power and vulnerability of water to visitors and to show the importance of the dams that have shaped its history and geography.

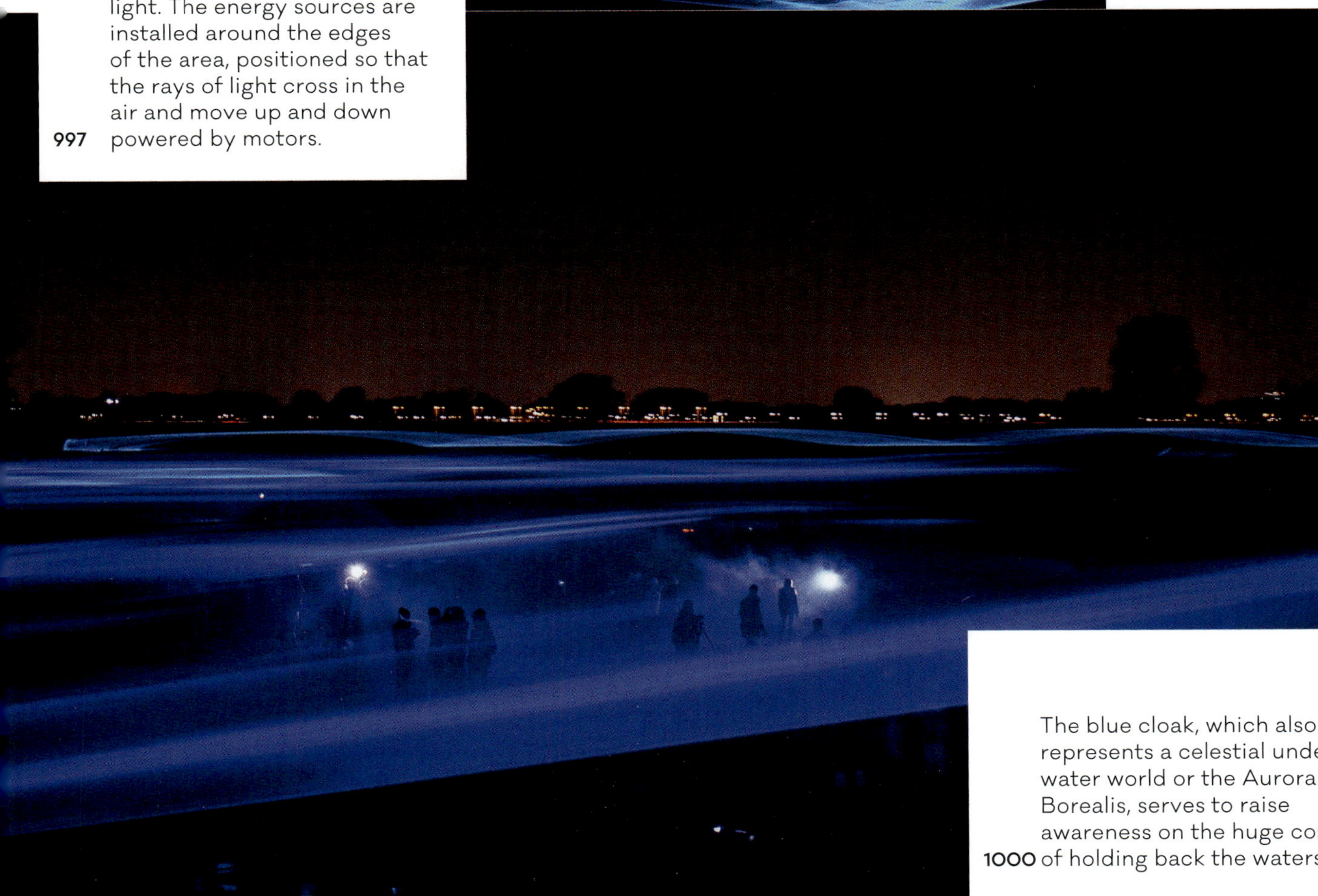

1000 The blue cloak, which also represents a celestial underwater world or the Aurora Borealis, serves to raise awareness on the huge cost of holding back the waters.

Index of Authors